Copyright as Personal Property

Copyright as Personal Property

POORNA MYSOOR

Fellow in Law, Lucy Cavendish College, University of Cambridge, UK

OXFORD
UNIVERSITY PRESS

OXFORD
UNIVERSITY PRESS

Great Clarendon Street, Oxford, OX2 6DP,
United Kingdom

Oxford University Press is a department of the University of Oxford.
It furthers the University's objective of excellence in research, scholarship,
and education by publishing worldwide. Oxford is a registered trade mark of
Oxford University Press in the UK and in certain other countries.

Published in the United States of America by Oxford University Press
198 Madison Avenue, New York, NY 10016, United States of America.

British Library Cataloguing in Publication Data
Data available

Library of Congress Control Number: 2025935311

ISBN 9780192864420

DOI: 10.1093/9780191954962.001.0001

The manufacturer's authorised representative in the EU for product safety is
Oxford University Press España S.A., Parque Empresarial San Fernando de Henares,
Avenida de Castilla, 2 – 28830 Madrid (www.oup.es/en or product.safety@oup.com).
OUP España S.A. also acts as importer into Spain of products made by the manufacturer.

For Anup

Preface

The seeds of this work were sown when I was working on my doctoral thesis on copyright licences. Looking at the provision in the Copyright Designs and Patents Act 1988 that copyright licences bind successors in title in a similar way to beneficial interests in a trust made me wonder what the rationale behind this provision may have been. My initial investigation revealed that this is simply what the statute says and has no impact on the conceptualisation of copyright licences as a property interest. It seemed to me that there should be a better explanation than this, especially one drawn from property theory. Upon further investigation, it became clear to me that there may be a more fundamental question to be addressed—that of copyright itself as a property right—before attempting to answer whether copyright licence is a property interest. Whilst copyright lawyers could work with the statutory provision confirming copyright as a property right, personal property lawyers only saw copyright as a chose in action, with neither group wanting to see a different picture.

It became clear to me further that if one were to attempt a work to explore the true nature of copyright that is historically supported, conceptually justifiable, and normatively tenable, it is inevitable that a deep dive not only into copyright law but also land law and personal property law would be required. It was also clear that it would not be possible to address it within the length and breadth of a journal article. This challenge appealed to be immensely, not least because it fits so well within the intersection of private law and intellectual property law—an area I find to be most fertile mining ground for ideas, connections, and investigations. This is how my journey with this book began. I hope to have done justice to the objectives I have set forth for this monograph, and to have imparted even a fraction of enthusiasm I have for this area.

Poorna Mysoor
30 December 2024

Acknowledgements

This work would not have been possible without the Leverhulme Trust Early Career Fellowship. The three years of this generous fellowship helped me to dive deep into this area and travel around the world meeting many of the academics cited in this work and to have fruitful conversations with them. My thanks are also due to the Faculty of Law, University of Cambridge, for their generous support with the Yorke Fund for research assistance. I am grateful to the Centre for Research in the Arts, Social Sciences and Humanities (CRASSH) for their generous support of a term's sabbatical. I extend my thanks also to the two research centres with which my work deeply engaged—the Centre for Intellectual Property and Information Law and the Cambridge Private Law Centre. Many thanks are also due to the Faculty of Law, University of Oxford where I held the Fellowship, Oxford Intellectual Property Research Centre and The Queen's College, Oxford.

My research was enriched by my affiliation as a visiting scholar at many a research centre across the globe: the Intellectual Property Research Institute of Australia at Melbourne Law School, the EW Barker Centre for Law & Business at National University of Singapore, the Berkman Klein Centre for Internet & Society and the Project on the Foundations of Private Law at Harvard Law School.

I'm overwhelmed by the support, attention, and encouragement given by Henry E Smith. Thank you, Henry! I also extend many thanks to Lionel Bently, Henning Gross-Rouse Khan, David Erdos, Nick McBride, Stephen Watterson, Sarah Worthington, Amy Goymour, Ernesto Vargas Weil, Ben McFarlane, Louise Gullifer, Jonathan Morgan, William Swadling, Simon Douglas, Luke Rostill, Aruna Nair, Rory Gregson, Lionel Smith, Dev Gangjee, Michael Bridge, James Penner, Tham Chee Ho, Jonathan Griffiths, Christopher Newman, Shyamkrishna Balganesh, John Goldberg, Andrew Robertson, Wendy Gordon, Ruth Okediji, Molly Schaffer Van Houweling, and Adam Mossoff, all of whom helped me hone my arguments on different ideas presented in the book at different points in time over the last six years. The initial guidance and support I received from my doctoral supervisor, Graeme Dinwoodie, will always be the foundation for every work I publish.

At Lucy Cavendish College, I'm deeply grateful to our Senior Tutor, Jane Greatorex, and the Assistant Senior Tutor, Mark King, for creating an environment where my research can flourish. I'm deeply grateful to Nabil Khabirpour for always believing in my abilities and for being the most perfect colleague one could ever have. Many thanks also to my students in Land Law and Law of Torts at Cambridge, who keep my knowledge of these areas of law fresh, current, and, importantly, sharp!

I extend special thanks to Rosa Matarewicz for her excellent research assistance. Rosa's meticulous work, exceptional work ethic, and infectious enthusiasm made all the difference in my ability to complete this work. Thank you, Rosa! I also extend my heartfelt thanks to my copy-editor, Caroline Valia-Kollery.

I'm deeply grateful to Anup for all the sacrifices you have made and for standing by me throughout. I'm thankful to my parents whose unshakable faith in me gives me all the strength I need.

Contents

Figures

Tables

Table of Cases

UNITED KINGDOM

COURT OF JUSTICE OF THE EUROPEAN UNION

EUROPEAN COURT OF HUMAN RIGHTS

AUSTRALIA

NEW ZEALAND

UNITED STATES

Table of Statutes and Treaties

UNITED KINGDOM

Statutes

REGULATIONS

AUSTRALIA

CANADA

NEW ZEALAND

UNITED STATES OF AMERCIA

EUROPEAN UNION DIRECTIVES

INTERNATIONAL TREATIES AND INSTRUMENTS

Abbreviations

A1P1	Article 1, Protocol 1, ECHR
ACA	Australian Copyright Act 1968
BC	Berne Convention for the Protection of Literary and Artistic Works
CCA	Canadian Copyright Act 1985 [Officially, The Copyright Act RSC 1985 c. C-42]
CDPA	Copyright, Designs and Patents Act 1988 (UK)
CFREU	Charter of Fundamental Rights of the European Union
CJEU	Court of Justice of the European Union
ECHR	European Convention on Human Rights
ECtHR	European Court of Human Rights
EEA	European Economic Area
HRA	Human Rights Act 1998 (UK)
Infosoc Directive	Directive 2001/29/EC on the harmonisation of certain aspects of copyright and related rights in the information society
TRIPS	WTO Agreement on Trade-Related Aspects of Intellectual Property Rights
WCT	WIPO Copyright Treaty
WIPO	World Intellectual Property Organization
WTO	World Trade Organization

Introduction

1. Why Does it Matter—Objectives

'Copyright shall be deemed personal property', declared section XXV of the Copyright Act of 1842.[1] About a century and a half later, the Copyright, Designs and Patents Act 1988 (CDPA) was enacted, which opens with a similar and unequivocal statement that 'Copyright is a property right . . .'.[2] The historical trajectory of copyright is replete with references to it being or being like personal property, either expressly or tacitly, in statutes as well as case law. As such, one may legitimately ask whether we need another book to tell us that copyright *is* a personal property right.[3] While the answer may be in the negative, a more incisive question to ask is what does it mean for copyright to behave *as* a personal property right—that is, what specific attributes make copyright a personal property right? For example, copyright statutes require certain works to be 'original' to qualify for copyright protection,[4] and we expend much effort in ascertaining what is and is not original. But we pay little attention to why we need originality in the first place, and what, if anything, it means within the context of copyright as a property right. The CDPA states that certain works must be recorded for copyright protection to arise.[5] Again, we do not sufficiently dwell on the question as to what role this plays in copyright as a property right. We have statutes in several common law countries that state that copyright licences are binding on successors in title.[6] But we overlook the question as to whether this might say anything about the nature of copyright licences as a property interest. Similarly, we give only slight attention, if any at all, to the question whether copyright should acknowledge the *numerus clausus* principle, and if so, to what extent.

[1] Copyright Act, London (1842) in Lionel Bently and Martin Kretschmer (eds), *Primary Sources on Copyright (1450–1900)* <www.copyrighthistory.org> accessed 10 November 2024. This provision appears in the context of transmission of copyright.

[2] CDPA, s 1(1).

[3] The relationship between personal property and property rights is addressed later in the introduction.

[4] CDPA, s 1(1)(a); Australian Copyright Act 1968 (ACA), s 31.

[5] CDPA, s 1(3); ACA, s 22.

[6] CDPA, s 90(4); ACA, s 196(4).

The paucity of analysis at a conceptual level might make copyright seem much less of a property right than might be the case. One may assert that since copyright is a creature of statute, the legislature is at liberty to label any right a property right. But one does wonder whether there might be certain core characteristics without which a right will not behave like a property right, no matter what the legislature labels it to be. We will then be back to asking the same question—what are the doctrinally significant characteristics that make copyright a property right? This monograph aims to answer this question in its various manifestations within copyright law and to answer it with more granularity than may have been attempted in the extant literature. It utilises the length and breadth of this monograph to unpack the question step by step and to answer it to its logical end, offering the required continuity to the answer.

Why does it matter that we analyse copyright as a personal property right? It matters because not only does the analysis reveal the truer nature of copyright but it also promotes a more coherent understanding of copyright within the larger context of property theory. In effect, this monograph has two objectives: an objective that is internal to copyright law and its conceptualisation within the context of the statute and its interpretation, and an objective that is external to copyright, engaging with the larger context of copyright within the law of personal property. Let us look at each of these objectives.

As regards the internal objective, there is a belief that conceptualising copyright as a property right only results in stronger and more expansive protection for copyright owners at the expense of the other stakeholders.[7] However, an analysis of copyright as a property right reveals that the contrary is true. In many instances, the expansive reach of copyright is because copyright has not stayed true to its roots as a property right, but has grown beyond the legitimate boundaries commonly known to circumscribe property rights. The boundaries in relation to which property rights operate are as much about regulating the conduct of the rest of the world as they are about precluding the copyright owner from over-claiming. Given the intangible nature of copyright, it is even more essential that the boundaries—whether these relate to the kind of subject matter, the extent of originality, the scope of the exclusive rights, or the design of the lesser interests that can be granted from copyright—are defined with this limiting nature of property rights in mind. As counterintuitive as it may sound, a deeper influence of property torts on copyright infringement could make the

[7] eg Mark Lemley, 'Property, Intellectual Property, and Free Riding' (2004–05) 83 Texas L Rev 1031, 1032; Neil W Netanel, 'Why Has Copyright Expanded? Analysis and Critique' in Fiona MacMillan (ed), *New Directions in Copyright Law* (Edward Elgar 2008) 1, 11–15.

latter achieve a better balance between competing interests. The first objective, therefore, is to dissect copyright into its constituent components and analyse the property logic behind it, to reveal the limiting, and therefore balancing, effect that can be achieved within the copyright system.[8]

The external objective of this monograph is to situate copyright contextually amidst other property rights. Doctrinally, English law has been guided by the binary classification of property rights into choses in possession and choses in action. Lumping all intangible assets including copyright in one category of choses in action is analytically problematic. To be sure, Fry LJ's words in relation to shares, in *Colonial Bank v Whinney*, that the law 'knows no *tertium quid*',[9] have been squarely rejected by Bryan J in *AA v Persons Unknown* in relation to Bitcoin.[10] While it is clear from the Law Commission Report that newer subject matter vying for protection by property rights is forcing a debate on this traditional taxonomy,[11] intellectual property rights, and in particular copyright, had already begun this debate at least a century and a half ago.[12] Bridge has tried to offer a more elaborate classification of property rights by separating land and chattels on one hand, and intangibles on the other, classifying copyright together with debt and shares among pure intangibles.[13] Again, the issue with this is that, other than intangibility, copyright has nothing in common with debt and shares. Even if the purpose of classification is simply to facilitate orderly study of an area, the danger of a bright-line divide between tangible and intangible assets is to create silos with little or no cross-fertilisation of concepts, principles, or doctrines. Copyright being enshrined in a statute gives it the shroud of specialism that only adds to the resistance to examine it from the perspective of property theory and common law.

The analysis of copyright as a property right helps fill an important evolutionary gap between property rights in tangible things and intangible assets. It is possible to demonstrate that despite being an intangible asset, copyright is closer to choses in possession than it is to choses in action, if one were to insist

[8] Others who share this view include Michael Carrier, who argues for expansion of the fair use doctrine in the context of the US law. See Michael Carrier, 'Limiting Copyright through Property' in Helena Howe and Jonathan Griffiths (eds), *Concepts of Property in Intellectual Property Law* (CUP 2013) 185, 202–04; Emily Hudson and Robert Burrell, 'Abandonment, Copyright and Orphaned Works: What Does It Mean to Take the Proprietary Nature of Intellectual Property Rights Seriously' (2011) 35 Melb U L Rev 971.

[9] (1885) 30 Ch D 261, 285.

[10] [2019] EWHC 3556 (Comm).

[11] Law Commission, *Report on Digital Assets* (Law Com No 412, 2023).

[12] Spencer Broadhurst, 'Is Copyright a Chose in Action?' (1895) 11 LQR 64; Cyprian T Williams, 'Property, Things in Action and Copyright' (1895) 11 LQR 223; Charles Sweet, 'Choses in Action' (1895) 11 LQR 238.

[13] Michael Bridge, *Personal Property Law* (4th edn, OUP 2015) 16.

on this classification. Yet, because of the rigidity of the existing taxonomy, many of the beneficial crossover of concepts, principles, and doctrines rarely takes place between the categories. Instead of categorising property rights within these fixed designations, this monograph proposes the idea of a spectrum of property rights as a more robust and apposite conceptualisation of property rights. It locates copyright along this spectrum, without having to classify it within a fixed category. It takes a stand against a static and binary conception of property rights in favour of a dynamic and pluralistic one. The idea of all property rights along a spectrum foregrounds the incrementalism underlying the application of *numerus clausus* to property rights.[14] Developing the spectrum in this manner also helps a more systematic assessment of newer subject matter as to their eligibility for protection by property rights,[15] for which this book, with the example of copyright, lays the foundation.

The soundness of the spectrum of property rights depends on how it is constructed. Let us look at the starting point of this spectrum. Classically, property rights have been conceptualised with tangible things at their centre. On the spectrum, however, instead of locating these rights at the centre, it helps to locate them at one end. This makes property rights to tangible things only the starting point of the spectrum. This provides a less controversial starting point for the conceptualisation of property rights because no one can dispute that property rights can arise in relation to tangible subject matter.[16] But at the same time, it will mean that property rights in tangible things are not the only kind of property rights, as some may still like to believe,[17] but only one of the many kinds, even if a paradigmatic kind. Furthermore, property rights have a protean face with multiple and contextual meanings. For instance, bankruptcy laws might have a more instrumentalist understanding of property, whilst tax laws might push for a more functional meaning of property. Having property rights in tangible things, as understood in their classical sense, as the starting point instead could help maintain a level of objectivity and stability. Thus, even if doctrinally a property right means one thing under, say, insolvency law and another under the law of conversion, the coherence of our foundational understanding of property rights can be maintained.

[14] See Chapter 1, Section 6 for further discussion on *numerus clausus*.

[15] See eg Timothy Chan, 'The Nature of Property in Crypto-assets' (2023) 43 LS 480, 484–91, where the author explores the question of what the thing in crypto-assets is.

[16] This starting point is not unusual. See Jeremy Waldron, *The Right to Private Property* (OUP 1988) 33, 59, where he posits that there are 'good reasons for discussing property in material resources first before grappling with the complexities of incorporeal property' and that material resources 'give[] us the raw material on which the analogies' with incorporeal property are based.

[17] Simon Douglas and Ben McFarlane, 'Defining Property Rights' in James Penner and Henry Smith (eds), *Philosophical Foundations of Property Law* (OUP 2013) 223–26.

The next important aspect to consider is the metric one should use to develop the spectrum. It is envisaged here that the spectrum will be guided by the core characteristics of property rights in tangible things as the framework for the rest of the spectrum. An attempt is made in this work to distil these core characteristics. The academic divergence on what these core characteristics are cannot be overstated. However, prominent property theorists largely converge on certain common themes for examination. Birks has described land law as rules dealing with the nature, creation, and protection of interests in land.[18] In a similar vein, while examining the structure of property law, McFarlane categorises property law into the content question, acquisition question, defences question, and remedies question.[19] One can see significant overlaps between these approaches. On this basis, it is possible to identify four salient aspects of property rights—their nature, the way they are acquired, the manner in which they are enforced, and to this one may also add how one transacts in these rights. Each of these aspects reveals certain characteristics which can be used as the metrics to help calibrate the construction of the spectrum. These metrics are then compared by analogy from property rights in tangible things to copyright to analyse the manner and extent to which copyright responds to these metrics. If convincing analogies can be drawn with copyright from a starting point that is stable and objective, then other property rights can be mapped along this continuum.

But this is not to say that this monograph regards the metrics applied to property rights in tangible things as being identical to those relating to property rights in intangible subject matter. Some differences are inevitable, and it is important to appreciate the impact of these differences.[20] One must also acknowledge that the extent to which copyright responds to these metrics may be only a matter of degree. As this book will show, copyright has a certain conceptual proximity to property rights in tangible things, which might justify a similar treatment of copyright as a property right taking into account the doctrinal consequences that might flow from these similarities. To demonstrate this and to ensure that the spectrum develops in a rationally defensible manner, this monograph uses analogical reasoning instead of simplistic comparison. Developing the analogy along the spectrum avoids making simplistic comparisons, and ill-informed

[18] Peter Birks, 'Before We Begin: Five Keys to Land Law' in Susan Bright and John Dewer (eds), *Land Law Themes and Perspectives* (OUP 1998) 460.

[19] Ben McFarlane, *The Structure of Property Law* (Hart 2008) 40.

[20] eg Balganesh regards the law of tangible property and copyright law as having a dialectic relationship. See Shyamkrishna Balganesh, 'Alienability and Copyright Law' in Helena Howe and Jonathan Griffiths (eds), *Concepts of Property in Intellectual Property Law* (CUP 2013) 161, 187.

development of the law. The use of analogy opens up the possibility of cross-application not only of concepts and principles but also doctrines from the law of tangible property to copyright, as the context permits.

2. Response to Sceptics

Sceptics may raise several objections against the arguments put forward in this monograph. First, whether it is necessary at all for copyright to be conceptualised as a property right. In particular, this question may be posed in the light of continental European regimes which conceptualise copyright more as a regulatory regime to protect authors' rights rather than as a property right.[21] One may also point to the attempts made to reimagine a world with a completely different copyright regime altogether–not as a property right, nor as authors' rights.[22] However, these regimes are characterised by reliance on the legislature for regulatory design and response to the needs of other stakeholders within the copyright system. This exposes the regulation not only to the vagaries of legislative process but also to the political tensions at both national and international levels, especially when any limitations or exceptions to the rights are to be imposed. As an illustration, it was only in 2016 that making accessible copies of copyright works was regarded a defence to copyright infringement, when the international community voted for this within the context of treaty-making, despite this defence being unquestionably worthy and the international treaty on copyright being in existence for over a century. When the legislature has expressly recognised copyright to be a property right it opens up the possibility of the inbuilt limits of property rights developed by common law to be reflected in the copyright regime. This monograph, therefore, argues that if copyright is regulated as a property right, it prevents the singular reliance on the legislature for any and every balancing need of the copyright system. It might instead help the copyright system to benefit from the best of both worlds—stability from the statute and flexibility from common law. Additionally, in England the historical underpinnings of copyright have shown a strong inclination towards property rights. Therefore, developing the property right discourse of copyright is a more organic way of exploring the potential of the limiting mechanisms inherent in property rights.

[21] Caterina Sganga, *Propertizing European Copyright* (Edward Elgar 2018).

[22] eg Rebecca Giblin and Kimberlee Weatherall, 'If We Redesigned Copyright from Scratch, What Might it Look Like?' in Rebecca Giblin and Kimberlee Weatherall (eds), *What if We Could Reimagine Copyright?* (ANU Press 2017).

Secondly, even if it is accepted that copyright is better analysed as a property right, is it safe to accept property rights in tangible things as a default starting point uncritically, for this analogy? Some might doubt that property rights have any limiting role at all. These fears, however, are overstated. No one believes that we have in modern times anything close to the absolute despotic dominion that Blackstone spoke of. There have been several inroads carved into property rights over the years. Although the concept of private property has its flaws, it has endured though millennia, morphing and evolving, progressing and regressing, but most importantly, thriving as an institution. Instead of starting our discussion by challenging the institution, it would be sensible to see how the aspects of the institution that have helped it balance the interests of various stakeholders might be reflected in copyright. Historically there is much to support the argument that the copyright regime was developed with property rights in tangible things as the basis.[23] However, there are many limiting aspects of land law and personal property law that have not found their way into copyright law. Doctrines of adverse possession, finders of goods, and prescription are only some examples. The analogy taken seriously can bring some of these balancing aspects into copyright.

Thirdly, even if property rights in tangible things are the correct starting point, does the non-rivalrous nature of the thing in copyright not pose a hurdle for the analogy? Rivalrousness in relation to a resource means that its use by one person deprives others of its use at the same time.[24] Rivalrousness of a resource is relative. Clearly, a bracelet is more rivalrous than a large tract of land. Nevertheless, land law makes use of symbolisms and legal fictions to cope with the factual non-rivalrousness of land. For example, in order to take possession of a large tract of land it is sufficient to put up a fence and a lockable gate; one does not need to build an impregnable fortress to prevent anyone else from using the land at the same time. Land law can work with the symbolism of the fence and the gate, and the legal fiction that this is sufficient to take control of the land. If symbolism and legal fictions work in relation to land, they could be made to work in relation to copyright too. Undeniably, rivalrousness has an impact on the kind of legal regulation that surrounds a resource. But non-rivalrousness on its own does not take away the eligibility of a resource from being regulated through property rights.

[23] Brad Sherman and Lionel Bently, *The Making of Modern Intellectual Property* (CUP 1999) 45. See also *Millar v Taylor* (1769) 4 Burr 2303, 98 ER 201, 224, where the language of real property such as invasion is used.

[24] Joseph E Stiglitz, 'Economic Foundations of Intellectual Property Rights' (2008) 57 Duke LJ 1693, 1699–700.

Fourthly, even if non-rivalrousness of copyright is not a big hurdle, is the use of analogy a legitimate method to adopt? Despite criticisms, analogies are ubiquitous in private law. Examples include the cautious expansion by analogy of the subject matter of grant of an easement and the determination of novel cases where duty of care may be imposed in the law of negligence.[25] Analogies help build analytical correlations systematically and meaningfully in a way that furthers the values of private law of certainty and coherence, with the underlying logic being maintained.[26] Weinreb describes analogy as 'reasoning by example', that is, 'finding the solution to a problem by reference to another similar problem and its solution'.[27] It consists of 'an observed similarity between two phenomena, the source and the target', and the identification of 'some further characteristic of the source, and the conclusion that the target (probably) also has that characteristic'.[28] It must be acknowledged that some analogies are closer than others, and a comparison with analytical correlatives must bear in mind the distance from the source to the target. If these factors are borne in mind, an analogical method could be of immense help in developing the spectrum of property rights. Even those who argue that property rights can extend only to tangible things, such as Douglas and McFarlane, accept that copyright does bear some similarities with property rights to tangible things by analogy.[29]

Fifthly, even if the legitimacy of analogy as a tool is accepted, is copyright only a property right by analogy and not a property right as such? Property rights in tangible things already accommodate a great deal of malleability, which has been made possible by arguments based on analogy. Take, for example, the concept of possession. The manner in which possession of land is understood is very different from the way possession of a ship is understood; and the latter is very different from the way the possession of a bracelet is understood.[30] Underlying this remarkable progression of the concept of possession, therefore, is the extensive use of analogy. However, the same terminology of possession is used, despite the conduct required to take possession in

[25] For easements, see Robert Megarry and others, *The Law of Real Property* (10th edn, Sweet & Maxwell 2024) para 26-015. For duty of care in negligence cases, see *Robinson v Chief Constable of South Yorkshire* [2018] AC 736 [21].

[26] This avoids the risks that Balganesh warns of in his work. See Balganesh (n 20) 167.

[27] Lloyd L Weinreb, *Legal Reason: The Use of Analogy in Legal Argument* (CUP 2005) 4.

[28] Scott Brewer, 'Exemplary Reasoning: Semantics, Pragmatics, and the Rational Force of Legal Argument by Analogy' (1996) 109 Harv L Rev 923, 967.

[29] Ben McFarlane and Simon Douglas, 'Property, Analogy, Variety' (2022) 42 OJLS 161, 176–77.

[30] Frederick Pollock and Robert S Wright, *An Essay on Possession in the Common Law* (Clarendon Press 1888) 11, where the authors recount the differences in the way factual control is exercised over a pen, a chair, a table, and the books around a room.

each of these scenarios being by no means identical. Similarly, when one says that copyright is a property right by analogy, it need not imply that copyright is any less of a property right. Analogy in this context only promotes a more coherent and rational comparison between copyright and property rights in tangible things based on common features, rather than detracting from such a comparison. Ultimately, the use of analogy fulfils the aim of establishing that property is not used as a hollow metaphor in relation to copyright, but there are substantive reasons and doctrinal consequences that flow from the property attributes of copyright.

Undeniably, there are challenges to drawing these analogies. Despite the initial inspiration for copyright law from property law relating to tangible things, in its later avatar copyright law has developed into an independent discipline, appearing to have moved away from its origin. This book aims to bring copyright law closer to property law relating to tangible things and to make them communicate with each other more effectively. These areas of law are rarely examined in depth in a full-length monograph. A difficulty in attempting a work like this is that the vocabulary of property law derives its meaning in the context of tangible things. Terminology such as thing-relatedness, title, possession, exclusive rights, and so on, have their distinct meaning in the context of tangible property law. Some scholars believe that one cannot speak meaningfully of many of these concepts in relation to intangible assets.[31] Similarly, there is vocabulary such as a 'work', 'originality', and 'restricted act', which have a meaning only in the context of copyright. While it is uncommon to use the vocabulary of tangible things to explain copyright, this book attempts to establish analytical equivalents of these concepts by analogy, in order to bring these two disciplines closer. This is sought to be achieved by detaching the concept from its context of tangibility and examining its ontological purpose at the conceptual level. Once the purpose is ascertained, it can then be analysed within the intangible context whether there is a concept that achieves a similar purpose. In doing so, the monograph tries to be sensitive to the doctrinal implications of this analysis and its limitations, ensuring that the analysis does not lead to confusion or conflation. This analysis is undertaken only in situations where copyright law can meaningfully benefit from the analogies with property rights in tangible things, and not simply as an exercise in semantics.

[31] eg William Swadling argues that it is inappropriate to use the word 'title' in relation to intangible assets such as shares and debts. See William Swadling, 'Property—General Principles' in Andrew Burrows (ed), *English Private Law* (OUP 2013) para 4.131.

3. Extant Literature and Moving the Needle

This book does not claim to be the first to shed light on copyright as personal property. There have been many that have adverted their attention to this. And when that is the case, it becomes even more important to show where this book fits and how it takes the argument further. Let us begin with the textbooks. On one hand, we have the textbooks on intellectual property law generally and copyright in particular. Most of these keep the discussion of copyright as a property right brief, with the acknowledgement that copyright is now expressly recognised to be so under the statute.[32] As we shall see in the rest of the monograph, it is not one singular characteristic of copyright that makes it a property right, but rather that many aspects of copyright can be explained by analogy to property rights in tangible things. To be fair, these aspects are discussed in the textbooks, but without reference to their connection with property rights or recognising them as characteristics of property rights. On the other hand, we have textbooks on personal property law, some of which do discuss intellectual property generally, but briefly.[33] Bridge et al provide a slightly more detailed account than other textbooks.[34] They conceptualise copyright as a chose in action in as much as they regard copyright as a property right in the exclusive rights themselves. Since the other aspects of copyright, such as acquisition, enforcement, and so on are dealt with by the statute, they do not deal with these aspects.

Although the conceptualisation of copyright as a chose in action reigns as the dominant view,[35] this book fundamentally disagrees with it. Since this conceptualisation supports the view that there is nothing more to copyright than the rights themselves, it helps copyright to be analysed in the same manner as other known entities within the category of choses in action. This impacts almost every other aspect of copyright discourse, starting from the understanding of the rights themselves to their acquisition, enforcement, remedies, and defences. Challenging the very basis of the classification between choses in possession and choses in action, this monograph argues that the essence of copyright as a property right lies in its conceptualisation as an intangible thing, which is the 'work'. This conceptualisation helps this monograph to shed new light on how the rights as well as powers and privileges in copyright are to be

[32] eg Adrian Speck and others, *The Modern Law of Copyright* (5th edn, LexisNexis 2018) 20.

[33] Duncan Sheehan, *The Principles of Personal Property Law* (Hart 2017) 3–5.

[34] Michael Bridge and others, *The Law of Personal Property* (3rd edn, Sweet & Maxwell 2022) chs 9 and 10.

[35] The Law Commission also regards copyright as a chose in action. Law Commission, *Digital Assets: A Consultation Paper* (Law Com No 256, 2022) para 3-59.

understood, how they are enforced, and how the remedies and defences can be understood. Another significant departure from the extant literature enabled by this conceptualisation is to regard copyright as being capable of giving rise to derivative interests and to analyse these interests. This is what makes this exposition deserving of the length and breadth of a monograph. By situating copyright within the larger context of the existing literature, this monograph seeks to provide a narrative of copyright accessible to those versed in the vocabulary of property rights in tangible things, exercising care and caution in drawing the analogies. It moves the needle by bridging the gap from where the personal property texts end and copyright textbooks begin, creating a segue between the two.

There are monographs focusing on the intellectual property laws of other jurisdictions being analysed within the property rubric. Notable mention may be made of Rognstad's *Property Aspects of Intellectual Property*.[36] In addition to being directed towards intellectual property rights in general, Rognstad's conceptual leanings and legal conclusions are more towards Scandinavian and continental European disciplines, although he does consider American jurisprudence in this regard.[37] Also worthy of mention is the work of Sganga, *Propertizing European Copyright*.[38] While Sganga does deal with UK law briefly, she takes it as settled that common law has a wide notion of property accommodating both tangible and intangible assets.[39] While these are excellent examples of monographs drawn from different legal traditions, they focus largely on the nature of copyright. The impact of property aspects or propertisation on acquisition, rights, enforcement, and so on is not explored in as much depth as it is in this monograph. In other words, this monograph sheds light on aspects of copyright that are not normally discussed from the point of view of property rights. In addition, by developing the idea of a spectrum of property rights and by locating copyright on this spectrum, this monograph takes a unique approach to the understanding of copyright as a property right, and to realising in relation to copyright the limiting potential of property rights.

There is immense literature in the academic journals addressing specific aspects of copyright as a property right from various perspectives.[40] Although

[36] Ole-Andreas Rognstad, *Property Aspects of Intellectual Property* (CUP 2018).
[37] ibid 47–51, 60–66.
[38] Sganga (n 21).
[39] ibid 9.
[40] Examples include Henry E Smith, 'Intellectual Property as Property: Delineating Entitlements in Information' (2007) 116 Yale LJ 1742; Wendy Gordon, 'Copyright as Property' (1989) 41 Stan L Rev 1343.

the arguments in many of these articles are drawn from US law (fair use, for example), to the extent that there is a comparable context within the United Kingdom, this literature is considered here. There is a certain continuity to the manner in which the property aspects of copyright can be explored and analysed at each stage in the copyright life cycle, from its nature to acquisition to enforcement to transactions. Capturing this within a monograph enables this continuity to be shown within one connected analysis.

4. Focus—'Personal Property' and 'Copyright'

The title 'Copyright as Personal Property' calls for an explanation of both copyright and personal property. Let us begin with personal property. Personal property is used in its taxonomical sense. Classically, personal property consists of all tangible things that are not land. Copyright being regarded as personal property conveys an argument that copyright should be classified alongside chattels as personal property. Of course, in the context of transmissibility of copyright, s 90(1) of the CDPA describes it as personal property.[41] Scholars have ascribed to copyright the further taxonomic category within personal property of pure intangibles together with debts and shares.[42] While this book accepts this classification at a high level of abstraction, it endeavours to establish how copyright is closer by analogy to tangible things than pure intangibles.

To the extent that land, personal property, and copyright are all regarded as property in this monograph, the meaning ascribed to property needs to be clarified. Property can mean the thing itself or the property right.[43] This monograph favours the meaning of property as property rights. Other than in the title of the book, the expression 'property right' is adopted for clarity. Two points need to be made in relation to the term 'property right'. First, it is shorthand for many consequences that follow when the title to a thing is acquired for the first time in a manner prescribed by law. The strict Hohfeldian meaning of a right on its own in this context might only mean the imposition of corresponding duties on the rest of the world. When the law lays down rules of acquiring title to a thing, what one acquires is not limited to placing duties of non-interference on the rest of the world. One also acquires powers, privileges,

[41] Australian Copyright Act 1968, s 196(1) also refers to copyright as personal property.
[42] Michael Bridge, *Personal Property Law* (4th edn, OUP 2015) para 1.1.4.1
[43] Swadling (n 31) para 4-02.

and immunities in relation to the thing. Depending on whether the property right acquired is the ownership interest or a lesser interest, the corresponding rights, powers, and so on will be more open-ended or more constricted. The terminology of property rights hides all these complexities. In general, the term property right is used in this broader sense, except when discussing property rights as a claim right in the relevant chapter analysing the exclusionary rights and corresponding duties imposed by copyright.[44] Secondly, when this book claims that copyright is a property right it does not mean that copyright is nothing but a right. This may lead to a mistaken understanding of copyright as a chose in action.[45] When one describes property rights in land it hardly means that the property right is merely a right and nothing more. One acknowledges that land is the resource to which the property right relates. In the same way, copyright conveys not only the right that is a property right but also the resource, namely, the work, which the property right protects.

While on the subject of property rights, it may also be noted that this book relies extensively on Hohfeldian analysis for the examination of property rights. Scholars attribute the Hohfeldian notion of property to the much discredited bundle of rights theory.[46] Nevertheless, scholars who do strongly believe in thinghood also use Hohfeldian analysis, arguing that Hohfeld's approach to fundamental legal conceptions is in itself helpful.[47] Hohfeldian analysis is used here in a similar vein. Hohfeld's conceptualisation of ownership as a complex aggregate of rights, powers, privileges, and immunities[48] is a helpful way to analyse the constituents of ownership, but not without an understanding of the nature of the thing. While it is acknowledged that Hohfeldian approach is not without criticism, Hohfeldian analysis is used only to the extent that it brings analytical clarity.

Turning to 'copyright', the book focuses not on intellectual property in general, but specifically on copyright, and within copyright, economic rights and not moral rights. Copyright is an outlier in abandoning all requirements of registration towards the end of nineteeth century. There is a marked difference in the way property rights are acquired between rights that arise by registration (trade marks and patents, for example) and those that need no registration,

[44] In Chapter 4, Section 2(a), property rights are understood in the Hohfeldian sense.

[45] See Chapter 2 for a discussion on why the description of copyright as a chose in action is misconceived.

[46] Henry E Smith, 'Property is Not Just a Bundle of Rights' (2011) 8(3) EJW 279, 279–80.

[47] Simon Douglas and Ben McFarlane, 'Defining Property Rights' in James Penner and Henry Smith (eds), *Philosophical Foundations of Property Law* (OUP 2013) 220.

[48] Wesley N Hohfeld, 'Fundamental Legal Conceptions as Applied in Judicial Reasoning' (1917) 26 Yale LJ 710, 746.

such as copyright. In this sense copyright can be seen as a more intuitive example to illustrate the characteristics of property rights. One must accept that it is more common for scholars writing on property theory to focus on intellectual property as a whole.[49] However, the subject matter of protection and the rationale behind it are wholly distinct between different types of intellectual property rights. If the focus of an argument is intellectual property generally, the analogies will have to be at a higher level of abstraction, which results in lumping together and loss of analysis, leading to generalisations about individual types of intellectual property that may not always be justified. By focusing only on copyright, this book provides a granular assessment, resulting in closer and deeper comparisons between the law governing tangible things and intangible things. The analysis not only extends to theoretical and conceptual levels but also proceeds to demonstrate the analytical correlations in the doctrine through specific statutory provisions and their judicial interpretations.

5. Scope and Coverage

The main jurisdictional footprint covered in this work jurisdictionally is UK copyright law. Doctrinally this monograph relies on the English common law of tangible property, and for conceptual analysis of property rights this monograph draws on Anglo-American scholarship. This work also references other common law jurisdictions such as Australia and Canada, where additional strength may be drawn to support the relevant argument. The choice of these jurisdictions is also based on the fact that although these jurisdictions have substantially amended their statutes over time, historically they have modelled their basic copyright statute directly or indirectly on one of the erstwhile versions of UK copyright statute—Australia on the UK Copyright Act 1956, and Canada on the UK Copyright Act 1911. This monograph does not cover US case law or statutes, as US law has historically charted a different path. However, the scholarly writings of American authors on conceptual issues surrounding the copyright and property debate do form part of the analysis in this monograph. This book does not seek to engage in a comparative study of copyright as a property right between common law and continental European jurisdictions. As already mentioned, experts in continental European law have previously adverted to this debate.[50] However, this book does engage with EU

[49] Rognstad (n 36).
[50] Sganga (n 21).

copyright law to the extent that the harmonisation project has had its impact on the matters covered here.[51]

Sherman and Bently have provided a deep dive into the history of copyright until the end of the nineteenth century.[52] They capture the remarkable journey of the law in recognising property rights in relation to outputs of the 'labour of the mind'.[53] They analyse the sources that reveal a comparison between the property concepts known at the time and 'literary property', that is, a kind of common law copyright. Based on this analysis they demonstrate how intangible subject matter came to be identified, how the rules of acquisition of property rights in intangible subject matter came to be formulated, and so on.[54] While this journey is entirely explicable, this monograph argues that the time may now be apt to re-open these debates. The original bases for protection afforded by copyright and reinforcing these might not only assist in resolving some of the conceptual and doctrinal issues in copyright but also serve as a guiding light for the formulation of protection regimes for other types of intangible assets.

The monograph supplements conceptual and doctrinal analysis with the historical underpinnings when examining the nature of copyright subject matter. An eye on history helps because it will reveal the epistemology of why and how copyright came to be conceptualised as a property right. These answers have a bearing on establishing analogies with property law governing tangible things. Bently and Sherman have explored in great detail copyright history until the end of nineteenth century in the lead up to the UK Copyright Act 1911. However, some of the formative developments of copyright that we see today took place in the twentieth century, especially those that relate to the mass production of sound recordings and broadcasting. These have had a tremendous impact on shaping the 1956 Act, and eventually on the CDPA. Taking these historical influences into account, this monograph provides an additional dimension to the analysis, bolstering the conceptual and doctrinal arguments.

Given the vastness of this subject, it is also important to explain what this work does not set out to achieve. This work deals only with the private property debates in relation to copyright, and not public ownership or commons.[55] This book takes property rights and intellectual property rights as having a

[51] See Chapter 1, Section 2 on the impact of EU directives on UK copyright law.
[52] Sherman and Bently (n 23).
[53] ibid chs 1 and 2.
[54] ibid.
[55] Private property in the sense used by Jeremy Waldron (n 16).

justifiable place in the modern world. It is not a detailed exposition on every aspect of copyright law, but rather a work focusing on the areas of copyright where one can see analogies with property rights in tangible things. Copyright responds more intuitively to some analogies than the others. But building an argument analogously makes the analysis more robust in revealing the missing pieces of the puzzle and drawing conclusions on what this means to the copyright system. In this sense, the main thrust of the arguments in this work is on theory and concept, and the resulting doctrinal dividend is posited as directions for future elaboration.

6. Structure of the Monograph

This work is a normative exploration of how copyright as a property right should be conceptualised by analogy with property rights in tangible things, and what are the theoretical, conceptual, and doctrinal benefits that can be derived from this. Before starting with the substantive chapters, the stage must be set for copyright, situating it in the context of influences that are external to property rights as well as those that are internal to it. The key external influences come from international treaties relating to copyright, EU directives before Brexit, and the human rights perspective. Chapter 1 helps ascertain the extent to which these external influences have an impact both on the assertion that copyright is a property right and on the analogy being drawn in the rest of the book with property rights in tangible things. A matter that is internal to property rights is the principle of *numerus clausus*. The chapter demonstrates the ways in which *numerus clausus* affects the conceptualisation of copyright as a property right. It shows how the progression of the spectrum of property rights draws legitimacy from the application of *numerus clausus* and the idea that property right develop in an incremental way.

Once the stage is set, Chapter 2 dives into exploring the thing-relatedness of copyright. Thinghood is one of the most quintessential aspects of property right in tangible things because the core concepts, principles, and doctrines that govern land and chattels all coalesce around the 'thing'. This monograph seeks to unpack thinghood in relation to tangible things and apply the findings to copyright by analogy, arguing for the possibility of an 'intangible thing'. This helps to counter the argument that there is nothing more to copyright than the rights, and to oppose the conceptualisation of copyright as a chose in action. Many of the analogies in the subsequent chapters cannot be developed successfully if it cannot be established as a foundational matter that the work demonstrates characteristics of a thing.

If we can establish the existence of a thing, the title to it can be acquired independently for the first time. Chapter 3 deals with the acquisition of copyright in this context. Copyright statutes provide for a method of first acquisition of copyright, which is different from entering into a contract. By analysing the rules of acquisition, this chapter shows that the method of acquisition of copyright is analogous to a combination of acquiring title to a tangible thing for the first time through accession by manufacture and the act of taking possession. The chapter argues that this is another reason why copyright can be distinguished from choses in action. This also enables the development of doctrines such as adverse possession and finders of goods by analogy.

While the Chapter 3 deals with the method of acquisition, Chapter 4 deals with the title that is acquired. It divides the chapter into exclusionary rights, exclusive powers, and exclusive privileges, all of which relate to the thing in copyright, that is, the copyright work. Of these, it regards the exclusionary rights as chronologically the first aspect to be acquired, because only once the rest of the world comes under an exclusionary duty can one speak of the ability to control or use the thing. This chapter provides a conceptualisation of exclusionary rights that is commensurate with the thing being intangible, by analogy with tangible things. This helps establish that the rights are separable from the thing. It goes on to examine the powers and privileges that the copyright owner acquires in relation to the copyright work, all of which again reinforce the argument that copyright should not be conceptualised as a chose in action.

Having examined the exclusionary rights, exclusive powers, and privileges, Chapter 5 examines what happens if these are infringed, by analysing the statutory tort of copyright infringement. Property rights, powers, and privileges in relation to tangible things are enforced by various torts, such as trespass, private nuisance, conversion, and negligent damage to property. In land law and personal property law, liability is strictest if the interference is direct and voluntary. But if the interference is indirect, even if it is voluntary the liability will only arise if the claimant can show undue interference. If the interference is involuntary, then only a liability in negligence is seen as apposite. However, in copyright infringement, whether the interference is direct or indirect, voluntary or involuntary, the liability arises without any variation of the fault element. Together with certain powerful remedies, such as account of profits and negotiating damages, copyright enforcement risks leading to unjust and unfair results. Chapter 5 examines the deficiencies of copyright infringement and proposes the doctrinal changes that can bring it in line with the property torts.

Whilst copyright lawyers point to the statutory defences as an *ex post* mechanism to balance competing interests, property theorists point to the number and nature of these defences to argue that these defences diminish the proprietary nature of copyright. Chapter 6 examines both statutory and non-statutory defences to copyright infringement and compares them to the defences to trespass and private nuisance. It argues that the justification for the defences to copyright infringement lies in the need for sharing in the use of copyright works due to their socio-cultural and educational significance, which is not too different from the need for sharing land due to its socio-economic significance. While private nuisance captures the balancing of competing interests *ex ante*, copyright defences engage in the balancing act *ex post*. This chapter also demonstrates that the limitations on the exploitation of copyright are comparable to limitations placed on the use of land and chattels by statute and common law. It drives home the point that neither the defences nor the limitations prevent copyright being a property right by analogy with tangible things.

One of the most important implications of thing-relatedness is the possibility of granting derivative interests. This embodies the power to carve out interests that are less than ownership. The design and content of these interests acknowledge the principle of *numerus clausus*. Chapter 7 deals with derivative interests that the copyright statutes themselves acknowledge, namely licences (exclusive and non-exclusive), assignments (partial and total), and security interests (by an extension of assignments). It also examines other interests less commonly discussed, namely the right to receive royalties, and options and rights of pre-emption. It assesses the ability of all these derivative interests to bind successors in title and impose trespassory liability on strangers from the perspective of *numerus clausus*.

The book ends with certain final remarks which bring together the discussions from the preceding chapters. It evaluates whether the twin objectives of the book were achieved. With the first objective it establishes how copyright being conceptualised by analogy with property rights in tangible things helps limit, curb, and contain the scope of copyright, from the conceptualisation of the work to its acquisition and enforcement, and the derivative interests. With the second objective it demonstrates how copyright being analogous to property rights in tangible things helps conceptualise a spectrum of property rights, with copyright being mapped closer to tangible things. It seeks thereby to pave the way for newer and more esoteric subject matter to undergo a similar analysis to be protected by property rights.

1
Setting the Stage

1. Introduction

Copyright is perceived as a specialised area of law with its own theoretical justification and internal logic to its statutory regime. To some extent, this is true, especially given the impact of technologies such as the gramophone, cinematography, and broadcasting in the twentieth century and the internet in the twenty-first century on copyright law. However, the specialised nature of copyright is not without external influences. History reveals that copyright has been the object of international treaties for more than a century. Furthermore, copyright law in the United Kingdom has also evolved in the context of the European harmonisation project. Over the years, copyright has also been viewed from the prism of human rights law. While these influences provide a context, at its core this book argues that the inner workings of copyright law have been developed with much the same deference to property theory as land law and personal property law. It is further argued that many of the doctrinal issues in copyright law can be addressed by maintaining a close analogy with land law and personal property law.

A discussion of copyright in the larger context of land law and personal property requires that the discussion is accessible to those less familiar with copyright law. Since much of the analysis in this book is about the analogies being drawn from land law and personal property law into copyright law, it makes sense to provide a primer on copyright law to assist a property theorist to appreciate the analogies being made. Copyright law has a vocabulary of its own and its semantics are doctrinally bound. In copyright we speak of 'works', 'originality', 'fixation', all of which are terminology derived from the statute and its interpretation in the case law. In copyright, we do not necessarily speak of a 'thing', 'possession', 'title', and so on, which are commonly used in the context of tangible assets. Before establishing conceptual connections between these vocabularies, it helps to provide a brief account of the salient features of copyright. Accordingly, Section 2 provides a primer on copyright law.

Copyright as Personal Property. Poorna Mysoor, Oxford University Press. © Poorna Mysoor 2025.
DOI: 10.1093/9780191954962.003.0001

The copyright law that we see today is the result of many external influences. Many aspects of UK copyright law are a result of the EU harmonisation process. The EU directives with the most sweeping effect on UK copyright law, namely the Information Society Directive (Infosoc Directive),[1] do not refer to the nature of copyright as personal property. But the case law of the CJEU has characterised copyright in a way that does not necessarily align with the conceptualisation of copyright under UK legislation and case law. The dynamic with EU law has changed since Brexit. Nevertheless, it is essential to appreciate this context and the impact of Brexit on copyright law. Section 3 gives a brief account of this context.

Copyright began attracting international attention in the latter part of the nineteenth century. Since then, international treaties and trade agreements have proliferated. In situating copyright in the international context, a concern arises as to whether asserting any of the characteristics of copyright as a personal property right derogates from any of the treaty obligations of the United Kingdom. Although the international treaties have generally been agnostic as to the manner in which copyright is conceptualised, it is worth noting their influence in shaping the subject matter that is covered by copyright laws worldwide. This is dealt with in Section 4.

The one context where copyright is recognised as personal property, or more accurately as a possession, is under article 1 of the First Protocol of the ECHR (A1P1).[2] Although A1P1 only refers to possession in general, the European Court of Human Rights has interpreted this provision to include intellectual property rights including copyright. The impact of this on copyright law is worth examining. This is dealt with in Section 5.

Once the boundaries with the other significant areas of law are drawn, Section 6 of this chapter looks inward and explores one of the most foundational principles of property theory, *numerus clausus*. Land law and personal property law in the United Kingdom only tacitly acknowledge the existence of *numerus clausus*, and therefore the very suggestion that intangible assets may need to adhere to *numerous clausus* can become a fraught issue. This necessitates a discussion on the issue at the outset, such that once the application of *numerus clausus* to copyright is established, the influence it exerts on different themes within the monograph can be laid out.

[1] Directive 2001/29/EC of the European Parliament and of the Council of 22 May 2001 on the harmonisation of certain aspects of copyright and related rights in the information society [2001] OJ L167/10.

[2] European Convention on Human Rights, Protocol No 1 to the Convention for the Protection of Human Rights and Fundamental Freedoms (Council of Europe Treaty Series No 005, 1950) art 1.

2. Copyright—a Primer

In the United Kingdom, the Copyright, Designs and Patents Act 1988 (CDPA) is the statute that governs the core aspects of copyright. It opens with the provision that asserts copyright as a property right.[3] This means that copyright can be described in the same way as a property right can be described in relation to land or personal property, which is as a composite of rights, powers, privileges, and immunities, and not merely claim rights in the Hohfeldian sense. Just as property rights in tangible assets relate to a tangible thing, copyright also relates to a thing that is a statutory construct called a 'copyright work'.[4] A work can be within any of the eight categories of works, namely, literary, dramatic, musical, and artistic works, together called authorial works, and sound recording, films, broadcasts, and typographical arrangements, together called entrepreneurial works. These works become copyright works when a person acquires copyright in them. It is important to appreciate that copyright is the name given to property rights that relate to copyright works as things, just as property rights can relate to land or chattels as things.

How does one acquire copyright? A person acquires copyright in authorial works if the person expresses them in an original way, and if these works are recorded in writing or otherwise.[5] A person acquires copyright in entrepreneurial works by investing resources and producing them in such a way that they are not copies of existing works.[6] Authorial works receive deeper protection in that it is not just the recorded expression that is protected but also the non-literal elements such as the theme, the story, and so on. For entrepreneurial works, only the work as it has been recorded is protected. The author is the first owner of copyright in the work they create, and the person who produces the entrepreneurial work is the first owner of that work.

The CDPA enumerates certain acts which it refers to as 'restricted acts'. These are copying, issuing copies to the public, performing in public, lending to the public, communicating to the public, and making an adaptation of the work.[7] The rights, powers, and privileges are all defined with reference to these restricted acts. This means that when a person acquires copyright, they have the right to preclude the rest of the world from exercising any of these restricted acts, and they have the power and the privilege to exercise these restricted acts

[3] CDPA, s 1(1).
[4] CDPA, s 1(2).
[5] CDPA, s 1(2) and (3).
[6] CDPA, ss 5A(2), 5B(4), 6(6), 8(2).
[7] CDPA, s 16(1).

at their own discretion. Therefore, copyright means a composite of rights, powers, and privileges, made up of acts exclusively reserved for the copyright owner. If any of the rights are infringed, the copyright owner can sue for infringement.[8] A court can grant the same remedies for copyright infringement as it would grant for the infraction of any property right.[9] The CDPA and copyright statutes generally in many jurisdictions provide for a wide array of defences. Some of the most important defences are the fair dealing defences. The CDPA identifies certain defined circumstances under which, if the dealing with the copyright work is fair, it can be put forward as a defence for copyright infringement. These circumstances include criticism, review, news reporting, parody, pastiche, instruction in a classroom, and so on.[10] Courts have developed a multifactorial approach to determining when a certain dealing with a copyright work by the defendant is fair.

The power to exercise the restricted acts enables the copyright owner to grant licences or any other interest in copyright. The privileges to exercise these restricted acts allow the copyright owner to do with their copyright work as they please. Copyright owners can grant exclusive or non-exclusive licences to perform any of the acts in relation to their works. They can also grant partial or complete assignment of their copyright interest. It is also possible for them to grant a security interest such as a mortgage or a charge.[11] In general, there are no restrictions on copyright owners to exploit their copyright. It is open to them to organise themselves to form collecting societies that help enforce their rights and provide efficient means to grant licences to their works. If these collecting societies refuse to grant a licence or charge too high a fee, it is possible for the affected parties to challenge this before the Copyright Tribunal. The Copyright Tribunal has a wide range of powers, including dictating a fair licence fee that the collecting societies can charge.[12]

3. Relationship with EU Law

When the United Kingdom was a member of the European Union, the CDPA was greatly impacted by the harmonisation of the laws in the internal market.

[8] CDPA, ss 17–21.
[9] CDPA, s 96.
[10] eg CDPA, ss 29, 30, and 30A.
[11] CDPA, s 90.
[12] CDPA, ss 149–51A.

EU directives are prescriptive in that they place an obligation on the member states to transpose the provisions into domestic law. EU directives, and in particular the Infosoc Directive,[13] have influenced to a great extent the way copyright legislation in the United Kingdom is shaped. However, post-Brexit, the directives that have been implemented into the domestic law as of the Implementation Period (IP) completion date, that is, 31 December 2020, have become part of the 'EU derived domestic legislation', unless amended by an act of Parliament.[14] Also, the case law of the Court of Justice of the European Union (CJEU) and its application by the domestic courts before the IP completion day, will be regarded 'assimilated case law' and will continue to apply to the United Kingdom, unless the Supreme Court decides to depart from it.[15]

Therefore, it is important to understand the background of the impact of EU law. The Infosoc Directive does not declare copyright to be a property right. As regards the nature of copyright, there are four salient aspects worth mentioning here. The first relates to thing-relatedness. The Infosoc Directive does not prescribe a closed list of protected works, whereas the CDPA categorises works and allows open-endedness of these categories in a limited way. Furthermore, one of the most important aspects of thing-relatedness of copyright, namely, fixation, is not required by the Infosoc Directive: a work does not have to be fixed in a material form for copyright protection to subsist. The CDPA, however, has always had a provision requiring copyright works to be recorded. Chapter 2, Section 3 discusses the implication of this divergence. Secondly, as regards exclusive rights, the CJEU's interpretation of the right of communication to the public has left us with questionable boundaries of this right. Chapter 4 examines the consequences of this. Thirdly, in finding infringement, the CDPA regards the taking of a substantial part as necessary. However, the Infosoc Directive has been interpreted by the CJEU case law to mean 'any part' being taken so long as it is original.[16] Chapter 5 examines the implications of this. Fourthly, Recital 32 of the Infosoc Directive declares that the directive contains an exhaustive enumeration of statutory limitations and exceptions, whereas the CDPA recognises a general public interest defence. Chapter 6 examines this apparent conflict.

[13] Infosoc Directive (n 1).

[14] European Union (Withdrawal) Act 2018, s 2. The IP completion date is defined in the European Union (Withdrawal Agreement) Act 2020, s 39(1) as 31 December 2020 at 11.00 pm UK time.

[15] European Union (Withdrawal) Act 2018, s 6(4)(a) and (7).

[16] Case C-5/08 *Infopaq International A/S v Danske Dagblades Forening* ECLI:EU:C:2009:465, paras 48–51.

4. Copyright and International Treaties

Let us begin with the international treaties that have a bearing on the nature of copyright. In terms of the content, the international treaties first set out to protect authorial works, namely, literary, dramatic, musical, and artistic works. The oldest of the treaties to do so was the Berne Convention (BC), first adopted in 1886 with the objective of bringing a degree of parity in the copyright legislation across the imperial powers.[17] In the following years, as the world saw innovation that affected copyright significantly, such as the gramophone, cinematography, and broadcasting technology, the BC was amended and expanded, such that authors in the signatory nations were protected against unauthorised exploitation of their works by these technological means. Protection of copyright was also extended to cinematographic films as authorial works.[18]

However, a more significant change took place when the investment made in enabling these technologies to disseminate authorial works was also sought to be rewarded with a property right. The focus was no longer authorial input in bringing about a work, but rather the entrepreneurial input in producing a sound recording and a broadcast that was going to be recognised as sufficient to attract copyright protection. The inclusion of sound recordings and broadcasts as protectable subject matter under the Rome Convention in 1961 has been one of the most controversial decisions in international copyright treaty-making.[19] The political influences on their inclusion for copyright protection cannot be denied. Whether and the extent to which the subject matter satisfies the requirements of a property right is a matter worth exploring. This discussion is also taken up further in Chapter 2.

The BC is not prescriptive on whether copyright is to be characterised as a property right under domestic law. However, a couple of points are worth noting. Article 2(2) of the BC leaves it 'for legislation in the countries of the Union to prescribe that . . . works shall not be protected unless they have been *fixed in some material form*'.[20] The United Kingdom has chosen to include it expressly under s 3(2), CDPA, in relation to literary, dramatic, and musical

[17] Berne Convention for the Protection of Literary and Artistic Works (1886).

[18] The CDPA recognises a cinematographic film as an entrepreneurial work, meaning it is not subject to the originality requirement. This makes acquisition of copyright easier under the CDPA than envisaged under the BC. The effect of this is discussed in Chapter 4.

[19] International Convention for the Protection of Performers, Producers of Phonograms and Broadcasting Organizations (UK accession date 26 October 1961) <www.wipo.int/wipolex/en/text/289757> (accessed 20 December 2024).

[20] Emphasis supplied.

works. As we shall see in Chapter 2, this provision has a profound impact on conceptualising copyright as a property right.[21] This book argues for this provision to be applied more strictly in relation to copyright works and defends this requirement as being an essential aspect of copyright subsistence.

Another provision that has an impact on copyright as a property right is art 5(2) of the BC, which provides that that the 'enjoyment and the exercise' of copyright shall not be subject to any formality. Formalities play a significant role particularly in relation to land. Formalities imbue property rights with essential qualities such as making them known to the public at large (publicity function). One cannot emphasise enough the importance of formalities such as registration in improving the tangible property systems, be it title by registration for land or the registration of secured transactions for personal property. Formalities can bring a great deal of certainty to the subsistence of rights and publicity to transactions. Indeed, the scholarly support for the bar on formalities appears to be dwindling.[22] In discussing copyright derivative interests, Chapter 7 provides further discussion.

Another treaty of great significance is the Agreement on the Trade-Related Aspects of Intellectual Property Rights (TRIPS), within the World Trade Organization (WTO) suite.[23] Among its provisions, one of the most important that impacts the thing-relatedness of copyright is art 9(2) that speaks of what cannot be protected. It states that copyright protection shall extend to expressions and not to 'ideas, procedures, methods of operation or mathematical concepts as such'. Not all copyright statutes embody this provision expressly. But this principle is well entrenched within the case law.[24] This provision goes a long way in demarcating the thing in copyright, and in the rules of acquisition of copyright. These aspects are discussed further in Chapters 2 and 3, respectively.

The arrival of the internet brought about further significant changes in the way copyright works are disseminated. As a result, the World Intellectual Property Organization (WIPO) Copyright Treaty was enacted expanding the exclusive rights granted to copyright owners to control dissemination of their works in the digital environment.[25] Among other things, it introduced

[21] See generally Poorna Mysoor, 'Form in Conceptualising Copyright as a Property Right' (2020) 67(1) J Copyright Soc'y USA 79.

[22] Stef van Gompel, *Formalities in Copyright Law: An Analysis of Their History, Rationales and Possible Future* (Kluwer Law International 2011).

[23] Agreement on the Trade-Related Aspects of Intellectual Property Rights (1995).

[24] eg *University of London Press v University Tutorial Press* [1916] 2 Ch 601; *Ladbroke v William Hill* [1964] 1 All ER 465.

[25] WIPO Copyright Treaty (adopted 20 December 1996).

the right of communication to the public under art 8. Member states implemented this provision, as did the United Kingdom under s 20, CDPA. As we will see in Chapter 4, this has been one of the most difficult exclusive rights to interpret.[26]

The principle that governs the remit of statutory limitations and exceptions is the so-called three-step test. It requires that limitations or exceptions to exclusive rights can only be recognised in certain 'special cases, provided that such reproduction does not conflict with a normal exploitation of the work and does not unreasonably prejudice the legitimate interests of the author'.[27] This provision has been interpreted to mean that the limitations and exceptions to copyright cannot be open-ended. One may argue that open-ended defences to the infringement of property rights dilute the property rights by widening the defences available, and therefore, to this extent, one can say that the international treaties strengthen the property rights approach to protection of copyright. This discussion is carried further in Chapter 5.

One of the greatest achievements of these international treaties is in enabling copyright enforcement across national borders. Under s 153(1), CDPA, a person qualifies for protection of their works under the CDPA if they satisfy the qualification requirements as regards the authorship, first publication of their work, or first transmission of their broadcast. A person qualifies as an author if at the material time they were connected to the United Kingdom by citizenship, domicile, or residence, and a corporation by its incorporation under the UK laws, but also to a person so connected with a signatory country of the BC, the WTO, or the Rome Convention.[28] A work qualifies for protection under the CDPA if it was first published in the United Kingdom or in any of the signatory countries of the BC, the WTO, or the Rome Convention.[29] A broadcast qualifies if it was first transmitted in the United Kingdom or a signatory to the Rome Convention.[30] In this way, what is essentially a nationally recognised property right can be enforced internationally. The reason for the international treaties to agree on minimum levels of protection is explained by the possibility of copyright enforcement transnationally.

[26] Poorna Mysoor, 'Unpacking the Right of Communication to the Public: A Closer Look at International and EU Copyright Law' [2013] IPQ 166.

[27] Berne Convention (n 17) art 9(2). Other treaties also provide for this. For example, the Agreement on Trade-Related Aspects of Intellectual Property Rights, art 13; the WIPO Copyright Treaty, art 10.

[28] CDPA, s 154(1) read with s 159(1) and (2).

[29] CDPA, s 155(1) read with s 159(1) and (2).

[30] CDPA, s 156(1) read with s 159(2).

5. Human Rights and Copyright

A1P1 states that all persons are 'entitled to the peaceful enjoyment of [their] possessions'. The European Court of Human Rights (ECtHR) has interpreted possessions in this context widely. It is no surprise that copyright qualifies as a possession under A1P1.[31] One may query whether this means that human rights discourse accepts copyright as a property right. It is worth noting that A1P1 does not appear to have used the term possessions in the strict property law sense. This is because the ECtHR has held, for example, that the economic interest in the running of a restaurant to serve alcoholic beverages can be regarded as a possession for the purposes of A1P1.[32] Furthermore, A1P1 is the provision that extends protection to property rights also in tangible things, including land.[33] This is even more compelling in demonstrating that A1P1 does not discriminate between tangible and intangible assets. The ECtHR's holding applies to copyright regardless of the way in which it is conceptualised. Peaceful enjoyment of possessions in the copyright context would be non-interference with the exercise of exclusive rights. Since an interference with the exercise of exclusive rights amounts to copyright infringement, a copyright owner can plead the A1P1 right in support of a claim of copyright infringement.

A1P1 is not an absolute right. It provides for two scenarios of justifiable state interference—the more invasive 'deprivation' of possessions, which can be only justified in the 'public interest', and less invasive 'control of use', which can only be justified by a law in the 'general interest'. The deprivation of possession could lead to copyright being denied altogether in a particular subject matter, by way of a state action, if it is justified in the public interest. Even if there is justifiable public interest, it is more likely that the exercise of copyright is denied rather than the very subsistence of copyright. To this extent, the difference between deprivation and control of use lies in the extent to which the copyright owner still has the ability to exercise any of the exclusive rights. An interference with the exercise of exclusive rights amounts to copyright infringement, in addition to the violation of the copyright owner's ability to control the use of their copyright. Therefore, the assertion of A1P1 can be justifiably resisted by showing general interest as being subsumed within one of the defences to copyright infringement.

In addition to relying on the justifiable interference that is built into A1P1, one can also rely on the interference with another right guaranteed under the

[31] *Dima v Romania* App no 58472/00 (ECtHR, 26 May 2005) para 78.
[32] *Tre Traktörer Aktiebolag v Sweden* (1991) 13 EHRR 309, para 53.
[33] *JA Pye (Oxford) Ltd v United Kingdom* (2008) 46 EHRR 45, para 38.

European Convention on Human Rights (ECHR) as the reason why the exercise of the A1P1 right should be denied or restricted. One of the most common competing rights put forward is the right to freedom of expression under art 10(1) of the ECHR. Article 10 protects not only the freedom to hold opinions but also to 'receive and impart information and ideas without interference by public authority and regardless of frontiers'. Although one can be seen to assert one's right to free speech in creating the copyright work, more often than not free speech is claimed as a defence against the assertion of copyright. Chapter 6 discusses the ways in which free speech arguments inform a successful defence and the ensuing remedy for copyright infringement.

Like the A1P1 right, there are grounds on which an interference with art 10(1) may be justified if prescribed by law and necessary in a democratic society. Article 10(2) sets forth a variety of circumstances, including the interests of national security, territorial integrity, or public safety; protection of reputation or *rights of others*; protection of confidentiality or impartiality of the judiciary, and so on, where the interference with the art 10(1) may be justified.[34] It can be difficult for a person to assert their right to freedom of speech against another person's copyright, because protection of copyright is justified as protecting the rights of others under art 10(2).[35] In this sense, copyright and free speech appear to have a dialectic relationship. Chapter 6 provides further discussion on the oscillation between assertion of copyright and defence of free speech.

6. The Abiding Principle of *Numerus Clausus*

The moment one speaks of a property right, the question of *numerus clausus* arises. *Numerus clausus* literally means the 'number is closed' and embodies the principle that the content and the number of property rights are limited.[36] Some courts have held that *numerus clausus* is a civilian concept having limited relevance to English property law.[37] Worthington supports this argument and lauds English law for having taken a different direction, as she is unconvinced about the benefits of this principle.[38] She argues that when applied

[34] Emphasis supplied.

[35] *Ashby Donald v France* App no 36769/08 (ECtHR, 10 January 2013) and *Frederik Neij v Sweden* App no 40397/12 (ECtHR, 19 February 2013).

[36] See generally, Bram Akkermans, 'The Numerus Clausus of Property Rights' in Michele Graziadei and Lionel Smith (eds), *Comparative Property Law: Global Perspectives* (Edward Elgar 2017).

[37] A recent example is *Bucknell v Alchemy Estates* [2023] EWHC 683 (Ch) [80].

[38] Sarah Worthington, 'Revolutions in Personal Property: Redrawing the Common Law's Conceptual Map' in Sarah Worthington, Andrew Robertson, and Graham Virgo (eds), *Revolution and Evolution in Private Law* (Hart 2018) 228, 234, 243.

in civilian jurisdictions, *numerus clausus* limits what things become property and what interests become property interests, although she believes that scholarly writing is unclear on these questions. She posits that this principle could be used to limit property rights only to tangibles, making a strict distinction between what is property and what is obligation. Yet, she rightly points out many instances in UK law where both the legislature and the courts recognise intangible things as property, giving the example of intellectual property and debts.[39]

Worthington's assertion that *numerus clausus* makes scholars confine their exploration to property rights in tangible things is certainly true. Most of the scholarly writing on *numerus clausus* supports limiting the number of property interests protected by law and prohibiting parties to a transaction from creating whimsical property interests. There is much less discussion on whether *numerus clausus* affects property rights in intangible assets in general and copyright in particular. This author agrees with Worthington on the fluidity in English law's understanding of property rights. Indeed, the idea of a spectrum of property rights that this book proposes is impelled by a pluralistic notion of property rights as opposed to a monolithic one. But it begs the question whether the principle of *numerus clausus* itself should be understood as rigidly as Worthington suggests. Importantly, is the notion of a spectrum of property rights incompatible with the principle of *numerus clausus*?

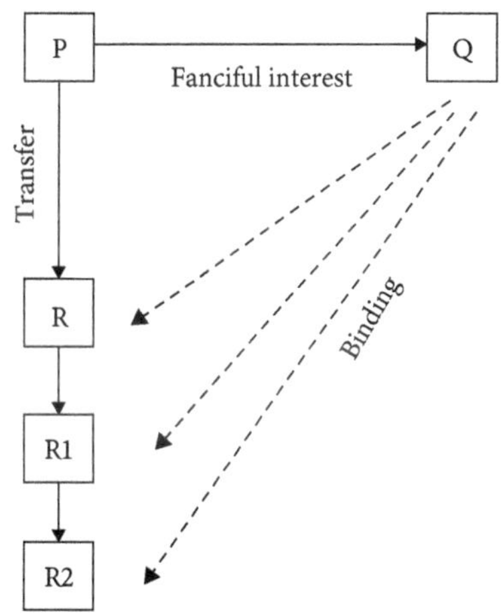

Figure 1.1 Successors in title and *numerus clausus*

[39] ibid.

It is not necessary for our purposes hereto rehearse the immense body of literature that exists on the meaning and logic behind *numerus clausus*.[40] To situate this principle in the context of copyright, a brief summary of the salient aspects of this debate would be sufficient. The basic idea generally put forward by scholars is that a property owner, P, should only be able to grant derivative interests in their property to another person, Q, that are recognised by law as one of a small number of interests (such as a lease, easement, and so on if the resource in question is land). Instead, if P can grant an interest to Q based on their whims and fancies, since property rights affect third parties, when P transfers her property right to R, a successor in title, the corresponding duty will be enforceable against R without their notice and without their consent. Rudden points to philosophical justifications for why this should not happen based on the Kantian theory of personhood and the Hegelian will theory that no duty should be imposed on a person without that person's consent.[41] The economic argument is that if there was no *numerus clausus*, then there could potentially be any number of interests, resulting in fragmented and burdened property rights, reducing their marketability to further successors in title, R1, R2, R3, and so on, as shown in Figure 1.1. However, as Epstein points out,[42] there are problems with each of these justifications, not least of which is the unavoidable interference with the autonomy of the transacting parties and their freedom of contract. He further argues that a robust registration system could deal with most of the difficulties with information costs and transaction costs.[43]

McFarlane foregrounds his arguments on *numerus clausus* beyond the context of property interests. He argues that rather than focusing on the effect of *numerus clausus*, a more convincing justification can be arrived at by focusing on the principle underpinning *numerus clausus*.[44] The principle, in his view, is that neither the parties to a transaction nor the courts can impose duties on persons without their consent. He points out that this allows us to make sense of *numerus clausus* not only in relation to successor liability arising from the duty imposed by a property right on the successors in title (R in the above

[40] For an extensive discussion of *numerus clausus* from a comparative perspective between English and German legal systems, see Ernesto Vargas Weil, *Stability and Change in Modern Property Law. A Comparative Approach to the Principle of Numerus Clausus* (Hart 2025) (forthcoming).

[41] Bernard Rudden, 'Economic Theory v. Property Law: The Numerus Clausus Problem' in John Eekelaar and John Bell (eds), *Oxford Essays in Jurisprudence: Third Series* (Clarendon Press 1987) 239.

[42] Richard A Epstein, 'Notice and Freedom of Contract in the Law of Servitudes' (1981) 55 S Cal L Rev 1353, 1360.

[43] ibid.

[44] Ben McFarlane, 'The *Numerus Clausus* Principle and Covenants Relating to Land' in Susan Bright (ed), *Modern Studies in Property Law*, vol 6 (Hart 2011) 311, 314.

example) but also trespassory liability arising from the duty imposed against the rest of the world, say S, when P grants the property right to Q, as shown in Figure 1.2. He argues that property rights binding successors in title focus only on those third parties who are connected with the holder of property rights either through a transaction or by the operation of the law (such as intestacy and bankruptcy). However, there is another more obvious class of people who are affected by the third-party effects of a property right. They are the rest of the world who have a duty of non-interference in relation to the thing. It is, after all, in the nature of property rights that they impose corresponding duties on the rest of the world. McFarlane posits that the scholarly writings of the past have not sufficiently appreciated the significance of *numerus clausus* in resisting the imposition of trespassory liability.[45]

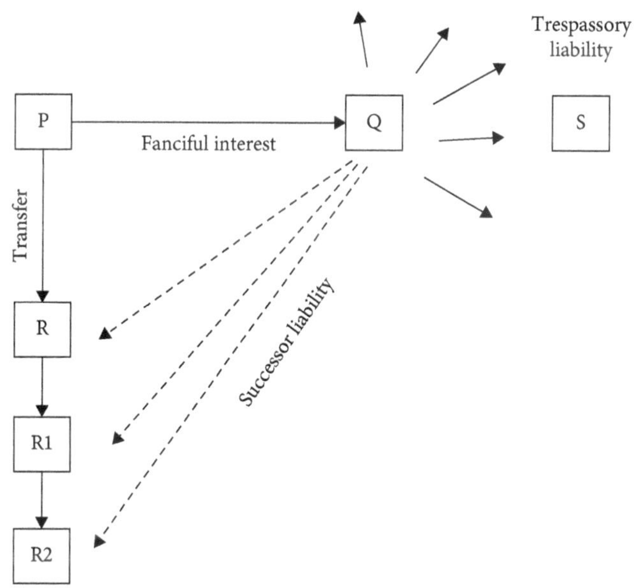

Figure 1.2 Trespassory liability and successor liability

McFarlane, and indeed other scholars, argue that English law should acknowledge the principle of *numerus clausus*.[46] In addition to the statutory embodiment of *numerus clausus* under s 1(1) of the Law of Property Act 1925,

[45] ibid 315.

[46] William Swadling, 'Property—General Principles' in Andrew Burrows (ed), *English Private Law* (3rd edn, OUP 2013) paras 4.09–4.11; Chris Bevan, 'The Doctrine of Benefit and Burden: Reforming the Law of Covenants and the Numerus Clausus "Problem"' (2018) 77 CLJ 72.

McFarlane argues that *Keppell v Bailey* supports *numerus clausus* as it relates to successor liability, and *Hill v Tupper* supports the principle as it relates to trespassory liability.[47] In *Keppell v Bailey*, the court refused to recognise a promise made by a certain group of persons that they and their successors in title would not procure limestone for their ironworks from any quarry other than the claimant's. The court held that this promise was not binding on the successor in title of that person. The basis was that 'great detriment would arise and much confusion of rights if parties were allowed to invent new modes of holding and enjoying real property'.[48] In *Hill v Tupper*, the court refused to recognise a right to put pleasure boats on a canal granted by a contract in favour of the claimant to be enforceable against a third party. The basis was that '[a] new species of incorporeal hereditament cannot be created at the will and pleasure of the owner of property'.[49] McFarlane also emphasises the role of analogy in incrementally expanding the applicability of property rights in newer contexts, giving the example of easements where the content is developed by analogy.[50]

Incrementalism points to some flexibility in the application of *numerus clausus*. Does English law take a different approach to the civilian jurisdictions? Swadling points to *National Provincial Bank v Ainsworth* as providing a different approach to *numerus clausus*.[51] In that case, the question was whether a deserted wife's right to stay in the matrimonial home was binding on the bank. Lord Wilberforce famously listed the criteria which must be satisfied before a right can be admitted to the list of property rights. These are that the right should be 'definable, identifiable by third parties, capable in its nature of assumption by third parties, and have some degree of permanence or stability'.[52] This meant that the list of property interests is closed only conditionally, with a possibility of the list being expanded if the conditions are met. However, Swadling points out that these criteria have been used only to reject new interests as property interests, and not for accepting them. While recognising that the list of equitable property rights is slightly longer as provided under s 4(1) of the Law of Property Act 1925, he

[47] Ben McFarlane, 'Tulk v Moxhay (1848); Hill v Tupper (1863)' in Charles Mitchell and Paul Mitchell (eds), *Landmark Cases in Equity* (Hart 2012) 2–3, where he points to cases which have not followed the principle of *numerus clausus*.

[48] (1834) 2 My & K 517, 536.

[49] (1863) 2 H & C 121, 127–28.

[50] McFarlane, 'The *Numerus Clausus* Principle' (n 44) 318.

[51] Swadling (n 46) paras 4.26–4.31.

[52] *National Provincial Bank v Ainsworth* [1965] AC 1175, 1247–48.

argues that it may not be possible for a new equitable property right to come into existence now.[53]

Nevertheless, it may be possible to argue that between the incrementalism highlighted by McFarlane and Lord Wilberforce's criteria, English common law does recognise some flexibility with the application of *numerus clausus*. Property rights are not envisaged to be as writ in stone as they might be in civilian jurisdictions. The principle may have more of a pragmatic and less of a dogmatic flavour in English law. That *Ainsworth* has not given rise to new property interests thus far does not mean it will be the case in the future, even if by setting forth only the bare minimum threshold requirements.

If one were to accept this, the next relevant question for this monograph is whether there are justifiable reasons for copyright law to embrace this principle by analogy. In their groundbreaking work on the economic justifications of *numerus clausus*, Merrill and Smith offer one of the most compelling and influential justifications in support of *numerus clausus*.[54] Their argument is based on the ability of *numerus clausus* to bring about optimal standardisation of property rights that reduces information costs associated with having to investigate the content of property rights and transaction costs for successors in title. For Merrill and Smith, it is not even a question that intellectual property in general and copyright in particular are subject to *numerus clausus*, although they do acknowledge that intellectual property demonstrates a weaker form of *numerus clausus*.[55] Mulligan also argues that normatively copyright should be subject to *numerus clausus*, but that in reality one does not find this to be the case.[56]

These scholars have demonstrated that there is nothing inherent in the principle of *numerus clausus* that necessitates the physicality of property, and that the principle applies in all situations where *in rem* rights are recognised in relation to a resource. Based on these observations, this book argues that as one of the most foundational limiting principles of property law, copyright should be governed by *numerus clausus*. It agrees with Mulligan that *numerus clausus*

[53] Swadling (n 46) paras 4.26–4.31.

[54] Thomas W Merrill and Henry E Smith, 'Optimal Standardization in the Law of Property: The Numerus Clausus Principle' (2000) 110 Yale LJ 1.

[55] ibid 19. Their focus is on the creation of new forms of intellectual property such as hot news and publicity rights, and the power of courts to create these rights. Others who have developed *numerus clausus* in the sphere of Law and Economics include Henry Hansmann and Reinier Kraakman, 'Property, Contract, and Verification: The Numerus Clausus Problem and the Divisibility of Rights' (2002) 31 JLS 373, emphasising the role of *numerus clausus* in aiding verification of property rights.

[56] Christina Mulligan, 'A Numerus Clausus Principle for Intellectual Property' (2013) 80 Tenn L Rev 235.

is of even greater significance in copyright than in relation to tangible property rights. It proceeds to demonstrate that the current copyright law at least in the United Kingdom is not agnostic to the principle of *numerus clausus*, though more could be done to ensure its compliance.

To justify why *numerus clausus* should underpin copyright, let us begin with the premise that duties cannot be imposed on third parties without their consent, whether the duties give rise to trespassory liability or successor liability. Even those who challenge the view that copyright has characteristics of a property right accept that copyright imposes duties on the rest of the world.[57] Let us unpack this using Figure 1.3.

The *in rem* nature of these duties is borne out by the copyright statutes.[58] These *in rem* duties can give rise to something akin to trespassory liability.[59] Copyright also gives rise to derivative interests such as partial assignments and exclusive and non-exclusive licences, and it would be worth examining whether these are property interests imposing successor liability. It should, therefore, be possible to argue that such duties cannot be placed on third parties without their consent, which means that copyright should also embrace *numerus clausus*. Each of trespassory and successor liability deserves examination.

Trespassory liability for copyright infringement is based on two components: first, what the infringer takes, that is, the subject matter, and secondly, how the infringer takes it, that is, the conduct of taking. Regarding the first component, this monograph argues that these exclusionary rights are mediated by the subject matter of copyright, which can be conceptualised as an intangible thing by analogy with tangible things. In case of tangible property rights, the subject matter is the physical thing to which the exclusionary right relates and is generally stable and well defined. Since the copyright subject matter, that is, the copyright work, is intangible, it requires the assistance of the law to determine the substantive content of the subject matter and to give it certainty of form, such that property rights may attach to it. As van Erp argues in relation to data as property, limiting the content of property rights means limiting the 'type of objects related to those property rights'.[60] Therefore, the

[57] Simon Douglas and Ben McFarlane, 'Defining Property Rights' in James Penner and Henry Smith (eds), *Philosophical Foundations of Property Law* (OUP 2013) 240.
[58] CDPA, ss 17–21.
[59] See Chapter 5, Section 2(a) for a discussion on why copyright infringement is akin to trespass.
[60] Stef van Erp, 'Ownership of Data: The Numerus Clausus of Legal Objects' (2017) 6 Brigham-Kanner Prop Rts Conf J 235.

content of the intangible thing that this monograph proposes to develop by analogy should also be limited.

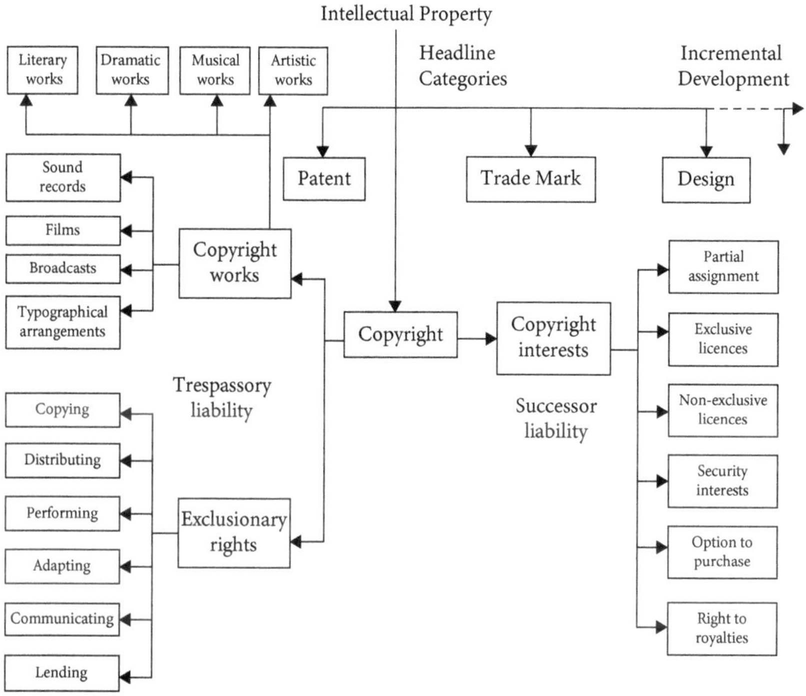

Figure 1.3 *Numerus clausus* in intellectual property and in copyright

Such limitation can be imposed in two different ways. The first is in relation to the number of types of things. The UK copyright statute provides for a closed list of categories of content that can be the subject matter of copyright, with some categories being developed *ejusdem generis*. One may liken this to how common law defines the headline requirements of an easement, leaving the substantive content of the easement to be developed incrementally by analogy.[61] This is an important limitation placed on copyright and any arguments to remove this should be resisted. The second limitation is in ensuring that if the law is stress tested to include a new entrant, the intangible thing should be defined based on the threshold attributes described by Lord Wilberforce in *Ainsworth*, such as definable, identifiable by third parties, and so on. Although

[61] McFarlane notes that the development of easements in an incremental way and by analogy is also an illustration of *numerus clausus*. McFarlane, 'The *Numerus Clausus* Principle' (n 44) 318.

Lord Wilberforce declared these to be the characteristics of property rights, it can hardly be argued that this description applies only to rights and not to the thing. After all, rights are in relation to the thing, and in particular this is the way in which this monograph conceptualises copyright. If the thing does not satisfy these characteristics, it would be difficult to regard a right relating to it as a property right. This idea can be further explored to help conceptualise the thing in copyright.[62] This is dealt with in Chapter 2, Section 3(a)(ii). In discussing thinghood in copyright, Chapter 2 provides the first insights into the application of the *numerus clausus* principle in copyright.

Regarding the second component, an infringer takes the thing in copyright context by exercising one or more of the exclusionary rights. The rest of the world has a duty not to exercise these rights. If a person were to avoid infringing copyright, they must know what they need to do, or, more precisely, what they should avoid doing. With tangible things the overarching duty involves the conduct of non-interference with the physical thing. Although the term 'interference' encompasses diverse actions, whether a person has interfered with a physical thing to invite liability is a factual matter that can be generally ascertained from the physical world. In case of copyright, the statutes enumerate specific rights in relation to the copyright work, which impose corresponding exclusionary duties. Courts can only interpret these rights according to their statutory remit clarifying the exclusionary conduct that one must engage in to avoid liability for infringement. If the courts' interpretation is so expansive that it makes infringers out of unsuspecting users of copyright works, then this could give rise to a *numerus clausus* problem. This will have to be fixed by interpreting the exclusionary right in an incremental way by analogy with pre-existing interpretations, and not in an indiscriminate way. This is discussed in Chapter 4.

Regarding successor liability, one must investigate whether it is possible to grant a property interest that is less than ownership—called a derivative interest. Copyright statutes state that copyright licences bind successors in title if they have notice. If a parallel were to be drawn with the law of tangible property, copyright licences are akin to equitable interests that only impose successor liability but not trespassory liability. However, exclusive licensees have the right of action to proceed on their own to sue infringers without having to join the copyright owner as a party. Further, copyright statutes also provide

[62] The Law Commission also uses these criteria extensively in relation to digital assets, another category of intangible assets. See Law Commission, *Digital Assets: A Consultation Paper* (Law Com No 256, 2022) para 5.39.

for partial assignment, seemingly permitting the copyright owner to slice and dice the copyright interest in any manner they wish. These provisions make it necessary for the *numerus clausus* principle to be examined also in relation to successor liability in copyright. To this extent, this monograph develops on Mulligan's work. It goes a step further to examine whether other interests such as the right to receive royalties, options and rights of pre-emption, and security interests need to also be brought under the principle of *numerus clausus*. The principle of *numerus clausus* affects the contours of all property interests including security interests. Further discussion on this is found in Chapter 7.

There are certain additional reasons why *numerus clausus* is particularly apposite as a guiding principle for copyright. Foremost is that there is no registration system in copyright. This means that the information costs in the operation of copyright are already higher than for other registered intellectual property rights. In addition, if *numerus clausus* has no role to play, this would result in unacceptable information costs. Rudden and others' arguments that a robust system of registration negates the need for *numerus clausus* does not apply to copyright. On the contrary, the principle of *numerus clausus* can help bring about much-needed stability in the content of the subject matter, exclusive rights, and a predictable definition of property interests.

Furthermore, one must appreciate the peculiarities of the trespassory liability in copyright. The moment a person acquires a property right, the rest of the world comes under a duty to engage in certain exclusionary conduct. In the tangible property context, although the person on whom this duty is placed could be an absolute stranger, the only time they interact with the property right is when they are in physical proximity to it. The physicality of the subject matter lends itself to a more limited number of interactions with the world at large, that is, with those who are in physical proximity to the thing. However, with copyright, since its subject matter can exist in digital form and be disseminated via the internet, third parties against whom the duty arises can be anyone across the globe. Therefore, the size of this class of third parties that is affected by the recognition of a new property right is much larger than in tangible property rights. This makes it imperative that the property rights are defined much more astutely.

Not only is *numerus clausus* more relevant to copyright, *Ainsworth* gives the required approach appropriate to copyright. As in land law, *Ainsworth* can also guide in copyright to reject aspects of a property right not in compliance with *numerus clausus*. If no new property interests have been approved in recent times in relation to tangible assets, it does not necessarily follow that no property interests will be admitted to the list also from among the intangible assets. Further, the design of property interests around newer forms of intangible assets can also give rise to newer situations unlike those confronted by land or chattels. The commercial importance of intangible assets in modern economies for their ability to create wealth makes it plausible that our legal systems could give birth to newer subject matter of property and newer property interests. *Ainsworth* as a celebrated case of English common law has a historic opportunity to guide the evolution of these property interests.

In the grander scheme of things, it is possible to argue that the development of intellectual property from the foundations of tangible property law itself is a demonstration of *numerus clausus.* Merrill and Smith attribute 'considerable stability in the recognized forms of intellectual property' such as copyright, trade marks, patents, and so on, to the principle of *numerus clausus.*[63] Accordingly, this monograph seeks to demonstrate that moving from tangible subject matter to intangible subject matter also shows the application of *numerus clausus.* It posits that *numerus clausus* is by no means contrary to the idea of a spectrum of property rights, but indeed a guiding light for the development of the spectrum. Although various forms of intellectual property have been introduced by way of legislative action rather than by the courts, it is arguable that the legislature is also led by the incremental way of developing property rights in relation to various subject matter. It is possible to show that in developing each of the different forms of intellectual property, the legislature may have had the threshold criteria of *Ainsworth* as the guiding light, even if it may never have been acknowledged to be so. Through the upcoming chapters, one will be able to see that copyright law in various aspects does abide by *Ainsworth* principles and, where it does not, it should do so such that the benefits of *numerus clausus* are fully achieved.

7. Summary

This chapter provides a context within which to situate the discussion in the chapters which follow and sets the stage by discussing the aspects of these influences that have a bearing on copyright as personal property. The relevance of this chapter lies in connecting the seemingly tangential strands drawn from disparate areas of law but still having some connection with copyright. There have been powerful external influences on the development of copyright, some from international treaties, some from EU directives, and indeed some from

[63] Merrill and Smith (n 54) 19.

human rights law. An analysis of these influences is not the focus of this book, but their existence should be acknowledged. Predictably, these influences may give rise to a certain scepticism as to the extent to which copyright can retain its nature as personal property. The rest of the chapters in this book argue that despite all these influences, copyright does retain its characteristic as personal property. The discussion on *numerus clausus* demonstrates the extent to which copyright can be examined by analogy with property rights in tangible things.

2
Thing-Relatedness in Copyright

1. Introduction

The centrality of the thing-relatedness to the conceptualisation of property rights is frequently questioned. At one extreme, we have scholars who believe that for a right to be a property right it must relate only to a physical thing,[1] and at the other we have scholars who believe that a right can be a property right even without it relating to a thing.[2] However, if there are a large number of duty holders, Smith argues that thinghood makes most sense because the thinghood's simplicity 'reduces the processing costs that would be high for such a large and anonymous audience'.[3] This explains why Pretto-Sakmann believes that one cannot misinterpret rights *in rem* as rights against persons generally.[4] They are rights to or in the thing or the *res*. When one views them along the spectrum of property rights that this book proposes, rights that relate to a thing demonstrate more convincingly the parameters for a property right than those that do not relate to a thing. The purpose of this chapter is to demonstrate that copyright is located closer to property rights in tangible things on this spectrum than to other intangible assets which cannot be meaningfully explained as relating to a thing. Doing so captures the characteristics of copyright more faithfully than if copyright were to be simply regarded as a right and nothing more. It also renders definite doctrinal benefits. The manner in which this can be achieved is by drawing an analogy between a tangible thing and the intangible thing that copyright protects.

Some scholars believe that it does not matter one way or another how copyright is conceptualised 'given the modern awareness of the specialised statutory regimes'.[5] It is also not common among copyright lawyers to ascribe thinghood

[1] eg Ben McFarlane, *The Structure of Property Law* (Hart 2008) 132.

[2] eg Chris Essert, 'Property in Licences and the Law of Things' (2014) 59 McGill LJ 559.

[3] Henry E Smith, 'Exclusion Versus Governance: Two Strategies for Delineating Property Rights' (2002) 31 J Legal Stud S453, S455.

[4] Arianna Pretto-Sakmann, *Boundaries of Personal Property: Shares and Sub-Shares* (Hart 2005) 92–93. In her view, the right to bodily integrity, though held against persons generally, is not a right *in rem*.

[5] Michael Bridge and others, *The Law of Personal Property* (3rd edn, Sweet & Maxwell 2022) para 9-006.

Copyright as Personal Property. Poorna Mysoor, Oxford University Press.
DOI: 10.1093/9780191954962.003.0002

to copyright explicitly. Instead, a popular way of addressing the nature of copyright is to bring it under the broad heading of 'subject matter' or 'subsistence' of copyright, and describe the categories of works that copyright protects, such as literary works, artistic works, and so on, and to explain the requirements such as originality, the need for works to be fixed, and so on.[6] Each of these attributes has a context when examined from the perspective of property theory which can help demonstrate that copyright indeed relates to a thing, albeit an intangible thing. By not appreciating precisely how these attributes align with thing-relatedness, the true nature of copyright will be masked.

It will not be an exaggeration to assert that thinghood has an impact on our understanding of the entire statutory framework within which copyright operates. Just as all aspects of the ontology of tangible property coalesce around the thing, all aspects of the ontology of copyright also coalesce around the intangible thing by analogy. In other words, establishing thing-relatedness of copyright convincingly enables the consequences of thing-relatedness of tangible property rights to follow by analogy. Arguments as to how title to copyright is acquired (Chapter 3),[7] what it means for exclusionary rights to arise in relation to copyright and what their content of the corresponding duties would be, and what it means to have exclusive powers and privileges in copyright and what it means to put copyright to use (Chapter 4), and what modes of enforcement and remedies are available (Chapter 5) are all predicated on an astute understanding of the thinghood of copyright. The centrality of this chapter to the subsequent chapters cannot be underestimated.

There are many theorists who have stepped back from the statute and have analysed copyright within the larger context of personal property. On the one hand, there are theorists who describe copyright as nothing more than a right, and therefore a chose in action.[8] On the other hand, there are those who acknowledge that the conceptualisation of copyright is inspired by the law governing tangible things. Bently et al describe intellectual property rights as property rights over intangible things.[9] The authors of *Cornish Llewelyn & Aplin* also acknowledge that intellectual property rights were developed by analogy with tangible property rights, although they argue that the analogy is incomplete because of the non-rival nature of information.[10] There are

[6] eg Lionel Bently and others, *Intellectual Property Law* (6th edn, OUP 2022) 62ff.
[7] See generally Poorna Mysoor, 'Possession in Copyright by Analogy' (2024) 140 LQR 277.
[8] Bridge and others (n 5) para 9-005.
[9] Bently and others (n 6) 3.
[10] David Llewelyn and Tanya Aplin, *Cornish Llewelyn & Aplin Intellectual Property: Patents, Copyrights, Trademarks & Allied Rights* (10th edn, Sweet & Maxwell 2023) paras 1.04–1.05.

certainly attributes that set copyright and indeed other types of intellectual property rights apart from tangible property rights. The non-rivalrous nature of information, which enables it not to be diminished by the simultaneous use of it by several persons at the same time, is one of the most important among these attributes. However, this monograph does not seek to establish copyright as being identical to property rights in tangible things. Its objective is to demonstrate that the true nature of copyright places it closer to property rights in tangible things on the spectrum of property rights, based on the analogies that can be drawn from them.

Some judges and jurists support the taxonomy of property between choses in possession and choses in action. Chose in possession or thing in possession refers to a thing of which one can take possession, have it, and use it. Classically, the idea of possession is also connected closely to taking physical control, and therefore a chose in possession only refers to tangible things. A chose in action refers to a thing in relation to which a person can have no possession or enjoyment but is a mere right enforceable by action.[11] Based on this classification, some theorists have argued that since copyright cannot be a chose in possession, it should be a chose in action. Section 2 examines the basis and the binary nature of this classification. It argues that even if one were to accept that copyright does not fit within choses in possession, it cannot be characterised as a chose in action either. It posits that the singular focus on the actionability of rights to the neglect of the actual resource being protected by copyright renders this conceptualisation inadequate.

The inadequacies of the chose in action conceptualisation pave the way for Section 3, where the thing-relatedness of copyright is considered. Property theorists have resisted the idea of an intangible thing. To them, the idea of a thing is so entrenched in the physical things in their mind that it may appear to them to be contrived to extrapolate the attributes of a thing to intangible assets. Section 3 drives home the argument that the existence of an intangible thing in copyright is not a figment of anyone's imagination but is indeed based on close analogies with the salient characteristics of tangible things. It argues that just as tangible things consist of substantive content that is separable and has a form, copyright subject matter is also made up of substantive content that is separable and has a form.

Section 4 deals with the benefits of the analysis of the intangible thing in copyright. It takes each of the components of the intangible thing analysed

[11] Howard W Elphinstone, 'What is a Chose in Action' (1893) 9 LQR 311, 312.

in Section 3 and demonstrates how it can make a difference to the doctrinal understanding of copyright.

2. Copyright as a Chose in Possession?

In the 1890s, an influential debate ensued between property theorists as to the definition of choses in action, and importantly, what resources qualify as choses in action, penned as a series of articles in the *Law Quarterly Review*. Copyright was a particular focus of some of these articles. Of these, it is worth considering the arguments put forward by Williams as they pertain to copyright. He argues that copyright is not a chose in possession because no one can have and take physical possession of copyright.[12] Williams essentially asserts that all incorporeal things are of the nature of things consisting in action because no one can take physical possession of them.[13] In effect, his argument is that copyright is a chose in action because it is not a chose in possession. Let us investigate the strength of these arguments.

The classification of chose in action and chose in possession boils down to separating tangible and intangible things, which is a crude basis for this classification. While physicality certainly impacts the manner of regulation, it cannot be the sole basis for classification, especially in modern times when intangible assets are of varied type and significance. Copyright is exactly the kind of resource that may not fit neatly within either chose in possession in the physical sense, or within chose in action despite being intangible. This makes the classification archaic, incomplete, and not fit for purpose.

The problem deepens when this classification is regarded as binary—the blinkered idea that there is no third category, ignoring the diversity among intangible assets. In *Colonial Bank v Whinney*,[14] Lindley LJ had observed that although debts, shares, and copyrights are all incorporeal personal property, 'they are so different in their nature and legal incidents, that care must be taken not to be misled by giving them all a common name which conceals their differences'.[15] However, Fry LJ famously insisted on the binary classification of all assets into choses in possession and choses in action, and nothing in-between, and the House of Lords agreed with him.[16] Despite this, the claim that choses

[12] T Cyprian Williams, 'Property, Things in Action and Copyright' (1895) 11 LQR 223, 225–27.
[13] ibid 224.
[14] (1885) 30 Ch D 261.
[15] ibid 284.
[16] (1886) 11 App Cas 426, 439–40, 447–48.

in possession and choses in action exhaustively cover all property rights should be examined more closely. The conclusion that all intangibles are the same is taxonomically and doctrinally incorrect. It is imperative that we have a more sophisticated classification of property rights where resources are assessed not based on the sole attribute of tangibility.

Whilst in recent times courts are waking up to the fallacy behind this classification,[17] this classification still holds much sway.[18] The inadequacies of the binary classification of choses in action and choses in possession have received much attention. The Law Commission's Consultation Paper on Digital Assets has challenged the classification, arguing for the digital assets to be accommodated in a third category. However, the Paper does not regard copyright as relating to a thing, because in their view copyright subject matter is 'pure information'.[19] This is conceptually and doctrinally incorrect as there cannot be any copyright in pure information. This will be further elaborated in Section 3 below.

At the centre of the argument of taking possession is the physical thing. If the possibility of the existence of an intangible thing is acknowledged, then the fallibility of the binary classification becomes immediately apparent. It has been a struggle for property theorists to conceptualise or support the existence of an intangible thing. In their view, since a coherent understanding of an intangible thing is not possible, anything intangible is indistinguishable from the rights themselves.[20] Copyright is a good example of this. Pretto-Sakmann has argued that these theorists fear that recognising these rights as property rights risks impinging on the boundaries carefully drawn between what qualifies as property as opposed to obligations.[21] This is because all rights, including rights that arise from a contract, look the same to these theorists. This line of thinking appears to underlie the conceptualisation of all intangibles as choses in action. To correct this, as a starting point, we need a conceptualisation of an intangible thing that can help distinguish between the thing and the right, although both are intangible. We also need this conceptualisation to help distinguish the intangible things from assets that consist only of rights, such as contractual debt for example. This requires the appreciation of the defining features of a thing that can be extrapolated beyond its physical manifestation. Pretto-Sakmann

[17] *AA v Persons Unknown* [2019] EWHC 3556 (Comm).

[18] Bridge and others (n 5) para 9-003.

[19] Law Commission, *Digital Assets: A Consultation Paper* (Law Comm No 256, 2022) paras 1.13–1.17, 3.62.

[20] Bridge and others (n 5) para 9-005.

[21] Pretto-Sakmann (n 4) 105–06.

also agrees that that can placate the fears of the merging of property rights with obligations.[22]

The acknowledgment of the thing also makes copyright more like a chose in possession. During the 1980s debate on choses in action, there were theorists who also offered other reasons why copyright might be a chose in possession. The basis on which Williams asserted that copyright is a chose in action makes Elphinstone wonder whether copyright was regarded as a chose in action for 'want of better classification'.[23] Among the reasons Elphinstone gives are that the rights of the copyright owner do not arise from contract, nor do they arise over a specific chattel, nor against any particular person; rather, they are rights that are enforceable against the whole world.[24] As will be argued in Chapter 3, acquisition of copyright bears much closer analogy with taking possession of tangible assets than it does with the acquisition of any chose in action. Remarkably, Sweet posits that the essential quality of copyright is that it is 'permanent property' even if it is not necessarily perpetual, but 'wholly different from such transient things as debts and other rights of action'.[25] A debt may be paid off at any time, affecting the duration for which the right is in existence, but, once copyright comes into existence, it lasts for the whole duration set by the statute.[26]

Taking the instance of copyright assignment, Brodhurst argued that it is incorrect to characterise copyright as not being capable of possession and enjoyment. He argued that unlike creditors who have neither possession nor enjoyment of the money owed to them until they receive the money, a copyright assignee has enjoyment as soon as the assignment is executed.[27] It may be noted that even without assignment, copyright in the hands of the owners themselves behaves exactly the same way as it does in the hands of the assignee of that interest. The owner of copyright is able to enjoy copyright from the moment copyright arises in the same way as an assignee upon assignment. But since possession is understood as physical control and there is no physical control in copyright, Brodhurst argues for constructive possession. This is an expression used when a person does not have physical possession, but only a right to possession which the law allows him to exercise as if he were in

[22] ibid 105.
[23] Elphinstone (n 11) 312.
[24] ibid 314.
[25] Charles Sweet, 'Choses in Action' (1895) 11 LQR 238, 315.
[26] The duration stands at author's life plus seventy years in the United Kingdom for authorial works. The duration of entrepreneurial works differs depending on the kind of work. See CDPA, ss 12–15.
[27] Spencer Brodhurst, 'Is Copyright a Chose in Action' (1895) 11 LQR 64, 71–73.

physical possession. Brodhurst argues that this can be extended to a situation where a person is not in physical control owing to the nature of the resource, whereby the law might continue to recognise his control over the resource as if the resource were physical.[28] It may not be necessary to stretch the concept of possession beyond its physical connotation. As discussed in Chapter 3, a meaningful analogy can be drawn between possession of physical objects and acquisition of copyright.

Brodhurst has further argued that copyright is indeed a chose in possession on the basis that 'an action against an infringer is in respect of a new and distinct cause of action, and reduces into possession not the right but the damages for violating it'.[29] With a debt, one sues for the realisation of the debt, even if it is with interest, which in any event is calculated based on the amount of the debt outstanding. The right to this amount arises at the time the debt arises. However, for copyright infringement the damages awarded represents the redress for the right infringed, which may be anything from nominal damages to substantial ones. This is exactly the same as the consequences that ensue from the infringement of rights to tangible things. Furthermore, injunctions and proprietary remedies such as negotiating damages and accounts of profit can also be awarded to redress copyright infringement in the same way as they can be awarded for trespass, private nuisance, and conversion.

It is, however, acknowledged here that copyright may not be a chose in possession in exactly the same way as tangible things are. Nevertheless, the view of copyright as a chose in action at best portrays an incomplete picture of copyright as it suggests that one does not need to go beyond the exclusionary rights to find the asset being protected in copyright. It conflates the right with the subject matter. Copyright grants exclusionary rights, exclusive powers, and exclusive privileges in relation to works of literature, art, music, drama, film, and so on. However, the very purpose of copyright legislation across the globe is the protection of these works as the subject matter. The subject matter must mean something and have a place within the conceptualisation of copyright. This brings us to the discussion in Section 3, which deals with the subject matter of copyright and the manner in which it conforms to the requirements of a thing.

[28] ibid 73. Referring to the requirement of the markings of taking physical control, Brodhurst argues that the assignee of copyright registering himself at the Stationers' Hall would count towards this, ibid 73–74. But it is worth noting that this formality is no longer required.

[29] See the editorial note at the end of the article. Brodhurst (n 27) 75.

3. Work as a Thing

There are many theorists who have considered the question of what constitutes a thing. Some of their conceptualisation is deliberately at a high level of abstraction such that the description of the thing at this level holds good regardless of the resource under discussion—tangible or intangible. For example, Newman defines the thing as 'a discrete and intelligible nexus of human activity with respect to which actions by different persons are likely to come into conflict'.[30] Smith explores the thing-relatedness of property based on the modular theory from the perspective of information costs. He regards things as 'modules' that hide information and interact with other modules only in limited and standardised ways through their interfaces.[31] He argues that intellectual property is highly responsive to the modular theory.[32] Each conceptualisation has its own purposes. For Newman, the objective appears to be, among others, to respond to a conceptualisation of property rights that is neither too physically centred as argued by McFarlane nor too distant from it as posited by Essert. For Smith, the focus is the architecture of the property system as a whole.[33] The quest here is rather more modest—what constitutes the thing for copyright that serves as a coherent extension of a tangible thing. The focus is on the characteristics of a thing that can help describe the tangible as well as the intangible thing.

Some theorists have considered thinghood in copyright; prominent among them is Rahmatian. Rahmatian contends that a property right is an abstract concept created by law. As such, he argues that it does not matter whether the thing, or what is called the *res* in Roman Law, is tangible or intangible.[34] This also aligns with Pretto-Sakmann's arguments already recounted. Accordingly, Rahmatian asserts that the dematerialised property that copyright is, consists of an original work that is recorded in some permanent form.[35] While it cannot be denied that the law has the ultimate say in declaring something as property, it is doubtful whether the law can make any object a *res*, regardless of its characterstics. To take Penner's example, could the law declare property in our talents, our personalities, and our friendships?[36] The answer must be in the negative because there are certain irreducible characteristics that the subject

[30] Christopher Newman, 'Using Things; Defining Property' in James Penner and Michael Otsuka (eds), *Property Theory: Legal and Political Perspectives* (CUP 2018) 90.
[31] Henry E Smith, 'Property as the Law of Things' (2012) 125 Harv L Rev 1691, 1701–03.
[32] Henry E Smith, 'Intellectual Property as Property: Delineating Entitlements in Information' (2007) 117 Yale LJ 1742, 1748, 1782.
[33] Smith, 'Property as the Law of Things' (n 31) 1694.
[34] Andreas Rahmatian, *Copyright and Creativity* (Edward Elgar 2011) 3, 5.
[35] ibid 14.
[36] James Penner, 'The Bundle of Rights Picture of Property' (1996) 43 UCLA L Rev 711, 799.

matter of property should have before the law considers it as a *res*. Rahmatian does list the characteristics of copyright *res*, such as originality, fixation, and so on, but it is unclear why these characteristics matter to the recognition of the *res*. In particular, it is not clear how the conceptualisation of *res* progresses from tangible to intangible assets and what characteristics of copyright help make this journey. We need a conceptualisation which locates these analytically distinct requirements within the property discourse.

Without using the terminology of thinghood, Pila examines the subject matter of intellectual property using certain devices of philosophy such as categories, properties, types and tokens, and artefacts. She provides an exhaustive list of all the requirements for protection of copyright works, conceptualising the subject matter of copyright as a 'bounded expressive object' that satisfies the requirement of originality.[37] The Court of Justice of the European Union (CJEU) conceptualises the subject matter of copyright as an original expression that is sufficiently identifiable.[38] This is not analytically accurate. In simple terms, originality is what makes a work its author's own. As such, for analytical clarity, originality should be examined in the context of acquisition of copyright. As will be seen from Chapter 3, originality is discussed under the topic of acquisition, rather than under the nature of copyright as a property right. Some scholars, such as Gordon, regard the need for works to be fixed in a material form as drawing the boundaries of the subject matter, which then brings about the thinghood in copyright.[39] While this requirement does play a significant role also in the analysis adopted in this chapter, there is more to the intangible thing in copyright than the need for fixation. It is essential, therefore, to unpick each attribute of the thing from the context of tangible property law and give it a meaningful context within copyright.

What do land and personal property lawyers say about the thing? In the vast majority of cases involving tangible assets, courts do not have to analyse the characteristics of the thing. Its physical existence makes it a non-issue. Tangible things qualify as resources or things of value, the access and exploitation of which a legal system regulates. McFarlane speaks of a presumption that all physical objects can qualify as the content of subject matter of a property right, but he admits that the nature of certain physical objects may make the idea of having a property right to them 'distasteful, inappropriate or otherwise unwelcome'.[40] Speaking of the attributes of a thing, McFarlane

[37] Justine Pila, *The Subject Matter of Intellectual Property* (OUP 2017) 63, 142, 146.
[38] Case C–310/17 *Levola Hengalo v Smilde Foods BV* [2019] ECDR 2, paras 40–41.
[39] Wendy Gordon, 'Copyright as Property' (1989) 41 Stan L Rev 1343, 1380–83.
[40] McFarlane (n 1) 137.

states that at a minimum the thing must be an external object in that it must be capable of being physically located.[41] Being physically located means that the thing must have a form which defines its physical boundaries,[42] and as an external object a thing must exist outside the human body. This means that a person cannot have a property right over a human being's body,[43] despite the human body having a physical form independent of another human being. One may point to moral and ethical reasons, among others, as to why this is so. The question of the substantive content of the subject matter, therefore, must be resolved at a normative level, even if a thing has a physical form and an external existence. A legal system must ask these questions relating to the substantive content because the exclusionary mechanism of a property right relates to such content, and therefore its impact on society must be assessed.

How does this assist with copyright? As explained in Chapter 1, copyright protects both authorial and entrepreneurial works. Broadly speaking, authorial works such as a poem or a musical tune are products of the human mind. If these remain in the human mind, they cannot be regarded as an external object or a thing for our purposes. The law has simply no eyes to see what is within the human mind. For these works as products of the human mind to become things, they must be separated from the human body, meaning that they should be expressed. But not all expressions can become the subject matter of copyright. There are rules governing the substantive content of copyright in that the substantive content needs to pass certain normative tests. Once expressed, it should be capable of existing outside the human body, which means that it must acquire a form. The acquisition of the form plays a crucial role in completing the process of a thing coming into existence for copyright purposes, so that the duties owed by the rest of the world can be appropriately directed. Entrepreneurial works like sound recordings and films also need to satisfy these requirements. As this author havs argued elsewhere,[44] one can speak meaningfully of a thing in copyright called a 'work' because, at a minimum, it has the following characteristics, namely it:

(a) has a substantive content;
(b) which is separable; and
(c) has a form.

[41] ibid 4.
[42] Ben McFarlane and Simon Douglas, 'Property, Analogy, Variety' (2022) 42(1) OJLS 161.
[43] *Yearworth v North Bristol NHS Trust* [2010] QB 1 [30].
[44] Mysoor, 'Possession in Copyright by Analogy' (n 7).

There is no statutory definition of a work, although Sherman describes it as a 'common denominator' that can be used to describe those that are either authorial or entrepreneurial in origin.[45] Whilst (b) and (c) above describe the outward characteristics of the work, (a) refers to its inner constituent. It is arguable that many intangible assets might satisfy the characteristics (b) and (c), such as contractual debts, but the existence of the substantive content makes copyright distinguishable from these rights. The substantive content is the valuable resource, the access to which is at the heart of the statutory regulation, and which imbues copyright with the characteristics and consequences of a thing.

The Law Commission also identifies certain components for digital assets to be regarded as a thing,[46] some of which overlap with the criteria proposed above. Although copyright is not its central focus, it claims that a work is pure information, which is protected only to the extent the statute provides.[47] It is argued here that the normative requirements prevent pure information from being the content of copyright. In relation to digital assets, the Law Commission also proposes that the thing must be independent of the legal system.[48] In its Consultation Paper, the Law Commission argued that the thing in copyright is not independent of the legal system. This chapter welcomes this aspect of separability analysis but argues that the substantive content in copyright is not only separable from the legal system but also from the right. The Law Commission also lists rivalrousness as an essential criterion. It will be argued in the following paragraphs that rivalrousness is not a determinative characteristic of a thing so long as it has a form.

(a) Substantive Content of the Work

The importance of the substantive content of the thing to the property right cannot be underestimated. Tangible things also have substantive content, but because the substantive content cannot be separated from the tangible thing itself, it is not noticed nor is it theorised or analysed separately. Its effects are ubiquitous. For example, at a very fundamental level, if the substantive content is land, the regulation that applies is different from if the substantive content is a bicycle. The manner in which one takes and retains possession differs.

[45] Brad Sherman, 'What is a Copyright Work?' (2011) 12 Theoretical Inq L 99, 111.
[46] Law Commission, *Report on Digital Assets* (Law Com No 412, 2023) para 4.5.
[47] Law Commission Consultation Paper (n 19) para 3.62.
[48] Law Commission Report (n 46) para 4.5(2).

The content of the exclusionary rights, exclusive powers, and exclusive privileges and the manner of enforcing them change. The defences available for their enforcement differ and finally, the kind of derivative interests that arise from them also changes. Even within the category of chattels, the difference in substantive content matters significantly. The manner of taking possession of an aircraft, a car, and a pencil is markedly different, as are the rights, powers, and privileges that arise in relation to them. But the law still manages to extend rules of property law to different substantive content by conceptual analogy. The ambition in this book is to extend this conceptual analogy from the content that is tangible to content that is intangible. It is the intangible content that helps to establish an existence of the intangible thing independent from the right. Accordingly, the aim is to distinguish copyright from other intangible assets at the same time.

That work has substantive content is part of our everyday ontology. The intuitive meaning of a work in ordinary language also refers to something that has been presented to the rest of the world, such as 'work of art', 'body of work', and so on. Just as the substantive content determines the kind of rules of property law that apply as explained above, in the same manner the attributes of the work shape the rules of copyright. Therefore, it is imperative that one pays closer attention to the conceptualisation of the work. As Marinotti asserts, especially in relation to intangible things, the thinghood should be meaningful because all relevant parties must be able to 'discern and agree upon the lines drawn'.[49] The following paragraphs deal with these attributes.

(i) Work as a normatively acceptable entity

The exclusionary rights, exclusive powers, and exclusive privileges of the holder of the property right are in relation to this substantive content, whether it is land, chattels, or a work. Since the granting of these rights, powers, and privileges has an impact on the rest of the world and their access to the resource, it is important for the law to make normative choices. The assessment should pertain to whether such substantive content should be subject to the exclusionary rights and whether such powers of control and privileges of use should be privately vested, before taking any further step in formalising the law. Depending on the kind of substantive content, exclusionary rights are bound to have an impact on one or more of public policy, socio-economic, cultural, moral, and ethical considerations, to name a few. The impact will be different on different sections of society, all of whom are stakeholders whose interests

[49] Joao Marinotti, 'Possessing Intangibles' (2022) 116 Northwestern Univ L Rev 1227, 1257.

often compete with one another. The law should weigh these considerations and balance these interests. This may be regarded as a process of assessing the normative eligibility of the substantive content to be the subject matter of a property right.

The assessment of normative acceptability of the substantive content of a thing is not unique to copyright, or indeed intangibles generally. Even in relation to certain tangible things, the assessment as to the normative fitness of the content of the thing is examined. For example, with the parts or products of the human body, once separated, many considerations go into whether these should go on to become the subject matter of a property right. These range from moral, ethical, and philosophical considerations to public health and public policy considerations. This is a highly contested area of law (and philosophy) and competing views exist on this issue.[50] While it is outside the scope of this monograph to dwell upon the desirability of property rights in body parts, it suffices to state here that complex considerations go into deciding the normative eligibility of this and generally any subject matter. In *Yearworth*, courts in the United Kingdom have decided that body parts and products can be the subject matter of property rights for the limited purpose of granting relief in the tort of conversion.

Returning to copyright, let us begin the discussion with authorial works. Ideas cannot be the content of subject matter because the law seeks to leave these free as the building blocks of culture, communication, innovation, creativity, and expression.[51] Ideas in this context are those that exist in the external world and can provide the raw material for the human mind to create works.[52] Leaving ideas free enables these to be available to all, resulting in a greater amount of knowledge being created. Accordingly, the considerations that weigh against the protection of ideas are educational, socio-cultural, economic, and public policy reasons. Ideas can be embedded in the style of writing in a literary work (eg ballads) or its topic (eg land law), the genre of music (eg folk) or dance (eg ballet), or the style of painting (eg impressionist) or its topic (eg a courtroom), to name a few. If these abstract entities could constitute eligible content of copyright, then it would result in exclusionary rights, exclusive powers, and privileges being recognised in relation to these entities,

[50] See eg Stephen R Munzer, 'An Uneasy Case Against Property Rights in Body Parts' (1994) 11 Soc Phil & Pol'y 259. And see William Boulier, 'Sperm, Spleens, and Other Valuables: The Need to Recognize Property Rights in Human Body Parts' (1995) 23 Hofstra L Rev 693.

[51] Bently and others (n 6) 234.

[52] John Locke defines ideas simply as objects of thinking. For philosophical discussion, see John Locke, *An Essay Concerning Human Understanding*, (1689), bk II, ch I: Of Ideas in General. <www.gutenberg.org/files/10615/10615-h/10615-h.htm> accessed 10 November 2024.

preventing their free access and use. One can hardly think it acceptable to have one textbook on land law or one composition in folk and so on, for the duration of the copyright if these abstract entities were to be protectable.

The Law Commission states in its Consultation Paper that 'an underlying . . . work . . . [in] copyright . . . comprising [of] information is . . . not of itself property. It is instead pure information.'[53] The overall argument of the Law Commission is that the thing in copyright is the right itself, which will be addressed more fully in Chapter 4. For our purposes here, the claim that a work is pure information needs to be tackled. The law of copyright has always been clear that pure information can never be a work. The same dangers that arise if ideas as abstract entities are protected as works follow if pure information is protectable as a work. Pure information such as procedures, methods of operation, or mathematical concepts are expressly prohibited from protection under Art 9(2) of the WTO Agreement on Trade Related Aspects of Intellectual Property (TRIPS Agreement). Further decisions such as *Ladbroke v William Hill*[54] are very clear that pure information cannot be protected. The Law Commission uses the adjective 'pure' to distinguish the information from the medium in which it is stored and to distinguish that which looks like information but is more than information.[55] Indeed, both these aspects are dealt with in copyright law. A work is only protected when it acquires a form, as we will see in Subsection 3(c) below. As will be discussed in Chapter 3, what copyright protects is more than information because it is only when a person exercises their intellectual qualities to transform the information that copyright can be acquired in it.

As regards entrepreneurial works, the exclusionary rights do not extend to protection of the content of the entrepreneurial works. For example, if P produces a film based on Q's novel, and if R infringes the copyright in Q's novel by taking a scene from it in his play, then it is Q who has the right of action against R for copyright infringement, and not P. P's rights only extend to the record that film is. Chapter 5 discusses this further. For our purposes here, if the entrepreneurial works are a record of an authorial work, as P's film is in the above example, then the film as a work will have satisfied the normative requirements discussed above if the novel has satisfied these requirements. If the entrepreneurial works are made of content that cannot be protected, such as a sound record of a lion roaring, or the film or broadcast of a sporting event,

[53] Law Commission Consultation Paper (n 19) para 3.62.
[54] [1964] 1 All ER 465, 473 (Lord Evershed).
[55] Law Commission Consultation Paper (n 19) para 3.6(1) and (2).

it does not pose significant normative issues. This is because the copyright protection extends only to the record and not to the content itself.

Other than ideas and pure information, copyright does not exclude content on the basis of moral or ethical grounds. In the earlier part of twentieth century, there were cases where courts excluded immoral subject matter from being recognised as works in the first place.[56] In subsequent years, courts have not barred copyright substing in the work but might decline to enforce copyright in it if a claim for infringement is brought.[57] Even if ideas and pure information are left free, there is an acknowledgement within copyright law that copyright protection even for works may have a far-reaching impact on society. Given the socio-economic, cultural, and educational considerations, copyright does not grant perpetual protection, but its duration is and has always been limited by statute. Upon the expiry of the term, the property right disappears, and the content becomes part of the public domain, allowing it to be used by the public in whatever manner they please. Likewise, these normative considerations also influence defences to copyright infringement that exist in the form of statutory limitations and exceptions. These defences are considered in Chapter 6.

(ii) Categorisation of works and *numerus clausus*

Exclusionary rights that the law recognises in relation to the work impose corresponding duties on the rest of the world. As argued in Chapter 1, Section 6, it is essential that the work has characteristics that allow the rest of the world to know what it is that they owe exclusionary duties in relation to. Accordingly, the law recognises only certain categories of work as the eligible content for copyright protection. Authorial works can only fall into one of the four categories, namely literary, dramatic, musical, and artistic works, and entrepreneurial works can only fall into one of the four categories, namely sound recordings, films, broadcasts, and typographical arrangements.[58]

This categorisation was arrived at incrementally by historical events. The content that was the first to be considered for subject matter of a property right was 'books', whether under the Statute of Anne or under the licensing regime before then. As part of the natural evolution of common law, courts had interpreted 'books' under the Statute of Anne to include pamphlets, sheet music, maps, and so on.[59] During the literary property debate in the latter part of the eighteenth century, there was not only a recognition of mental labour, that

[56] *Glyn v Weston Feature Film Co* [1916] 1 Ch 261, 269.
[57] *Hyde Park Residence v Yelland* [2000] EWCA Civ 37, [2001] Ch 143 [64], [66].
[58] CDPA, s 1(1).
[59] Brad Sherman and Lionel Bently, *The Making of Modern Intellectual Property* (CUP 1999) 15.

is, the labour that flows from human intellect, but the privileging of it over physical labour as a defining feature of human existence. This debate is well captured in the arguments put forward by Blackstone and Yates in *Tonson v Collins*.[60] During this period, a raft of legislation was passed, all held together by the common thread of human creativity. The content of the subject matter was thus expanded by analogy with the pre-existing subject matter by noting the similarities.[61] Accordingly, the Engravers Act 1735 was passed to include engravings, the Calico Printers' Act 1787 to include the art of designing and printing linen, and the Models and Busts Act 1798 to include sculptures.[62] Onward into the nineteenth century, by the same methodology, additional content was recognised within the purview of the law by way of the Dramatic Literary Property Act 1833 and the Fine Arts Copyright Act 1862. 'Books' continued to be the content for written works in both the eighteenth and nineteenth centuries.

From the end of the nineteenth century to the turn of the twentieth century, various factors including international pressures led to the consolidation of the statutes in existence at the time that dealt with human expressions. It would have been possible for the consolidated statute to state that all products of mental labour are protected. After all, historically, that was the common thread that connected the various statutes being combined. Instead, the law makers chose to identify the categories into which the works would be put. There is property logic to the methodology of categorising the content of the subject matter. If there are categories, it is possible to lay down further descriptions of the subject matter, such that the statute can provide greater certainty as to the expressions that qualify. If, on the other hand, the statute simply stated that all products of mental labour qualify as works, it would have granted unguided discretion to the courts to fill in the details. Since recognition of a work by the law imposes exclusionary duties on the rest of the world, the uncertainties would have impacted third parties. A *via media* was arrived at, which was to name open-ended categories with inclusive definitions where required, such that works of particular types could be coherently classified. This left it to the courts to develop the meaning of these categories *ejusdem generis*, depending on the needs of the time and the type and category of work.[63] This is how the

[60] *Tonson v Collins* (1760) 96 ER 180. See also Ronan Deazley (2008) 'Commentary on *Tonson v. Collins* (1762)' in Lionel Bently and Martin Kretschmer (eds), *Primary Sources on Copyright (1450–1900)* <www.copyrighthistory.org> accessed 10 November 2024.

[61] Sherman and Bently (n 59) 15–18.

[62] See generally *Primary Sources on Copyright (1450–1900)* (n 60).

[63] See generally Poorna Mysoor, 'Does UK Really Have a "Closed" List of Works Protected by Copyright?' [2019] EIPR 474.

four categories of expression, namely literary, dramatic, musical, and artistic works, were identified in Copyright Act 1911, which continued under Copyright Act 1956 and the Copyright, Designs and Patents Act 1988 (CDPA).

One can witness the statute balancing flexibility and certainty by adopting the method of open-ended categories in relation to artistic works where artistic freedom is paramount. The law makers did not want the statute to be seen as restricting the manner of artistic expression. They seem to have recognised that while flexibility of the definition is important, a level of certainty is also imperative. Under s 35(1), Copyright Act, 1911, an expression qualified as an artistic work if it was a painting, drawing, sculpture, a work of artistic craftsmanship, architectural work of art, engraving, or photograph. Under this provision, not only was the definition of artistic work inclusive but also the definition of each mode of expression. Therefore, sculpture included casts and moulds, and engravings included etchings, lithographs, wood-cuts, prints, and other similar works. Section 3 of the Copyright Act 1956, on the other hand, provided for an exhaustive list of artistic works, although the definition of some of its ingredients, such as sculpture and engravings, had an inclusive definition under s 48(1). The same mechanism is followed in the CDPA where artistic work has an exhaustive definition under s 4, but its constituents, such as graphic work and buildings, have an inclusive definition. If a work does not fit into any of the recognised categories, it may be possible to fit it within the definition of graphic works. This would depend on how the courts have interpreted graphic works and whether the recognition of the work at hand as a graphic work amounts to an incremental development of the definition. An example with similar breadth of possible works is dramatic works. Given the diversity of the possible works of action, this category has always had an inclusive definition since the 1911 Act.

Apart from the definition and description of these works in the statute, case law has added rich doctrine, bringing in other socio-cultural considerations in conceptualising a work. There is plentiful scholarly literature exploring the judicial interpretation of different categories and expressions.[64] This monograph will not rehearse them here. However, to the extent that these may appear to be judicial interference with the certainty of the subject matter, a broader policy reason underlies the decisions of these courts. After all, it is legitimate for the statute as well as the courts as gatekeepers to filter the subject matter and permit only certain specific expressions to become eligible for copyright. For example,

[64] Pila (n 37) ch 3. See also Tanya Aplin, 'Subject Matter' in Estelle Derclaye (ed), *Research Handbook on the Future of EU Copyright* (Edward Elgar 2009) 50ff.

in the case of an artistic work, artistic intent has been held to be important for it to qualify as a work of artistic craftsmanship and a sculpture.[65] Especially in the pre-harmonisation decision of *Hensher*, works of artistic craftsmanship have been held to require artistic quality interpreted variously by their Lordships.[66]

The categorisation of entrepreneurial works is also the result of historical events such as the invention of the gramophone, cinematography, and broadcasting during the late nineteenth and early twentieth centuries. With the amount of investment that began to be sunk into these newer technologies, there was pressure on the law makers in the United Kingdom to protect these investments by giving them a level of exclusivity. The successive diplomatic conferences of the Berne Convention brought pressure on national governments to recognise newer works created using newer technologies. Eventually, in the Copyright Act 1956, whilst authorial works were dealt with in Part I, Part II was newly introduced, incorporating entrepreneurial works. The CDPA does not expressly use the definition of authorial and entrepreneurial works but recognises the distinction in the details of the statute.[67] Given that these are fairly stable categories and have stood the test of time for several decades, although they are not open-ended in their definition, this has not posed much difficulty with newer technologies, including digital filming and internet transmission.

(iii) A new category of works and the *Ainsworth* criteria

The above discussion shows that the categories are finite and are limited to literary, dramatic, musical, and artistic works. If the law is required to recognise newer works that do not fall into any of the existing categories, then, as argued in Chapter 1, Section 6, the criteria set forth by Lord Wilberforce in *National Provincial Bank v Ainsworth*,[68] can help guide the decision as to whether the categories need to be opened. The *Ainsworth* criteria, however, were developed with reference to rights which are themselves intangible, though in that case the right in question ultimately related to land. That the content of tangible things such as land and chattels meet this description is axiomatic. If it were possible to conceptualise the work as the content of the intangible thing to which copyright as a property right relates, then it follows that the work also should demonstrate the same characteristics as the right to promote certainty. Surely there can be no property right in a work that is not definable, not

[65] eg *Hensher v Restawile* [1976] AC 64; *Lucasfilm v Ainsworth* [2012] 1 AC 208.
[66] See Bently and others (n 6) 86–87 for a helpful summary.
[67] CDPA, s 1(1)(a)–(c).
[68] [1965] AC 1175, 1247–48.

identifiable by third parties, not capable in its nature of assumption by third parties, and which does not have some degree of permanence or stability.

The Law Commission in its Consultation Paper relies extensively on the *Ainsworth* criteria. They rightly point out that the *Ainsworth* criteria are negative in that if these are fulfilled, it does not necessarily follow that the right will be regarded as a property right.[69] It also means that the *Ainsworth* criteria do not necessarily tell us what constitutes a thing. Therefore, in addition to these criteria, one needs to show something more. For tangible things, when human body parts were put forward as a new thing, the *Ainsworth* criteria alone could not have helped decide whether property rights should or should not relate to them. This is why moral, ethical, and philosophical justifications were sought, among others. In copyright, when faced with newer works, the first effort should be to ascertain that they do not fall within the excluded category such as ideas or pure information. If they do not, then one should try and fit them within the designated categories, as described above. Only failing these, the *Ainsworth* criteria may be considered.

A distinction may be made between works that can be objectively perceived and those that are more subjectively perceived. The expressions that can be visually or aurally perceived are more objective than those perceived by smell, taste, or touch. Once perceived, they may (and do) invoke markedly diverse sentiments; but the concern here is the perception of these works at a more immediate and basic level. Literary, dramatic, musical, and artistic works can be perceived visually or orally or both, and therefore their existence can be more objectively ascertained. For example, a person looking at Van Gogh's *Sunflowers* sees yellow flowers no matter which part of the world they hail from. Similarly, with music the same notes are heard and with literary works the same words are seen. However, it is not the same with smell, taste, or touch. Even if one can broadly identify the smell of a perfume, the taste of a particular wine, and the touch of a fabric, there is no singular objective way of perceiving these. The lack of objectivity at such a basic level deprives them of certainty and consistency, thereby preventing them from qualifying to be works.

One may consider the case of the taste of cheese, which was claimed as a subject matter in *Levola Hengelo v Smilde*,[70] a CJEU decision. In declining to extend copyright protection, the CJEU explained that the subject matter protected by copyright must be expressed in a manner which makes it identifiable with sufficient precision and objectivity by the authorities that enforce the

[69] Law Commission Consultation Paper (n 19) paras 2.39, 5.39.

[70] Case C–310/17 *Levola Hengalo v Smilde Foods BV* ECLI:EU:C:2018:899; [2019] ECDR 2.

exclusive rights. Such expression, the CJEU held, enables individuals and economic operators to know the protection extended to others, especially their competitors. The CJEU further observed that in the process of identifying the subject matter, there should be no element of subjectivity, which the Court believed is detrimental to legal certainty.[71] Even if there is no express provision in the EU directives declaring copyright to be a property right,[72] the CJEU held that the subject matter of any exclusionary right should have a minimum level of certainty.

When one applies the *Ainsworth* criteria to a work of taste (or smell or touch for that matter), it is clear that it would be difficult to define it because of the varying subjective experience of the taste. It would be difficult for third parties to identify it because the taste buds of the third parties may be different. If such a work is to be assigned, the assignee will have the same difficulty of knowing whether the work that was transferred was the same as the work of the transferor. Such a work will also struggle to be stable because of lack of objectivity in perceiving it, though it may have a degree of permanence.

In addition to satisfying the substantive requirements discussed above, the work should demonstrate that it is separable and that it has a form. This leads us to the subsections below.

(b) Separability of the Work

As the Law Commission rightly identifies, there are two ways in which separability affects property rights. First, in the thing having to be separate from the human body; and secondly, in the thing having to be separate from the legal system. Together these ensure that the thing is truly independent and free-standing, such that property rights can be acquired in relation to it. The following paragraphs deal with each of these.

(i) Separable from human body

One of the clearest expositions of the need for separability is given by Penner. In his separability thesis he argues that for a person to have a right to a thing, there must be a distinguishable person and a distinguishable thing. He posits that what makes something property is that it is only contingently ours and for this relationship of contingency to exist, the thing must be separated from

[71] ibid [40]–[41].
[72] Caterina Sganga, *Propertizing European Copyright* (Edward Elgar 2018) 178–90.

us. Penner argues that there is no way of separating the right not to be murdered, the right to assemble, and the right to make binding agreements, from the person and that we do not stand in relation to these as we stand in relation to our property. He insists on the thing being freestanding such that anyone else might just as well own it.[73] The basic idea is that the thing must be separable from the person who comes to have the property right to it. In the words of Pretto-Sakmann, there is a spatial significance to the thing.[74]

Separability, or the need to have a spatial existence, is also required for tangible assets, but it is so obvious (eg land, bicycle) that it seems pointless to mention it as a requirement. Nevertheless, examples of tangible things that help us illustrate separability convincingly are human body parts and products. Although there is no property in the live human body, to the extent that certain parts or products can be separated from the human body, these can become things and an eligible subject matter if other requirements are satisfied. The desirability of body parts as the substantive content of the thing is a different discussion, which was explored above. The aim of this subsection is to point out how the courts have recognised the idea of separability.

A good example is the case of *Yearworth v North Bristol NHS Trust*.[75] In this case, six men who had been diagnosed with cancer gave their semen sample to the defendant to be frozen for future use, before the men went through treatment for cancer that might have had an impact on their fertility. Due to the negligence of the defendant, the sperm samples were destroyed. Claimants brought an action for conversion, among other claims. The court held that since the men had ejaculated the semen for the purpose of being frozen, they had the property right over it and could hold the defendant liable in conversion.

The decision of the Court of Appeal was analytically not as systematic as it could have been. The broader question of our concern was whether the claimants could have a property right over their sperm samples. This question can be broken up into (i) whether human sperm can be the content of the subject matter of a property right; (ii) when it becomes eligible for property rights to arise in relation it; and (iii) how the property right is acquired. The court skipped over (i) and (ii) and answered only (iii), from which we can gather by implication that (i) and (ii) were also answered in the affirmative. In considering whether a part of the human body can be a thing for the purposes of a property right, the Court of Appeal considered the example of a finger having

[73] Penner, 'The Bundle of Rights' (n 36) 802–05.
[74] Pretto-Sakmann (n 4) 106.
[75] [2010] QB 1.

been severed in an accident and a surgeon damaging it before it is grafted back on to the injured hand.[76] From this, it appears that the court did answer in the affirmative the question whether being separated from the human body, without more, gives the body parts and products the threshold eligibility to be the subject matter of a property right. While *Yearworth* is a case that raises the issues of acquisition of a property right, it is important to note that it also addressed a more preliminary question of separability, although the court did not use that specific expression.[77] The question of who gets ownership is a distinct enquiry, which will be considered in Chapter 3.

The above discussion demonstrates the application of separability to tangible things. How do we carry over this discussion to intangible assets? *OBG v Allan*,[78] where the issue was conversion of contractual rights, confirms that an attribute of property (though more specifically the thing) is in its existence independent of a particular person. With copyright, authorial works in a very broad sense are products of the human mind. Just as parts or products of the human body must be separated from the human body to be considered as eligible subject matter of a property right, products of the human mind also need to be separated from the human body. As stated in Subsection 2(a)(i) above, ideas are excluded from being the subject matter. But ideas can give rise to thought processes within the human mind which should be separated from that human mind for them to become eligible as works. A more coherent way of stating this is that these thoughts should be expressed for them to become works. The separability analysis gives a convincing explanation as to why copyright only protects expressions of ideas and not ideas themselves.

There is an additional reason why separability analysis makes particular sense in relation to copyright. The thoughts that remain in one's mind are discernible only subjectively, unlike a part of the human body that is objectively discernible. A fundamental tenet of private law is to rely on what is objectively discernible when regulating human conduct. Most notable is contract law's insistence on taking into account the intention of the parties to a contract that is objectively discernible, disregarding the subjective state of mind.[79] Expressing thoughts makes them objectively discernible, so that the law can then go on to formulate appropriate rules to protect them. Furthermore, the definition of a

[76] ibid [45](d).
[77] Douglas and Goold analyse *Yearworth* to demonstrate the conflation of the issues surrounding the subsistence of property rights and acquisition of property rights. See generally Simon Douglas and Imogen Goold, 'Property in Human Biomaterials: A New Methodology' (2016) 75(3) CLJ 478.
[78] *OBG v Allan* [2007] UKHL 21 [309] (Lady Hale).
[79] Ewan McKendrick, *Contract Law* (7th edn, OUP 2014) 20.

work as an expression is apparent in the colloquial use of the word 'work'. We can only refer something as a literary work if the words behind it are expressed. If the words remain within a person's mind, we cannot even perceive the literary work, let alone refer to it as one.

However, this does not mean that, despite being excluded, subject matter ideas never face the danger of being subsumed within the work. Ideas are discernible as a more abstract version of the expression. After all, there is always an idea behind an expression, even if at a rudimentary level. Although there is no way the law can protect what is inside a person's mind, in assessing non-literal copying courts are sometimes asked to push the boundaries of the expression towards its more abstract version, risking protecting the underlying idea. How the courts should guard against this is more fully considered in Chapter 5 when discussing the enforcement of copyright through the tort of infringement. For our purposes here, under the heading of 'idea-expression dichotomy', scholars discuss the undesirability of protecting ideas. The upshot is that copyright can only subsist in works that are expressions, and expressions are nothing but a manifestation of the requirement of separability.

That copyright's focus on expression and not ideas themselves is perhaps not appreciated sufficiently by land law and personal property scholars, and much less that it is a manifestation of separability. McFarlane and Douglas quote Yates J's dissenting opinion in *Millar v Taylor* stating that an assertion that a person holds a property right 'to the very ideas themselves, seems to me very difficult, or rather quite wild'.[80] They mention *Donaldson v Becket* to show that the minority view in *Millar* was confirmed. They use this quote to support their argument that one should not make a direct comparison between 'artistic expression' on one hand and land and chattels on the other, because in the former there is no physical thing like in the latter around which the duties of non-interference can coalesce.[81] Given the tenor of the remaining arguments on intellectual property rights, it appears that the thrust of McFarlane and Douglas's argument is that there can be no property rights in anything other than physical things. To come to this conclusion, they appear to equate ideas and artistic expressions; they quote a judge, Yates J, who was not speaking of copyright in its statutory form under the Statute of Anne; and, as will be explained below, McFarlane and Douglas omit to state the opinion of Yates J acknowledging the right under the Statute of Anne as a property right elsewhere in his dissenting opinion. Let us unpack these points.

[80] McFarlane and Douglas (n 42) 175.
[81] ibid 174–76.

Millar v Taylor was a case that arose in relation to the Statute of Anne, which protected 'books' for fourteen years and if the author was alive at the end of this period, for a further fourteen years.[82] The claimants had found the term of fourteen years too short and had brought several cases before the courts that there was a property right in common law akin to copyright but enjoyed in perpetuity. The majority in this case held that the common law rights akin to copyright did exist upon the expiry of the statutory term. This does not mean that the majority ruled in favour of protecting ideas. The majority did recognise that there must be a 'distinguishable existence' before a thing can be claimed as property. Accordingly, the majority found that when sentiments are 'communicated to the sight and understanding of every man, by the medium of printing, the work becomes a distinguishable subject of property, and not totally destitute of corporeal qualities'.[83] This clearly demonstrates that even when the court was dealing with nebulous rights akin to copyright under common law, they still required it to adhere to the severability principle. *Millar* was, of course, overturned by *Donaldson v Becket*, which held that the common law property did not survive the Statute of Anne. But the reason was not because there could be no property rights in ideas or expressions, but because the right in perpetuity was found undesirable. However, the point to note here is the undeniable role of separability in the reasoning of *Millar*.

In *Millar*, Yates J made one of the most powerful arguments against protecting ideas when he gave his dissenting opinion. Noting that the property claimed by the defendants was in ideas, he observed that 'their whole existence is in the mind alone; incapable of any other modes of acquisition or enjoyment, than by mental possession or apprehension'.[84] As stated above, he was not speaking of the statutory copyright under the Statute of Anne, but common law copyright, whose confines were murkier. Although it was not expressly stated in this way, the reason for Yates J's fears that ideas would become protectable is because upon expiry of the term under the Statute of Anne, the contents of the book would become part of the public domain; if a common law right still operates, it can only be seen to protect ideas. Clearly, this was not a critique of the Statute of Anne itself. Yates was fully in support of the right granted in the Statute of Anne and had no qualms in characterising it as a property right. Indeed, Yates J stated later in his dissenting judgment that '[t]he Legislature has *fixed the extent of his property*: they have allowed him twenty eight years;

[82] 4 Burr 2340–41, 98 ER 201.
[83] 98 ER 201, 221–22.
[84] ibid 233.

and expressly declared, he shall have it no longer.'[85] If Yates J was of the view, as McFarlane and Douglas seem to assert, that neither ideas nor expressions can be the subject matter of property rights, Yates J would not have characterised the statutory right under the Statute of Anne as a property right.[86] Reading his dissenting judgment in the round, one can gather Yates's objection to be that of common law being the source of copyright, resulting in a perpetual property right, rather than the eligibility of copyright to be a property right.

The Statute of Anne referred to 'books', which presupposes that the author's ideas must have been expressed. To the extent that the book is external to the writer, separability was at play under the Statute of Anne. As discussed in the previous section, during the eighteenth and nineteenth centuries, many statutes were passed relating to different subject matter—the Engravers Act 1735, the Models and Busts Act 1798, the Dramatic Property Act 1833, the Fine Art Copyright Act 1862, to name a few. All these related to works that had been expressed. As for literary works, the Copyright Act 1842 continued to focus on 'books', but extended the term of protection. Although these statutes did not have an express provision on separability, case law had consistently affirmed this. An example of this can be found in *Kenrick v Lawrence*.[87] Here, the plaintiff had created a card with the drawing of a hand holding a pencil in the act of completing a cross within a square for voting purposes. The defendant created a similar card, but with the hand in a slightly different position. The similarity between the two drawings was the idea and not the expression. Willis J held that with a drawing of this nature, 'copyright must be confined to that which is special to the individual drawing over and above the idea'.[88]

With the consolidation of all subject matter under one enactment in the Copyright Act 1911, the reference was not to books or sculptures, but to broader categories of expression such as literary works, artistic works, and so on, as explained in Subsection (a)(ii) above. This continued to be the case in the UK Copyright Act 1956 and the CDPA, thereby recognising the separation of ideas as expressions of these categories. In addition to the implied recognition of separability in this manner, the House of Lords has recognised as trite law the principle that there can be no copyright in ideas alone.[89] This principle is also recognised under Art 9(2) of the TRIPS Agreement. Despite the Treaty-level recognition, it does not mean that this principle is uncontroversial in its

[85] ibid 232 (emphasis supplied).
[86] ibid 235.
[87] (1890) 25 QBD 99.
[88] ibid 104.
[89] *LB (Plastics) v Swish Products* [1979] RPC 551, 160 (Lord Hailsham), 165 (Lord Salmon).

application. It may be reiterated that difficulties do arise when deciding what is a non-literal copy of a work, which is dealt with in greater detail in Chapter 4 when discussing infringement of copyright.

The above discussion relates to authorial works where the separability analysis is demonstrated by the separation of expression from the ideas that arise within human minds. Moving on from the focus on the human mind, the twentieth century was marked by certain technological innovations that resulted in films, sound recordings, and broadcasts being added to the copyright subject matter. These are not strictly products of the human mind in the authorial sense, but products of investment. As products of technology, from their inception, they have an external existence and can be located outside the human body. As such, separability analysis readily applies to these products. The concern here, therefore, was not whether ideas had been expressed, but whether the work has a record, which is dealt with under Subsection (c) below.

(ii) Separable from the legal system and from the rights

The Law Commission's Consultation Paper states that the thing in copyright is the right itself and that these rights only exist because the statute says so. Based on this, the Paper concludes that the thing in copyright is not separable from the legal system.[90] This book disagrees with this view. While Chapter 4 explains why the rights themselves are not the thing in copyright, this chapter has thus far been arguing why there is an identifiable thing in copyright of which the work makes up the content. In order to show that the work exists outside the legal system and is independent of the rights, the work needs to be conceptualised as a resource. A resource can be broadly defined as anything of value, be it economic, social, or cultural. Land and chattels are the resources regulated by land law and personal property law, and a work is the resource protected by copyright law. Harris refers to it as an ideational resource, given its origin in human minds.[91] With such a broad definition of a resource, it would appear that even contractual rights would qualify as resources. In general, contracting is also the product of human endeavour, as a work is, and it creates rights and duties that are to be performed by the parties to the contract. But it is only resources that are also independent of the rights themselves that go on to be the substantive content of a thing.

For example, if P lends Q £100 and Q agrees to return it in a month, then P's right to recover the £100 can be regarded as a resource. This resource is the

[90] Law Commission Consultation Paper (n 19) paras 3.57, 3.61.
[91] Jim W Harris, *Property and Justice* (Clarendon Press 1996) 139.

'ability' to demand the repayment of the £100 from Q that the right represents and nothing outside or independent of the right. This ability to demand can be assigned by P to R, and R will then be entitled to the repayment and nothing outside of the right. It should be noted here that the £100 itself is not the resource, but rather the right to receive the £100. Whether money represented by £100 on its own is capable of being the substantive content is not the issue here. The example can be changed to P's right to receive a car having paid Q for its purchase from Q. The car here is a separate resource from the right to receive its delivery. It is the right to receive the car, or be repaid the loan, which is being considered here, and not the object of such receipt or repayment.

By contrast, if P writes a poem, the poem itself has an inherent value without anyone else having to do anything for P to derive value from it. The Law Commission downplays the importance of value to a thing, but acknowledges that if the thing is valuable, property rights normally follow.[92] A poem's inherent value is economically, socially, and culturally as justifiable as that of land or chattels.[93] This value exists prior to the law recognising rights in relation to it and provides justification for such rights. Once the law recognises a right and imposes the duty on the rest of the world, including Q, not to copy the poem, then Q performing this duty will mean that P will become the only one with the ability to copy the poem. However, the existence of the poem is unchanged by Q's performance of these duties. In other words, the poem has an existence independent of the rights that the law confers in relation to it. Both the inherent value and an independent existence that the poem itself has remain unaffected by Q's performance of this duty of not copying the poem. Once the poem is separated from the human mind in the form of an expression, the independent existence of the poem is a reality as objectively discernible as the independent existence of land or chattels, even if through different senses. Those who regard copyright as a chose in action in the same way as a contractual right ignore the independent existence of the poem and the independent value it has without anyone having to perform any duty.

The arguments herein are not meant to undermine or devalue the exclusionary rights that the law recognises in relation to these works.[94] The intention here is to drive home the point that the works exist pre-law and can exist

[92] Law Commission Consultation Paper (n 19) paras 2.81, 3.13.

[93] Even those who are opposed to granting property rights over a poem would agree that a poem has economic, social, and political value. The objection is normally to the protection mechanism rather than to acknowledging the inherent value in the products of the human mind.

[94] Indeed, this book maintains that exclusionary rights are chronologically and intuitively the first to be acquired when a person acquires copyright.

without the protection of the law. If the Statute of Anne 1710 is loosely taken to be the first copyright legislation of its kind, it can hardly be said that prior to the Statute of Anne no one authored books or plays or music, not to mention the sculpture and art that thrived. It is because the value of these intangible resources to society was recognised as a benefit worth protecting that the Statute of Anne was passed. Nothing can be more evocative of the intention behind this statute than its long title, which read as 'A Bill for Encouragement of Learning, and for Securing the Property of Copies of Books to the Rightful Owners thereof'.[95] If the works and not the rights that copyright legislation recognised are taken to be the thing in copyright, it is not difficult to see that these exist independent of the legal system and of the rights.

The existence of the work gives certain benefits to the copyright owner that is more than merely going to law for the infringement of the right. Instead, it can be connected to the use of the resource. This also demonstrates why copyright is more like a chose in possession, if one still believes that there is merit in this classification. Choses in action are merely rights. They do not concern resources independent of the rights themselves. In the example above, the benefits that P will have if P has a right to the repayment of the £100 are (i) the repayment of £100 by Q; (ii) the ability to assign or create a charge over this right; and (iii) the ability to go to the court if Q does not repay £100 according to the terms of the contract. All of these benefits are still predicated on Q repaying the money to P or his assignee or chargee, or as a remedy if the right has to be enforced. If P wrote a poem, P can also enjoy the benefits of being able to assign or charge the rights in the poem to someone and being able to sue for infringement of the rights. In place of deriving a single benefit of being repaid the loan in the previous example, by contrast in the poem example, P here can benefit from a potentially open-ended set of privileges.[96] The benefits P can derive from the poem are to recite it, say in a podcast or a book club; to reproduce it, say on a poster or a greeting card; to compose it into a song or publish it in an anthology; and so on. These benefits arise because the poem has an inherent value which not only benefits P but also others in society who may want to engage with the work.

It is more common to explain this by using the distinction between *in rem* and *in personam* rights, and their exigibility or more simply, demandability.

[95] A Bill for Encouragement of Learning, London (1710) in Lionel Bently and Martin Kretschmer (eds), *Primary Sources on Copyright* (n 60).

[96] See Chapter 4, Section 4 for a discussion on the exclusive privileges to which copyright gives rise. There are other benefits to a copyright work which everyone can gain—such as being able to read a copyright protected novel.

Pretto-Sakmann foregrounds a similar idea when discussing 'locanda' in relation to rights *in rem*. The idea here is that all rights are intangible but those rights 'whose exigibility or demandability is defined by the existence and location of the thing to which they relate are rights *in rem*'.[97] In this sense, a right *in rem* is a right in a thing or to a thing. *Rem*, she explains, is a derivative of the word *res* in Roman law. Rights *in personam* are rights that are exigible or demandable only from the person against whom the right arose. In the language of Pretto-Sakmann, the thing in copyright counts as an ideational thing which can be located in the work of another person when it is copied. If there is a thing outside of the right itself, whoever has the thing is the one against whom the right to the thing is demandable. Therefore, an action for the infringement of copyright can be initiated by following the location of the infringing material.[98] Rights *in personam*, on the contrary, are only demandable against the person who originally granted the right. In other words, one depends on the person doing something for exigibility and not the location of the thing.[99] This distinction certainly helps. Exigibility arises when the right needs to be enforced, such as stopping someone else from copying. But even without having to do so, the person who creates a work can enjoy it in a similar way to a person who enjoys a bicycle or a parcel of land.

Separability from the human body and from the legal system is a necessary but insufficient condition to describe a thing. Once human thoughts have been expressed and the expression qualifies as the content of the subject matter, the expression must be capable of surviving outside the human body—meaning that the content must go on to acquire a form. This takes us to the subsection below.

(c) Need for Form to be Regarded as a Work

To be a work that truly exists independent of the human body, the legal system, and the rights, it needs a form. By acquiring a form, the work will be able to comply with all the *Ainsworth* requirements of definability, identifiability, and so on. The Law Commission asserts that it is also necessary for the thing to be rivalrous.[100] This chapter disagrees with this view and asserts that the work

[97] Pretto-Sakmann (n 4) 90–91.
[98] ibid 105–06.
[99] ibid 90.
[100] Law Commission Report (n 46) para 4.5.

acquiring a form is sufficient and it does not also have to be rivalrous. The following paragraphs deal with each of these aspects.

(i) Form as reification of the work

At the point of separation, tangible things acquire a form that is independent of the entity from which they are separated. In *Yearworth*, the court gave the example of a finger being severed from a person due to an accident and a surgeon negligently damaging the severed finger.[101] At the point of severance it is arguable that the finger acquired a form that is independent of the human body. One may also consider the example of extraction of minerals from the earth, where at the point of separation from the earth the minerals become a new and independent thing from the land. The separation gives rise to two important, but closely related consequences: first, a new subject matter of property comes into existence; and secondly, separation gives the body part or the minerals boundaries of their own, making them capable of being the subject matter in which exclusionary rights, exclusive powers, and exclusive privileges may arise.

Unlike in the case of body parts or minerals, in copyright the act of separation does not always mark a new subject matter coming into existence. Aside from the obvious difference of tangibility, there is an issue with the momentariness of certain expressions. Although thoughts being expressed denote their separation from human body, expressions that qualify to be in the category of literary, dramatic, or musical works are unique in that these can be expressed but may not necessarily remain as external entities capable of being located. As an example, one may think of an extempore speech, an impromptu dance move, or the humming of a tune. When these are expressed, they exist in the moment.[102] Because of this, their very existence can be called into question. If these expressions are so uncertain that they lend themselves poorly to objective proof, their boundaries are unclear or ambiguous, then exclusionary rights, powers, and so on cannot attach to them. To address these issues, a further requirement of such expressions having to acquire a specific form will have to be imposed. Accordingly, the act of giving the expression a form leads to the same two consequences as body parts and minerals explained above: the form gives rise to a new and distinguishable subject matter of property; and the

[101] [2010] QB 1 [45](d).

[102] eg in *Hadley v Kemp* [1999] EMLR 589, the words of the song and the music that was set to it had come into existence before these were recorded. *Sawkins v Hyperion Records* [2005] 1 WLR 3281 [53], is another example where Mummery, LJ recognises that a musical work can exist before it is recorded.

form demarcates the boundaries of the subject matter so that the exclusionary rights can apply.

Barring a few exceptions,[103] the need for form is not understood or appreciated sufficiently. Most scholars of copyright law lump together the need for form with other requirements such as the notion of a work, of originality, and indeed the duration of the right under the broad heading of copyright subsistence.[104] Others who do engage in a discussion of the nature of copyright regard copyright as relating to expressions, without more.[105] For example, Pretto-Sakmann, despite a clear exposition of separability, regards expressions as ideational entities in relation to which rights *in rem* may arise.[106] I have provided elsewhere an analysis of the crucial role played by the requirement of form in conceptualising copyright as a property right.[107] The following builds on the underlying conceptual arguments and provides a more detailed historical context.

The derivatives of the word form are 'formal' and 'formality'. Land law and personal property law, and indeed private law in general, are no strangers to the need for formalities. In these areas of law, form is bestowed by requiring certain formalities to be followed. Speaking of land, Birks explains that all land rights are invisible—one cannot see a fee simple or a lease, and therefore '[r]eal rights have to be made apparent through documents'.[108] It is not rights that relate to land alone that are invisible, but all property rights (and indeed, all rights). When formalities make these rights apparent, not only can their existence be objectively provable but also the boundaries or limits of these rights become apparent, addressing both evidential and demarcation functions.

Referring to contract law, Fuller explains the essential functions of formalities to include an evidentiary function where formalities provide evidence of the existence and purport of a legal relationship.[109] Fuller also refers to the channelling function, arguing that formalities serve to mark or signal a simple and external test of enforceability. To Fuller, formalities offer 'channels' for the legally effective expression of intention, or a legal framework into which a person can fit his or her actions.[110] While in the context of contract, following

[103] Smith, 'Intellectual Property as Property' (n 32) 1807; Gordon (n 39) 1380.

[104] Pila (n 37) 157–59; Aplin (n 64) 54–55; Sherman (n 45) 108–10, 115–19.

[105] eg James Penner, *The Idea of Property in Law* (OUP 2000) 119–20.

[106] Pretto-Sakmann (n 4) 106.

[107] Poorna Mysoor, 'Form in Conceptualising Copyright as a Property Right' (2020) 67(1) J Copyright Soc'y USA 301.

[108] Peter Birks, 'Before We Begin: Five Keys to Land Law' in Susan Bright and James Dewar (eds), *Land Law Themes and Perspectives* (OUP 1998) 483.

[109] Lon L Fuller, 'Consideration and Form' (1941) 41 Colum L Rev 799, 800.

[110] ibid 801.

a formality can be taken to signal an expression of intention, in the context of property rights, following a formality can be taken to signal exclusionary duties being imposed upon the rest of the world. Since a property right imposes *in rem* duties on the rest of the world, formalities also have publicity and information functions to ensure that the subject matter and the scope of protection are made known to third parties.[111]

In the copyright context, the concerns are that for property rights to arise in relation to a work, the work should be objectively provable, that is, an evidentiary problem; the boundaries in relation to which the exclusionary duties apply should be ascertainable, that is, a demarcation problem; and there should be an act that indicates to the rest of the world the exclusionary duty, that is, a signalling problem. In copyright, not only is the work invisible but also the rights that arise in relation to it. As such, it should come as no surprise that there is need for a formality. This formality can be nimble in requiring only writing or some other kind of record; or can be onerous in requiring a registration process, a deposit requirement, and so on. The expressions that comply with the formalities result in the imposition of the exclusionary duties on the rest of the world and the expressions that do not comply with the formalities are channelled to the public domain. The kinds of formality that bring about signalling and publicity functions could be publication, registration, and so on.

While the paragraphs above shed light on the rationale behind formalities, the need for formalities as a condition for property rights to arise should also be explained. A formality need not necessarily be a matter that affects substantive rights. Whether a formality affects substantive rights depends on the nature of the formality itself and the objective sought to be achieved by the formality. If the certainty that the formality brings about is fundamental to the exercise or enforcement of the relevant property right, the law can require that a property right cannot be substantively enjoyed unless a formality is complied with. These are constitutive formalities in that compliance with these is a constituent element of the substantive right itself. A good example is the act of registration in relation to land: though in itself a formal act, registration is what grants legal title to land.[112] The rationale is, inter alia, to eliminate the uncertainties associated with the conveyancing system that existed before (whereby title deeds had to be examined at the time of each disposition of land) and to provide publicity to rights in land by bringing them all onto the Land Register. Therefore,

[111] McFarlane (n 1) 100–04.

[112] Land Registration Act 2002 (LRA), ss 29 and 30, read with s 58, excluding overriding interests.

it is within the legislative remit to use a formal act as an essential aspect of acquiring substantive property rights.

In the copyright context, the statute makes the requirement of a work having to acquire a form constitutive of copyright arising in relation to it. As explained above, without a form, literary, dramatic, and musical works have such a degree of uncertainty that they cannot be regarded as the subject matter of a property right if they exist momentarily. Requiring these works to have a form helps to prove the work, demarcate its boundaries, and signal exclusionary duties. Therefore, if the requirement of form is imposed as a condition precedent for the exclusionary rights of copyright to arise in relation to the work, then the uncertainties explained above will have been addressed before the *in rem* consequences of copyright ensue. This has been the technique followed historically to address the uncertainties associated with the intangibility of copyright subject matter. It is only the nature of the formalities that have changed over the last three centuries, as the following paragraphs recount.

Historically, greater emphasis was laid on the signalling and publicity function of formalities. The act that marked the beginning of the term of protection shed light on the point at which the exclusionary duties came to be imposed on the rest of the world. One may see that the Statute of Anne made this act an overt act. As stated above, the content of the subject matter in the Statute of Anne was stated to be 'books'. A book is already a reification of the expression of its author. But the Statute of Anne went further to provide specifically that the book had to be published, registered at the Stationers' Company, and had to be deposited in certain libraries. While these overt actions played the role of bringing the new work to the attention of the public, the action that triggered the onset of the term of protection of the initial fourteen years was the publication of the book (which continued for another fourteen years if the author was alive at the end of this period).[113]

Support for the need for formalities was expressed in unequivocal terms in Yates J's judgment in *Millar* when he was trying to distinguish between the statutory right created under the Statute of Anne and the common law right to literary property. He noted as one of the specific concerns 'at what time, and by what act, does the author's common law property attach?' He went on to observe that the Statute of Anne 'very properly obviated this, by fixing the commencement of his property from the time of publication; first, entering it at Stationers Hall'.[114] As an aside, one may see that McFarlane and Douglas's

[113] See generally Ronan Deazley (2008) 'Commentary on the *Statute of Anne* 1710' in Lionel Bently and Martin Kretschmer (eds), *Primary Sources on Copyright* (n 60).

[114] 98 ER 201, 230–31.

quote from Yates J's dissenting opinion is misdirected, given that Yates J had so clearly acknowledged that the Statute of Anne had given rise to property rights.[115]

Such was the durability and usefulness of publication as the triggering point that it continued under section III of the Copyright Act 1842.[116] There was, however, no statutory definition of publication. Courts had interpreted it to mean publication in print and not in performance.[117] This meant that plays that had been written but not printed and published were open for any person to lawfully perform without the author's consent. This took away the very essence of economic value of the dramatic work from its authors, and therefore the Dramatic Literary Property Act 1833 was passed to extend the right to represent on stage an unprinted and unpublished play to its author for twenty-eight years. Curiously, the dependence of the statute on printing and publishing continued even in case of an act of performance. This shows that it is printing and publishing that give the play the form that is sufficiently certain.

Indeed, the question of aspects of a play that are not printed and published arose in *Tate v Fullbrook*.[118] This was a case where the non-verbal aspects of the plaintiff's dramatic piece, such as the scenic set-up and comic parts, had been taken by the defendant. The question was whether the protection of the 1833 Act extended to all aspects of a dramatic work or only to the aspects that complied with the twin requirements of form under the 1833 Act of being printed and published. The court held that the protection of the 1833 Act only extended to aspects that could be printed and published. In this context, Farwell LJ observed that 'the Act creates monopoly and in such a case there must be certainty in the subject matter of such monopoly in order to avoid injustice to the rest of the world'.[119] These words of Farwell LJ have been quoted in many cases over the last century, to support certainty of both content and form of the subject matter.[120]

[115] McFarlane and Douglas (n 42) 174–76.

[116] Statute of Anne, London (1710) and Copyright Act, London (1842) in Lionel Bently and Martin Kretschmer (eds), *Primary Sources on Copyright (1450–1900)* (n 60). An additional requirement to deposit any published book with the British Museum, in addition to the libraries, was also imposed under section VI.

[117] *Coleman v Wathen* (1793) 5 D & E 245.

[118] [1908] 1 KB 821.

[119] ibid 832–33.

[120] *Tate v Thomas* [1921] 1 Ch 503 where the Copyright Act 1911 was being considered; *Green v Broadcasting Corporation of New Zealand* [1989] RPC 700 (PC) where the New Zealand Copyright Act 1962 was being considered, *IPC Media Ltd v Highbury* [2005] FSR 20 [7]–[8] and *Baigent v Random House* [2006] EMLR 16 [156] both under the CDPA. Although in *Tate v Fullbrook* the reference was to the certainty of the form, in *Green* the quote was used to support certainty of the content of the subject matter, namely the need for unity in a reality show, for it to be a dramatic work.

It is no surprise that historically literary works were expected to be in print and needed to be published. More noteworthy are the requirements for other types of work, such as engravings and sculptures under the Engravings Act 1735 and the Models and Busts Act 1798. These were not required to be printed, being works that need a different medium for expression. However, the requirement was that the engraving and sculptures be published. Publication of an engraving or a sculpture had to be understood within the context of the respective works and, most likely, in the light of the conventions of the respective trade. The Fine Art Copyright Act 1862, which extended to paintings, drawings, photographs, and their negatives, on the other hand, specifically provided under s 4 for the registration of the respective work with the Stationers' Company as the action that triggered the benefit of the Act to be accrued to the artists. The benefit of the Act according to s 1 was the sole right of copying, engraving, reproducing, and multiplying the work during the lifetime of the author plus seven years thereafter. Thus, artistic works also had a combination of publication and registration as the overt act that triggered the respective rights.

As explained above, all the statutes that addressed different works were consolidated under the Copyright Act 1911. Due to the influence of the Berne Convention, the United Kingdom was required to eliminate formalities associated with copyright. This resulted in printing, publishing, and registration requirements being eliminated. With this, the signalling function has been diluted and publicity functions have been removed. The law makers took away publication and other formalities as a trade-off for authors to gain property rights more easily in the light of the ubiquity and spontaneity with which literary, dramatic, and musical works come into existence. Surprisingly, although the 1911 Act stated that the term of protection for authorial works lasted until fifty years after the end of the calendar year of the author's death, it did not say exactly when the work would come into existence. It could not have been that the term of protection began from the date of publication since the 1911 Act extended copyright to published and unpublished authorial works alike. It appears that the time of creating the authorial work was in itself the trigger for the exclusionary duties to be placed on the rest of the world. The need for dramatic works to be in writing was retained,[121] but ambiguities persisted whether this indicated that the same applies to literary and musical works. The Copyright Act 1956 applied the need for writing to literary, dramatic, and musical works,[122] but did not specifically state that the term of protection

[121] Copyright Act 1911, s 35(1).
[122] Copyright Act 1956, ss 48(1) and 49(4).

began from the time of writing. This anomaly has been set right in the CDPA in requiring some form of record uniformly for literary, dramatic, and musical works alike. The need for form, be it an authorial work or an entrepreneurial work, now only requires a record, which weakens the ability to publicise to the rest of the world when they become subject to the exclusionary duties. The law makers chose to retain the most fundamental function of formalities, which is the evidentiary and demarcation function, for which, as demonstrated below, the need for record is a sufficient formality.

For completeness, let us now turn to the statutory provisions in relation to different kinds of works under the CDPA. The CDPA has one of the simplest and clearest requirements of form. Literary, dramatic, and musical works acquire a form simply by being 'recorded, in writing or otherwise', as per s 3(2). Most authors, however, use the expression 'fixed in material form'.[123] The CDPA uses none of these expressions. Read with s 178 of the CDPA, writing includes digital form. The word 'otherwise' in s 3(2) provides possibilities of a record that is not necessarily in writing, nor in 'material' or permanent form. Section 22(1) of the Australian Copyright Act 1968 uses the expression 'reduced to writing or to some other material form'. As this author has argued elsewhere,[124] fixed does not mean permanent and material does not exclude digital form. A more helpful way to understand the need for record is that it is sufficient if the record is in a medium that is capable of being reproduced.[125]

Section 3(2) of the CDPA does not refer to artistic works, though s 22(1) of the Australian Copyright Act (ACA) does. This is not to say that artistic works do not need form under the CDPA. For an artistic expression to arise, a medium must have been used, even if it is digital and even if ephemeral,[126] so long as the form that artistic work takes is such that it can be reproduced.[127] Artistic works are expressed through one or more of the enumerated inclusive list of methods, such as painting, engraving, sculpture, and so on, which inevitably create a record of the work when the work itself is created. This does not mean that the content and form of an artistic work are indistinguishable. It confuses the form with the work itself. The work in a painting, for example, includes

[123] Gwilym Harbottle and others, *Copinger and Skone James Copyright* (19th edn, Sweet & Maxwell 2025) para 2-169; Mary Vitoria and others, *The Modern Law of Copyright and Designs* (4th edn, LexisNexis 2018) para 3.15.

[124] Mysoor, 'Form in Conceptualising Copyright' (n 107) 306–08.

[125] US Copyright Act 1976, 17 USC § 102(a) speaks of reproducible medium.

[126] *Abraham Moon v Thornber* [2012] FSR 17 [105]; *SAS Institute v World Programming* [2013] RPC 17 [29] held that that the record can be in a non-material form. *Islestarr Holdings v Aldi* [2019] EWHC 1473 (Ch) [48] (unreported). See also Estelle Derclaye, 'Debunking Some of UK Copyright Law's Longstanding Myths and Misunderstandings' [2013] IPQ 1, 12–17.

[127] Harbottle and others (n 123) para 2-170.

inter alia the configuration of the expression, the brush strokes involved, the choice of colours, and so on. It just so happens that the author may have chosen canvas as the reifier of the artistic expression. It is within the powers of the author to paint the same artwork, configuration, and brush strokes on any other surface—a ceramic plate for example. Thus, painting is an expression which is agnostic towards the form it takes. To some extent, the form which the work takes is controlled by the method through which the author chooses to express. For example, the form taken by a sculpture as an artistic work is likely to be three-dimensional and a drawing may be two-dimensional. Many of the definitions of expressions within artistic works are inclusive, leaving room for the author to decide the form that the work takes. Therefore, the absence of an express requirement of creating a record leaves it to the author's artistic freedom as to the kind of record that the author wants to create.

As regards entrepreneurial works, sound recordings and films by definition should create a record to become a work.[128] A typographical arrangement is protected not in isolation, but as part of a published edition, which means that it has a form in which it exists. Unlike authorial works there is no work without its record in case of these entrepreneurial works. For example, if P, a flautist, composes certain music and plays it aloud, the composed music is a musical work so long as it satisfies the definition of a musical work.[129] It will only attract copyright in favour of P if the composition is somehow recorded—either by notation or recording the notes when played (subject to it being original, for which see Chapter 3). If Q, a music producer, is the one recording P's composition, then P will still acquire copyright in the musical work, and Q will acquire copyright in the sound record so created (so long as it is not a copy of an existing record—again, see Chapter 3). P's musical work is separable from the record that can be created of it, whereas Q's sound recording is the work. In other words, the record merges with the work. Therefore, it is more in the nature of tangible things such as land and bicycles where the content of the subject matter is the same as its form.

A broadcast is not expressly required to be recorded. It is an electronic transmission of sound, images, and other information in the form of signals. It is possible for a live broadcast also to be a work without any record of the transmission having ever been created. The transmission is indistinguishable from its content. Balganesh has forcefully argued that if the content is an authorial work such as a play (dramatic work), then the signals carrying the work are

[128] CDPA, ss 5A and 5B.

[129] See *Hyperion Records Ltd v Sawkins* [2005] 1 WLR 3281.

indistinguishable from the work itself, creating concurrent rights of the author and the broadcaster in the work, and liability with the end-users.[130] If the content is not an authorial work, such as a sporting event, the broadcaster will indirectly be able to exercise exclusionary rights over non-protectable content in the signals. If a record is created of a radio broadcast it will become a sound recording, which is itself a separate work. Likewise, if a record is created of an audio-visual broadcast then it becomes a film—also a separate work. Why then is the transmission itself a work? Given the lack of a form, it would appear that almost none of the *Ainsworth* threshold criteria are satisfied—a live broadcast of which no record is made may not be definable, identifiable, not assignable, and most of all will have no stability, nor any permanence.

Balganesh has convincingly argued that in its origin the transmission is the result of a contract that the broadcaster enters into with the content providers, which results in property; and in its delivery the transmission is a service, which again is treated as property. He reveals the political dynamic of the United States being actively behind the international treaty negotiations to make other nations recognise broadcasts as works.[131] But the irony is that the United States itself has never recognised broadcasts as works. In the United Kingdom, broadcasts were recognised as works for the first time under the Copyright Act 1956. The lobbying groups that most powerfully argued for this were sports promotors who had no other way to protect sporting spectacles,[132] and the British Broadcasting Corporation, which did not want broadcasts of events such as the coronation to be aired in cinema theatres without their consent.[133] History seems to suggest that in the wake of these powerful forces vying for their economic interests to be protected, the conceptual qualifying factors for thinghood were completely overlooked. That broadcasts are simply electronic waves containing certain signals literally up in the air, was not regarded problematic. It would appear that in most cases when broadcasters allege infringement of their copyright, they may have a record of the broadcast to show what the work is. Since in that situation it may simply be a sound recording or a film, one may wonder what purpose the broadcast being a work really serves.

[130] Shyamkrishna Balganesh, 'The Social Costs of Property Rights in Broadcast (and Cable) Signals' (2007) 22 Berkeley Tech LJ 1303, 1320.

[131] ibid 1329, 1385.

[132] See generally Brad Sherman, 'Public Ownership of Private Spectacles' in Brad Sherman and Leanne Wiseman (eds), *Copyright and the Challenge of the New* (Kluwer Law International 2012) 221–49.

[133] BBC Memorandum, 'A Copyright in Broadcasting' (June 1949), submitted to the Broadcasting Committee (copy with the author, taken from the National Archives). In the run up to the passing of the Copyright Act 1956, the BBC engaged deeply with the consultation process and lobbied for broadcasts to be recognised as copyright works.

Ignoring broadcasts for the time being, in general, despite being minimalist, the requirement of form still performs the evidential and boundary roles. The need for record is inextricably linked to the exclusionary duties that copyright imposes on the rest of the world. Chapter 4 elaborates further on what these duties are made up of. Breach of this duty means performing any of these acts when not authorised, and this leads to liability for the tortious action of copyright infringement, as discussed further in Chapter 5. In an action for infringement, the copyright owner should be able to prove what the work is and where its boundaries lie in order to demonstrate that a restricted act has been performed in relation to the work. The existence of the record as a condition precedent for copyright to subsist in the work responds to both these needs—as evidence to prove the work and as an indicator of the boundaries of the work.

Some scholars argue that even if one accepts that a record is needed as proof, alternative evidence can be produced, so that the need for record prior to copyright subsistence can be done away with. Alternative evidence likely means oral evidence, since any other evidence documenting the work can count as record of the work, given that the law is not prescriptive about the manner of record. Despite the safeguards of cross-examination, oral evidence is a subjective recollection of the relevant witnesses. Even if we were to accept this, the oral evidence may not corroborate the existence of a work.[134] To piece together from bits of oral evidence the content of the work sufficient to enable comparison with the alleged copy of the work, or to assess if any other restricted act has been carried out, risks failure in most cases. The existence of a record resolves this issue and provides stability to the subject matter so that the exclusionary right can be enforced.

While form helps draw the boundaries of the work and alert the rest of the world about it, the nature of the work is such that if a person exercises the exclusionary right in relation to the work without the copyright owner's permission, the copyright owner cannot physically exclude them. This is because their exercise of the right does not diminish the copyright owner's ability to exercise the same rights at the same time. To the Law Commission this means that a copyright owner is not able to really exclude the rest of the world from the work. In its terminology, the work is non-rivalrous. The Law Commission argues that for a resource to qualify to be a thing it should be rivalrous. This brings us to the subsection below.

[134] For issues associated with lack of form in television programmes, see *Green v Broadcasting Corporation of New Zealand* [1989] RPC 700.

(ii) Form and non-rivalrousness of work

The proponents of the chose in action theory of copyright, such as Williams, argue that the benefit that one can derive from copyright is not the varied uses that can be made of the work, but rather the exclusivity in being able to exercise privileges over it. In their view, this is what makes copyright a property right—no one else but the copyright owner can exercise these privileges, which, if not complied with, the copyright owner must go to the court to enforce.[135] Balganesh argues that due to the non-rivalrous nature of copyright, there is no way that a copyright owner can ensure the factual exclusivity of the use of their resource in the same manner as the owner of a tangible resource can do. He further argues that the only way the exclusivity can be maintained is by going to law,[136] mirroring the argument of Williams above. Let us first examine the idea of a non-rivalrous resource. Then we can ascertain whether exclusivity is the singular essence of copyright. If it is not, then going to law is also not the only way that one can enjoy copyright.

A non-rivalrous resource is that which is not diminished by the simultaneous use of it by several persons at the same time.[137] Conversely, the use of a rivalrous resource by one person eliminates the simultaneous use of it by another person. But it is important to appreciate that the rivalrous nature of tangible resources is a matter of degree. The Law Commission's Consultation Paper also acknowledges this and refers to it as existing on a spectrum.[138] But the Paper nevertheless goes on to regard it as one of the defining features of a thing.[139] When the rivalrous nature of tangible assets is itself relative, it cannot be made the basis for a brightline and a binary distinction between tangible and intangible assets.

Let us take three examples and examine how the rivalrous nature of resources plays out. Suppose P owns a diamond ring. P adorning the diamond ring eliminates any other person's ability to use it as a finger ring at the same time. Indeed, P's use of it renders it factually impossible for everyone else to wear it at the same time. There is no meaningful way in which the diamond ring can be partially worn by Q, while P retains at the same time some use and enjoyment of the diamond ring as a finger ring. The very nature of the diamond ring enables complete factual exclusion from it. This coincidence makes

[135] Williams (n 12) 232.

[136] Shyamkrishna Balganesh, 'Alienability and Copyright Law' in Helena Howe and Jonathan Griffiths, *Concepts of Property in Intellectual Property Law* (CUP 2013) 178–79.

[137] For more discussion on what rivalrousness means, see Smith, 'Intellectual Property as Property' (n 32) 1758, 1779.

[138] Law Commission Consultation Paper (n 19) para 5.81.

[139] Law Commission Report (n 46) paras 2.60–2.61.

it seem that the only focus of property rights should be exclusivity. To the extent that rivalrousness enables a person to achieve this, it may also seem that only those resources that are rivalrous can be things.

A parcel of land, however, is less rivalrous than a diamond ring. Let us examine how. If P owns a thousand-acre pasture, a squatter, Q, occupying a small barn on the pasture does not diminish completely the enjoyment of the pasture as a pasture by P. P can still enjoy the land not occupied by Q in all the ways that an owner would enjoy it by exercising their powers and privileges over it. Similarly, Q can also exercise their own powers and privileges over the barn as an owner would do. This is why it is still possible for Q to adversely possess the same land while it is in possession of another person until such time as P's title extinguishes.[140] The exclusivity of the whole land does mean something to the landowner and the law does recognise their right to sue for repossession of the land up to a point.[141] The more land Q begins to occupy, the greater is P's concern for exclusivity. But until it reaches the tipping point where P cannot enjoy their land at all when Q is enjoying it, it is not possible to say that P's enjoyment is diminished completely. The landowner's ability to enjoy the land as a resource is, therefore, independent of whether they bring a suit, and indeed whether they are successful in that suit. The exclusivity is not the singular focus of a landowner's interest in their land.

Let us see how rivalrous nature applies to the content of copyright. If P writes a novel, potentially infinite copies of it can be made and each copy can be used by a user without affecting its use by P or someone else. Unlike if P owned a diamond ring which only P can wear at any given point in time, P's novel can be copied and each copy enjoyed without diminishing any single holder's use of it. The content of copyright subject matter is relatively less rivalrous in a similar way as land. Suppose, for simplicity, that Q copies 5 per cent of P's novel.[142] Q copying the novel in this manner may have an economic impact on P in losing some of the exclusivity to their novel, but the ability of P to go on to use the novel to derive benefit from it by publishing it, distributing it, communicating it, adapting it, and so on is not completely diminished. The law does recognise P's ability to go to the court to enforce the exclusivity by an

[140] Assuming that the land is in the United Kingdom and is unregistered.

[141] Limitation Act 1980, s 15(1). But in the United Kingdom, with the introduction of the LRA and the successive registration of much of the land, the approach to adverse possession has changed. See LRA, sch 6.

[142] Of course, the 5 per cent copied should represent a substantial part for it to amount to copyright infringement. More on substantiality in Chapter 5.

action of copyright infringement. But even if P does not go to the court, P can continue to enjoy all privileges and powers in relation to the novel. Exclusivity is, therefore, not the singular focus of the enjoyment of the resource, either if the resource is land, or if the resource is the work.

Another argument Balganesh makes is that the only way for a copyright owner to maintain the exclusivity is to go to law.[143] This may not be the case in relation to any of the resources discussed above. If Q sees a diamond ring even when P is not wearing it, there is no reason to assume that Q will always take it, such that the only way for P to maintain exclusivity over their ring is to bring an action in conversion. Similarly, even if P has left the boundaries of the thousand-acre pasture with nothing more than a wooden fence, there is no reason to assume that Q will remove the fence. It may not be that the only way P can maintain exclusivity to their pasture is by suing Q in trespass. In the same way, if P has written a novel, there is no reason to assume that the rest of the world including Q is out to copy their novel. They may enjoy the novel in ways other than making copies of it. Therefore, it is incorrect to claim that the only way to maintain exclusivity is to go to the court. Just as we do not live in a world where one needs to be constantly vigilant to protect one's tangible things, we have also reached a point where one can rest assured that a person purchasing a copyright protected novel, for example, will know better than to make copies of it. The rights in a novel may be more susceptible to being infringed in comparison to land or chattels, but this does not mean that the rights will necessarily be infringed.

Despite all this discussion, eventually, if the rights are infringed and P wants to take action, then P has to go to court, whether the resource is a diamond ring, land, or copyright content. Singling out copyright to argue that the only way of maintaining exclusivity is by going to the court paints a skewed picture. The rest of the world being prevented from exercising what an owner can exercise in relation to the tangible resource is an essential characteristic also of a property right in tangible things. For example, P, a landowner, has a privilege to grow red roses in her garden which no one else, including Q, R, S, and so on, can do, and if they did without her consent, it amounts to trespass the moment they enter P's land. Does P not have to go to law to enforce this exclusivity? Although Williams does not address this expressly, his argument seems to suggest that with property rights in tangible things the owner does not always have to go to law but can resort to self-help or self-redress. Even if this is true, the

[143] Balganesh, 'Alienability and Copyright Law' (n 136) 178–79.

extent to which an owner can turn to self-help is limited strictly to clear and simple cases (such as an overhanging branch in land law, for example) or situations of emergency where a court proceeding might be too slow to respond. Courts have cautioned that the remedy must be 'regarded with great jealousy' against wider application.[144] Self-help is not possible in copyright, but it would be incorrect to make this the basis on which to regard copyright as a chose in action, given the narrowness of the availability of self-help even in relation to tangible things.

The discussion above reveals that a work is closer in nature to land than it is to contractual rights. This leads to one of two conclusions: first, if land can be a chose in possession despite being relatively less rivalrous than chattels, so can a work if one moves away from chattels on the rivalrousness spectrum; secondly, if rivalrousness can move along such a wide spectrum, rivalrousness should not be the basis for classifying resources. The latter is a more convincing conclusion.

4. Benefits of Thinghood Analysis in Copyright

The discussion above is not merely confined to theory but can result in many doctrinal benefits. It drives home the point that the property regime places several safeguards against an expansionist tendency. Let us examine them in relation to each component of the intangible thing in copyright.

By insisting on evaluating the substantive content of the subject matter of property rights with normative considerations, the property regime prevents copyright being extended to everything that is a product of the human mind. The eligibility of a certain content to become a work is also a matter for *numerus clausus*. The categorisation of works is a result of historical developments, international treaty influences, and a reflection through the statute of what a society regards as worthy of protection. As they would do in relation to property rights in tangible things, courts should exercise restraint in recognising new subject matter that has not passed legislative scrutiny. The categories operate as a guiding light for the courts. This not only enables maintaining the objectively perceptible categories of works but also helps evaluate the definitional criteria for individual works. It is essential for courts to evaluate what

[144] *Moffett v Brewer* (1848) Iowa 1 Greene 348, 350 (Greene J). For a more recent discussion of the authorities, see *Macnab v Richardson* [2008] EWCA Civ 1631 [24]–[36] (Lloyd LJ).

amounts to a sculpture, for example, or a graphic work, separate from whether these works are original.

The insistence on separability of the subject matter helps leave ideas free. This leaves the building blocks of creation available in plenty to foster greater creativity and promote diverse works based on the same idea. Certain kinds of works may continue to push the boundaries of the definition of works. In this regard, difficulties may arise also in relation to works that exist only momentarily, such as a firework display or a laser show. Arguably, for their own benefit, those who claim copyright in this are better advised to record the sequence, variety, and configuration of the display in some other form, so that copyright protection can be extended.[145] Furthermore, conceptual art, which makes an art out of a concept or an idea, may raise controversial questions. Since ideas are not themselves protectable, if an argument is made that such art can somehow be protected as graphic works because of the inclusive definition under CDPA, s 4(2), courts should exercise caution because fundamentally the very definition of a work is not fulfilled. Dramatic works also have an inclusive definition under s 3(1), and therefore it is arguable that performance art should be included in it. Like conceptual art, performance art also conveys an idea and for similar reasons courts should exercise caution before protecting it as a dramatic work.

By requiring that only recorded expressions be protected, the CDPA achieves another objective—to also keep unrecorded expressions free. The law determining the timing of triggering property rights only after a record is created promotes oral traditions and sharing of expressions in sectors such as jazz music and improvised comedic acts. Requiring that a thing have a form is double-edged: as much as it provides boundaries for the rest of the world to exclude themselves, it also provides boundaries for the property owner not to claim beyond those boundaries. If expression alone was sufficient for the copyright owner to claim copyright protection, they could control the extent of the work based on largely subjective oral evidence to suit the needs of a potential infringement action *ex post*. The need for record seeks to limit such opportunistic behaviour by drawing an objective boundary on what a copyright owner can claim (either as a copy or as an altered copy).

The arguments on thinghood presented here go against the tide of the CJEU case law, which has substantially diluted the need for the definition of

[145] Here, parallels can be drawn with *Abraham Moon* (n 126) where a fabric design was described using letters and numbers.

a work. The CJEU has held that anything that is an identifiable original expression attracts copyright protection.[146] Even if this were to be read as subsuming the requirements of separability and form,[147] it does not require any assessment of the substantive content. Whilst originality will be discussed in Chapter 3, essentially any product of the human mind that is an expression and can be objectively identifiable is protected. This makes it possible to disregard the categories of works so meticulously drawn under the CDPA and the requirement of form as well as any definitional attributes developed by the courts in relation to specific works. These decisions are part of UK law until a higher court diverges from it. This was the issue in *Waterrower v Liking*, where Forsyth J acknowledged the conflict between *Hensher*, which required a work of artistic craftsmanship to have artistic quality as part of the definition of the work, and *Cofemel*, which required any criteria other than originality to be disregarded.[148] Having given due consideration to the historical reasons behind recognising artistic craftsmanship as a separate work under the CDPA, Forsyth J sought to interpret *Cofemel* harmoniously with *Hensher*. He held that the issue of originality should be dealt with first in conformity with *Cofemel*, and only if this step is passed, then the *Hensher* criteria can be applied.[149] In future, if an opportunity arose to diverge from the CJEU jurisprudence, the arguments put forward in this chapter could provide a strong rationale for separating the work from the requirement of originality.

5. Summary

The centrality of the thing in the law of tangible property cannot be overemphasised. The analogy indicates that the very notion of copyright as a property right begins with a clear and analytically explicable concept of an intangible thing. This chapter demonstrated that the thing in copyright consists of substantive content that can be referred to as a work, that is separable from the human body and from the rights, is independent of the legal system and has a form. It sought to argue that the existence of the thing in copyright should be able to counter arguments as to the nature of copyright, such as that the

[146] Case C–310/17 *Levola Hengelo BV v European Food Company BV*, EU:C:2018:899, paras 36–37; Case C–683/17 *Cofemel—Sociedade de Vestuário SA v G-Star Raw CV*, EU:C:2019:721, paras 22–24.

[147] *Wright v BTC Core* [2023] EWCA Civ 868, [2023] ECDR 18 [59]–[60], holding that identifiability of a work is not the same as the need for record under CDPA, s 3(2), though it may serve the same purpose.

[148] [2024] EWHC 2806 (IPEC) [146], [154]–[159].

[149] ibid [159].

thing in copyright is the right itself, that copyright relates to pure information, and that because copyright is non-rivalrous, copyright is a chose in action. In addition to clearing these misconceptions, this chapter also demonstrated the doctrinal benefits that can be gained in conceptualising the existence of a thing in copyright.

3
Acquisition of Copyright

1. Introduction

One of the most immediate consequences of establishing the existence of a thing for the purposes of property law is that a person can acquire title to it independently for the first time. Some scholars have argued that in relation to land, the title so acquired consists of a fee simple and in relation to chattels one can call the interest ownership.[1] This makes some scholars insist that the term 'title' can only be used meaningfully in relation to tangible assets because in both land and chattels title means exclusive possession forever.[2] Helpfully, there are also scholars who have described title as meaning generally an entitlement or an interest,[3] opening up the possibility of the title being acquired also in an intangible thing. Applying this to the copyright context, at the point of first acquisition the entitlement acquired is the entitlement to the fullest interest that can be acquired, which in other words is the ownership of the work of copyright.

Acquiring the title by a person has an impact on the behaviour of the rest of the world towards the thing and on the relationship of the acquirer to the thing. The act of acquisition places in relation to the thing duties on the rest of the world of non-interference, grants legal power over the thing that the acquirer can exercise at their discretion, and grants use privileges exercisable at the acquirer's discretion. Since these duties are imposed on the rest of the world without their consent, the rest of the world needs to know when it is that they need to alter their actions to comply with the duties. Given this impact, the conduct of acquisition gains heightened importance. Therefore, as a practical

[1] eg Ben McFarlane, *The Structure of Property Law* (Hart Publishing 2008) 140. Rostill challenges this by offering three different views on the interest that is acquired, namely a weak possessory interest, a strong proprietary interest and a presumed interest. Luke Rostill, *Possession, Relative Title, and Ownership in English Law* (OUP 2021) 27–36.

[2] William Swadling, 'Property—General Principles' in Andrew Burrows (ed), *English Private Law* (3rd edn, OUP 2013) para 4.131. To be sure, Swadling objects to using the word title in relation to debt and shares, and not necessarily to intellectual property.

[3] Anthony M Honoré, 'Ownership' in Anthony G Guest (ed), *Oxford Essays in Jurisprudence* (OUP 1961) 107, 134.

Copyright as Personal Property. Poorna Mysoor, Oxford University Press. © Poorna Mysoor 2025.
DOI: 10.1093/9780191954962.003.0003

matter, the conduct of acquisition must be an overt and observable act. As a legal matter, the conduct of acquisition can only be designated by the law and not by the parties agreeing between themselves. As a normative matter the conduct of acquisition should provide sufficient justification for the acquirer of the thing to exercise exclusionary rights, powers and privileges over the thing.

Given the express provisions of the copyright statutes, no one can deny that copyright places duties of non-interference on the rest of the world.[4] But scholars rarely turn their attention to how these duties come to be imposed. The duties are imposed on the world at large not simply because the relevant statute says so, but because copyright is also a right in an intangible thing, as argued in Chapter 2, and is acquired in a manner analogous to exclusionary rights that are acquired in a tangible thing. The existence of rules of independent acquisition makes copyright different from other intangible assets, such as contractual debt. The right to the repayment of a contractual debt is acquired for the first time by way of a contract. Because of its *inter partes* nature, it imposes only *in personam* duties, meaning only on the parties to the contract because the contracting parties are meant to have consented to these duties.[5] Copyright on the contrary is acquired for the first time by conduct that is not even remotely akin to entering into a contract. The rights and duties that arise with the acquisition of copyright are not mutually negotiated between the parties but imposed by the law. This has long been recognised as one of the most prominent reasons why copyright cannot be grouped in the same category of rights as contractual debts by describing them with the common terminology of choses in action.[6]

The act of acquisition of rights to a tangible thing independently for the first time is described as taking possession of it.[7] For this reason, possession as a technical term is only used in relation to tangible things. Since physicality of the thing is central to the conceptualisation of possession, one cannot take possession of intangible things.[8] So entrenched is this view to the ontology of property rights that theorists might regard it as abhorrent to even consider the

[4] McFarlane (n 1) 6; Simon Douglas, '*Kuwait Airways Corporation v Iraqi Airways Company*' in Simon Douglas, Robin Hickey, and Emma Waring (eds), *Landmark Cases in Property Law* (Hart 2015) 212.

[5] Contract law does problematise consent as the basis for contracting, and in many contracts it may be difficult to find a meaningful consent. However, the purpose here is limited to distinguishing between *in rem* and *in personam* rights.

[6] Howard W Elphinstone, 'What is a Chose in Action' (1893) 9 LQR 311, 312–14.

[7] Possession has many other meanings in different contexts, but the one that is used here is in the context of the first acquisition of title.

[8] Simon Douglas, '*Kuwait Airways*' (n 4) 213; Thomas Merrill, 'Ownership and Possession' in Yun-Chien Chang (ed), *Law and Economics of Possession* (CUP 2015) 25.

idea of possession of intangible things. In specific relation to copyright, courts have also held that one cannot take possession of copyright.[9] Therefore, there is no need to go against this tide and give the term possession an unnatural meaning. But one must avoid drawing inaccurate conclusions from the physicality of possession. It should not follow that the only way to acquire property rights is by taking possession or that only those rights that are acquired by taking possession are property rights. Taking possession is only one of the ways of acquiring property rights. If the thing is tangible, then property rights in it can be acquired by taking possession. If the thing is intangible, property rights can still be acquired by other means prescribed by law.

The concept of possession, therefore, should be separated from the broader question of the acquisition of property rights, with a focus on the 'conduct' that enables the acquisition. If we examine why the concept of possession is required at all, the answer lies in the allocative justice that possession brings about. In civilised societies, to ensure peaceful co-existence, we need an orderly way of allocating resources to persons that indicates shared acceptance of the rationale underlying the allocation. After all, the role of possession in this context is to demonstrate, as Epstein describes, 'how given bits of property are matched with given individuals'.[10] Surely the rules that match things with persons are not limited only to physical things. Indeed, it is arguable that the substantive content of the thing—be it land, chattels, or a work, determines the conduct that performs the allocative function. But the existence of the conduct of acquisition of property rights in relation to these things cannot be denied.

The upshot is that the preoccupation with the physical in the conceptualization of possession should not make us blind to the possibility that there are rules of acquisition also of intangible things.[11] A person P, for instance, singing a Beatles song, does not make the song (lyrics or music) theirs even if it is an expression and even if they record it. There must be something else that allocates the expression to P. Chapter 2 argued that it is possible to speak meaningfully of an intangible thing in relation to copyright by analogy with tangible things. When the thing-relatedness can be detached from the physical, *a fortiori* the process of acquisition of the rights in it will also be detached from the physical. As this author has argued elsewhere,[12] it is possible to explore the

[9] *Chaplin v Leslie Frewin (Publishers) Ltd* [1966] Ch 71, 94; *Performing Rights Society v London Theatres* [1924] AC 1, 26.

[10] Richard Epstein, 'Possession as the Root of Title' (1979) 13 Ga L Rev 1221, 1222.

[11] The Law Commission also argues that this is possible in relation to digital assets. Law Commission, *Digital Assets: A Consultation Paper* (Law Com No 256, 2022) paras 4.22, 4.24. Law Commission, *Report on Digital Assets* (Law Com No 412, 2023) ch 5.

[12] Poorna Mysoor, 'Possession in Copyright by Analogy' (2024) 140 LQR 277.

rules of acquisition of copyright by analogy with taking possession of tangible things. Let us examine what the conduct is, the engaging in which enables a person to acquire copyright.

Under the provisions governing the first ownership of copyright in the Copyright, Designs and Patents Act 1988 (CDPA), a person acquires copyright in an authorial work by expressing their thoughts in an 'original' manner.[13] Therefore, literary, dramatic, musical, and artistic works can become the author's own only if the author has expressed their thoughts in an original manner. Entrepreneurial works require the relevant efforts in creating a work that is not a copy of an existing work.[14] Therefore, for works such as sound recordings, films, broadcasts, and typographical arrangements, their maker should invest resources in creating a new work of the relevant kind. It is possible to argue that rules of acquisition of copyright are analogous to a combination of the rules of accession to a thing by manufacture and rules governing taking possession of a thing. Section 2 below deals with how the conduct in relation to these works can be studied by analogy with accession to tangible things by manufacture and taking possession of tangible things.

Scholars often make a connection between the rivalrousness of a thing and the ability to take possession of it. By this argument, a work being a non-rivalrous resource makes it impossible to be acquired by taking possession of it, or even be acceded to by manufacturing it. Section 3 deals with this debate and explains how rivalrousness is a matter of degree and that not all tangible things are perfectly and factually rivalrous. It shows how the law imbues factually less perfect things like land with characteristics such that it can function as a rivalrous resource. By extension, it demonstrates how in copyright the law imbues analogous characteristics.

Section 4 below goes on to discuss the conceptual and doctrinal benefits of exploring the analogy with possession. Although the CDPA does sufficiently provide for ownership, it still makes sense to separate the analogous concept of possession from ownership. First, the implications on the taxonomy of choses in possession and choses in action, since possession underpins this classification. Secondly, the teleological explanation that the analogy within the first acquisition context can offer to support the need for a work to be separated from originality. As a result, it can also offer guidelines as to the level of originality that would be normatively justifiable. Thirdly, and as an extension of this, the separation of the thing from a focus on the act of acquisition can bring the

[13] CDPA, s 1(1)(a). Classically, these are the works with human authors.

[14] CDPA, ss 5A(2), 5B(4), 6(6), and 8(2).

emphasis back to the act of acquisition as being the significant differentiator of copyright from other intangible assets. Finally, the analogy with first acquisition can inspire within copyright discourse a discussion in relation to subsequent independent acquisition, similar to tangible things.

2. Accession, Possession, and Copyright

Let us begin with the statement that the title can be acquired in tangible things by taking possession of them. The law recognises many ways in which one can take possession depending on whether the thing is a chattel or land, and whether the thing already exists in nature or has come into existence for the first time. In the world that we live in, there is not much land that is not currently owned. Therefore, scholars acknowledge that the conduct that results in adverse possession is consistent with first acquisition of title to land.[15] In this vein, English law identifies two elements necessary for legal possession: first, a sufficient degree of exclusive physical control of the thing; and, secondly, an intention to exclude the world at large.[16] With chattels that are already in existence, the rules on finders of goods are analogous in their elements to those of adverse possession. With chattels that come into existence for the first time as chattels, the rules of accession recognise mixing and manufacture as the conduct that grants title to the person engaging in the relevant conduct.[17] At an abstract level, physical control is a more general concept with significant malleability to its meaning, whereas accession is a more specific type of conduct. The difference lies in the focus on accession being the labour that goes into the creation of new things, whereas in possession the focus is on taking physical control of things that already exist in various ways.[18] Some scholars recognise that the process of accession is also one of the ways in which a person takes physical control over the thing to which one accedes.[19] This is because it is difficult to think of a mode of accession that does not result in some degree of physical control over the thing being manufactured. But it is entirely

[15] eg Luke Rostill (n 1)) 15–16. See also Henry E Smith, 'The Elements of Possession' in Yun-Chien Chang, *Law and Economics of Possession* (CUP 2015) 67.

[16] *JA Pye (Oxford) Ltd v Graham* [2002] UKHL 30, [2003] 1 AC 419 [32], [41]–[43] (Lord Browne-Wilkinson).

[17] McFarlane (n 1) 158–62

[18] eg *Aluminium Industrie Vaassen BV v Romalpa Aluminium Ltd* [1976] 1 WLR 676; *Borden (UK) Ltd v Scottish Timber Products Ltd* [1981] Ch 25; and *Re Peachdart* [1984] Ch 131 all support manufacture as an independent mode of acquisition of title.

[19] McFarlane (n 1) 161.

conceivable for a person to exert physical control over a thing without also manufacturing the thing.

What does this discussion mean for copyright? Works capable of attracting copyright that had hitherto not been in existence are created every minute. One may argue that the context most closely analogous to copyright is that of accession to chattels by manufacture, because first acquisition of copyright is to newly created works. Just as the property right in a thing manufactured does not exist before the process of manufacture in that form, a work does not exist on its own before copyright in it is acquired. Additionally, in copyright there is a boundary problem. Chattels by their very nature of being tangible acquire boundaries because of their shape and form when they are manufactured, enabling the exclusionary rights, exclusive powers, and privileges to arise in relation to them. When works are created, as intangible things, they have no physical boundaries. Interestingly, land can also have boundary problems. Consider taking adverse possession of a certain piece of land that has no visible boundaries (say a pasture) by putting up a fence, demarcating the boundary of the land being adversely possessed. Therefore, the analogy with both accession by manufacture and taking possession can be demonstrated in copyright.

It is not a surprise that both accession and possession have been developed only in relation to tangible things, and therefore extending them to intangible things may seem to be an insurmountable challenge. As regards accession, a product is said to be manufactured if the process leads to the ingredients losing their identity as such, resulting in a product that is different from its ingredients.[20] In the case law, not only are the ingredients physical things, but also the end product manufactured. The question that much of the case law on possession seeks to answer, be it in the context of finders of goods or adverse possession, is whether certain conduct amounts to exercising exclusive physical control.[21] Our purpose of extending these to intangible things would be a non-starter because these decisions only reinforce the preoccupation of the concept of both possession and accession with the physical. One needs to move beyond the specificity of the case law to ask the more conceptual question as to why physical control is necessary in the first place for establishing possession.

The following paragraphs begin by exploring the rationale behind the rules of manufacture and its relationship with the creation of works of copyright and the rules of taking physical control and its analogy with creating boundaries.

[20] *Borden (UK) Ltd v Scottish Timber Products Ltd* [1981] Ch 25, where the resin was held to have lost its identity in the manufacture of a chipboard.

[21] eg *JA Pye* (n 16).

The intention to exclude, some scholars argue, is manifest in the very conduct of taking physical control. One might argue that if physical control is proved unambiguously, the intention will have been proved on the back of it. It would be worth ascertaining what intention to exclude means in copyright. Table 3.1 below provides a summary of analogies being drawn at a conceptual level.

Table 3.1 Symbolism and signals behind certain conduct

Conduct	Symbolism	Signal
Manufacture of chattels	Ingredients being transformed	Relational signal to the rest of the world
Expressing in original way in copyright	Content in the public domain and other sources used to transform	Relational signal to the rest of the world
Taking physical control of land	Boundaries being drawn so that rest of the world knows what they should do	Exclusionary signal
Recording the expression in copyright	Boundaries being drawn so that rest of the world knows what they should do	Exclusionary signal

(a) Manufacture, Physical Control, and Copyright

Following the natural sequence, it makes sense to explore how the intangible thing is created first before we explore how the boundaries are drawn. Accordingly, we may begin with the rules of accession by manufacture. Manufacture as a process is said to be complete when the constituents are consumed, destroyed, or lose their characteristics or value as raw materials.[22] On the face of it, it is difficult to see this removed from the physicality. But the reason why the person manufacturing acquires title in the thing is not because of the disappearance of the raw materials, but because of the labour and skill that the person expends to transform the thing from its raw materials. There is an intuitive and jurisprudential connection between the person expending the labour and skill, and the entitlement to the thing the person manufactures, regardless of whether the thing or the ingredients are physical in nature.[23] Once the process of acceding to a thing by manufacture can be shown to be

[22] *Re Peachdart* [1984] Ch 131, 142.

[23] The Lockean labour dessert is often put forward in this context as a justification. For a detailed account of the application of Lockean theory to intellectual property, see Justin Hughes, The Philosophy of Intellectual Property (1988) 77 Geo L J 287, 296ff.

detachable from the physical in this manner, it can be conceptualised in the realm of the intangible.

When the intangible thing is created, boundaries need to be drawn for which analogies may be found in taking physical control. An attempt to understand physical control as anything outside the physical realm suggests impossibility and pointlessness. This is where most of the difficulty in establishing the analogy lies. However, the reason why the law requires the exercise of physical control is not because physically it achieves exclusivity of control. It is because of the symbolism attached to the conduct of taking physical control, which in turn achieves exclusivity in the eyes of the law. If the idea of exclusive physical control can be detached from the physical in this manner, then we can attempt to draw an analogy with intangible things. If we can find acts in relation to copyright that perform a similar role as taking exclusive physical control, we can establish by analogy what it means in copyright to take possession.

There is a vast diversity in the kind of conduct that courts find sufficient to exercise physical control. In their celebrated essay on possession, Pollock and Wright acknowledged that 'it is not possible, as a matter of fact, to possess a house, a wood, or a field in the same manner as we possess the money in our pockets'.[24] Clearly, some things lend themselves to greater physical control than the others. Whales, shipwrecks, and large tracts of land can be brought under exclusive physical control in the eyes of the law,[25] even in circumstances where the physical control exercised does not exclude someone else from the thing. Pollock and Wright acknowledge that physical control does not require unqualified power, and that all power is finite.[26] Writing in 1895, Brodhurst wondered whether the belief that possession only extended to actual physical control was a misapprehension.[27]

Whilst theorists generally acknowledge the symbolism behind the conduct of taking physical control, they show great resistance to moving beyond the physicality of the thing itself over which the control is exercised. Merrill posits that exercising physical control is an empirically observable way in which a person establishes a relationship between themself and a thing, although he insists that such a relationship is only possible with physical things.[28] Rose argues that physically restraining the rest of the world to exclude them is not the

[24] Frederick Pollock and Robert S Wright, *An Essay on Possession in Common Law* (Clarendon Press 1888) 30.

[25] For whales, see *Swift v Gifford*, 23 F Cas 558 (D Mass 1872) 560; for a case on shipwreck, see *The Tubantia* [1924] P 78 (PDA) 88–91 and for land, *JA Pye* (n 16) is a good example.

[26] Pollock and Wright (n 24) 12.

[27] Spencer Brodhurst, 'Is Copyright a Chose in Action?' (1895) 11 LQR 64, 74.

[28] Merrill (n 8) 11.

purpose behind the requirement of physical control, but to send a signal to the rest of the world that the person exercising control retains the thing for themself.[29] She argues that it is 'something like yelling loudly enough to all who may be interested' that 'This is mine'.[30] She argues that the signalling function is what allows even the most modest fence to perform this function effectively. Interestingly, Rose also insists that the physicality of the action is vital for possession. She asserts that there must be a physical thing to which possession can refer, and that 'the idea of possession carries little sway' in connection with intellectual property.[31]

Emphasising the expressive role of possession, Crawford argues that the significance of physical control lies in 'the message that particular factual relationships between people and objects of property send to other members of a particular interpretive community'.[32] He insists that the unacknowledged reasons for courts closely examining the actions involved in exercising physical control are to look for the messages that they convey to the relevant community. Doctrinally he demonstrates, using *Pye v Graham*, that the activities that were overwhelmingly influential in the adverse possessor being held to have exercised physical control were not that he had the key to the gate of the grazing land, but that he had done everything to use the land for cattle farming as if he were the owner.[33] Crawford argues that 'the sum total' of the adverse possessor's behaviour sent 'unmistakable claim-staking signals to all who cared to see'.[34] Nevertheless, Crawford dismisses intellectual property as 'analytically different' while discussing thing-relatedness,[35] leaving the possibility of an expressive role of possession in intellectual property unexplored.

One can see why theorists do not wish to separate possession of its connection with the physical realm. But the subordinate role of the physical power in physical control is quite clear. It may not be incorrect to suggest that courts insist on physical control not for its own sake, but to achieve symbolically the allocative function. It can hardly be argued that in case of a non-physical resource like a poem the law has no rules that perform the allocative function of demarcating them as belonging to persons. Even the scholars arguing most astutely that there is no concept of possession in intangibles go on to put their

[29] Carol M Rose, 'The Law Is Nine-Tenths of Possession: An Adage Turned on Its Head' in Yun-Chien Chang (ed), *Law and Economics of Possession* (CUP 2015) 50–53.
[30] Carol M Rose, 'Possession as the Origin of Property' (1985) 52 U Chi L Rev 73, 77, 81.
[31] Rose, 'The Law Is Nine-Tenths of Possession' (n 29) 60–61.
[32] Michael Crawford, *An Expressive Theory of Possession* (Hart 2020) 64.
[33] *JA Pye* (n 16) [58] (Lord Browne-Wilkinson).
[34] Crawford (n 32) 85.
[35] ibid 13. See Chapter 2 above for a discussion on what thing-relatedness means in copyright.

name down at the end of their scholarly piece to identify the literary work as theirs! Such empirical evidence aside, it is the relationship established through such demarcation of boundaries that enables a person to exercise their powers and privileges over the thing to use it and enjoy it, be it a physical or non-physical resource.

One may note that historically, the move of the rules of acquisition of title in the physical world towards the intangible world was one of the knottiest issues that the law had to deal with during the formative years of copyright law in the late eighteenth century. As Sherman and Bently explain, until about the mid-eighteenth century, the law had only known the manner of acquisition of property rights as they relate to tangible things, such as descent, purchase, occupation, and so on.[36] It had been argued that taking physical possession as in the case of occupancy was not the only way in which property rights can arise and that the law had to move with the times to respond to intangible subject matter. Following in the footsteps of Locke, it was argued that exerting labour could also be legitimately recognised for securing property rights, and such labour did not have to be only physical, but could also be intellectual,[37] marking a big leap in the conceptualisation of the ways in which the law can recognise the acquisition of title. Theorists who resist applying the symbolism behind taking physical control to non-physical things fail to appreciate this seismic change that took place nearly three hundred years ago.

The above discussion reveals that there are conceptual and historical reasons why it is possible to understand acquisition of copyright by analogy with acquisition of title to tangible things. Based on this symbolism an analogous signalling mechanism can be ascertained in copyright. At a conceptual level, the analysis of the process of manufacture gives out an important signal. One may call this the 'relational signal', which conveys to the world the relationship that the person manufacturing the thing establishes with that thing. This relationship underlies the ability to proclaim 'This is mine'. The second, and a related signal is the 'exclusionary signal', which entails an observable act that requires the rest of the world to exclude themselves from acting in a certain way in relation to the thing. This corresponds to a proclamation of 'Keep off' in relation to tangibles. For tangibles, the same act of taking physical control can send relational and exclusionary signals. However, in copyright, each of these signals is demonstrated by separate acts, as described below. It is, therefore,

[36] Brad Sherman and Lionel Bently, *The Making of Modern Intellectual Property Law* (CUP 1999) 20–21.
[37] ibid 22–24.

important to treat these functions as analytically distinct. Let us deal with each signal in turn.

(i) Relational signal

At the heart of the relational signal is the allocative significance of accession by manufacture, which demarcates things as belonging to persons. In the physical world, this relationship is established by a physical act. For things that have not yet come into existence, the act of bringing them into existence through the process of manufacture establishes the relational signal. Doctrinally, manufacture is defined as a process that makes the ingredients lose their identity and transform themselves into something different.[38] It is the labour and skill that a person puts in that makes the thing so manufactured their own.

A good example of cases where courts have been asked to examine how labour and skill perform the allocative function is in relation to body parts. Although common law frowns upon the human corpse being the subject matter of property rights, a person exercising labour and skill to transform human body parts in such a way that they can be differentiated from a mere corpse can acquire property rights in those body parts.[39] One may explore extending this rule beyond this context. If a person extracts genetic material from a living human cell by exercising labour and skill, arguably such person might acquire rights over such material. The skill and effort should be of a kind that make the body part lose the identity it had when it was part of the living human being. On this basis, Douglas and Goold also see the possibility of allocating rights over body tissue to the person who exerts skill and effort in excising it from the body.[40]

Pila uses this analogy to show that there must be a transformative act to give rise to a work in the copyright sense. For authorial works, she argues that the transformative act on the part of the author which results in creating the authorial work justifies the acquisition of property rights by the author.[41] For analytical clarity, the relational signal can be further divided into two parts—one that establishes the relationship and one that sends the signal to this effect to the rest of the world. In the case of tangibles, including body parts, the same observable act performs both functions. In copyright, by contrast, for authorial works, these two acts need to be separated. First, the act establishing the

[38] *Re Peachdart* [1984] Ch 131, 142.
[39] *Doodeward v Spence* [1908] 6 CLR 406 (High Court of Australia).
[40] Simon Douglas and Imogen Goold, 'Property in Human Biomaterials: A New Methodology' (2016) 75 CLJ 478, 500.
[41] Justine Pila, *The Subject Matter of Intellectual Property* (OUP 2017) 180–81.

relationship is a mental act involving the exercise of certain intellectual qualities, all of which can be explained together within the concept of 'originality'. A discussion on originality entails the kind of labour that goes into establishing this relationship. Secondly, the observable act that signals to the rest of the world that such a relationship has been established is the act of putting out or expressing the original work.

Let us begin with the first point. How exactly is the concept of originality to be understood by analogy with tangible things? In the context of human body parts, the use of skill and labour should be of such a kind that it has a transformative effect over what existed before. In the copyright context, what exist before the work is created are the ideas, the material in the public domain, the language, the rules of grammar, musical notes, and so on, and indeed anything that inspires, drives, or even just supports human beings to create a product of their mind. A true analogy with manufacture would only make sense if it could be shown that certain mental or intellectual labour was exercised to transform these ingredients to create a work that did not exist before. When we say that a work is original, conceptually it should capture this transformation by analogy. It follows intuitively that the person who brings about this transformation is the one who acquires the property rights. A person who 'comes up with' a song develops an attachment to it in such a way that they can claim 'I created it', which in other words is to claim 'This is mine'. The philosophical moorings drawn from Lockean labour theory and Hegelian personhood theory to offer normative justification for intellectual property are arguably rooted in the concept of originality.[42]

Regarding the doctrinal meaning of originality, as Bently explains, it is concerned with the relationship between the author and the work, not with whether the work is inventive, novel, or unique. In *University of London Press v University Tutorial Press*, where examination question papers were held to be original literary works, originality meant that the work must 'originate' from the author in the sense of not being copied.[43] For the law to recognise that a work originates from a particular person, that person should have put in certain intellectual qualities.[44] There is some dispute as to what these qualities are. The older English decisions identified labour, skill, and judgement.[45]

[42] For a historical account of copyright from the perspective of natural law, see generally Alfred C Yen, 'Restoring the Natural Law: Copyright as Labor and Possession' (1990) 51 Ohio St LJ 517.

[43] [1916] 2 Ch 601, 609.

[44] Lionel Bently and others, *Intellectual Property Law* (6th edn, OUP 2022) 100–02.

[45] *Ladbroke v William Hill* [1964]1 All ER 465, 473 (Lord Evershed). Different judges gave different formulations of this. The question in this case was whether football pools coupons with tables of

A question may still arise as to what kind of labour or skill is required. In *Interlego v Tyco*, the kind of labour and skill exercised was in production of a copy of a technical drawing, albeit with a high level of precision as to its measurements. It was held to be the wrong kind of labour because it ultimately only produced a copy.[46] As the work was the result of 'slavish' copying, involving no judgement on the author's part, no originality was found. To the extent that the notion of originality had been harmonised with EU law, it is part of the retained law in the United Kingdom. The formulation of originality under EU law is that the work must be the author's own intellectual creation.[47] Although there is some scepticism as to whether the harmonisation makes a practical difference to the outcome of a case on the issue of originality,[48] the courts in the United Kingdom have followed the EU formulation of originality.

Let us consider the second requirement of conveying to the world that a person has exercised the required transformative labour to establish the relationship with the work. While originality establishes the required relationship, the law further requires this relationship to be observable by way of an overt act so that it signals the relationship to the rest of the world. A consequence of the transformative nature of the intellectual labour exercised is that it is the 'work' that needs to be original, and not the underlying ideas. The underlying ideas together with the content in the public domain are the ingredients used to create a transformed entity which is the work. One may question the extent to which expressing one's thoughts in the form of a work is an overt or observable act. If, for example, a person, P, has a pencil on their desk, to declare their possession of it they do not need to take it out into the street and hold it in their hand where everyone can see it. The signalling function of possession is only such that the possession of a tangible asset can be empirically observed. The act of expression can be empirically observed in a similar manner and therefore perform the signalling function.

Another reason why the law requires that originality apply to works which are expressions is that if originality were required of the *ideas* themselves, then one person expressing an idea would have prevented another person from expressing the same idea as it would not be original even in the most basic sense

football teams to bet on were original literary works attracting copyright protection. The court held that the coupons were the result of a substantial measure to at least a non-trivial extent of labour, skill, and judgement, ibid 478 (Lord Devlin).

46 *Interlego v Tyco* [1989] AC 217, 263.

47 Case C–5/08 *Infopaq Int v Danske Dagblades Forening* [2009] ECR I–6569 (ECJ) para 45.

48 Although in most cases the UK and EU standards might produce similar results, scholars have identified a small number of situations when this may not be true. Bently and others (n 44) 102–07.

of having originated from the author. Therefore, in copyright one can only claim expressions to be one's own, not ideas. This is consistent with the arguments presented in Chapter 2 that as a normative matter ideas could not make up the substantive content of a work, and a work is separable from the right because it is captured within the expression. This ensures that a 'work' can only refer to an expression and not ideas themselves, such that ideas remain free as socio-cultural building blocks. Requiring originality of expression rather than ideas seeks to foster diversity of expressions. For example, a person can paint a still life of a basket of apples, even if the idea of a basket of apples is not original to that person. Copyright law will recognise the work as original so long as the components of the painting such as brushstrokes, the colour scheme, configuration, and so on are original in the sense that the person has used their creative choices and judgement in creating the painting. This ensures that anyone else can paint a basket of apples in any number of ways and styles, and each could be an original work.

Having signalled that the person has established a relationship with the work, the next step is to signal to the rest of the world what it is that they need to exclude themselves from, by drawing the boundaries. This brings us to the section below.

(ii) Exclusionary signal

In relation to tangible things, the exclusionary signal is an important aspect of control in that only the person exercising physical control should be able to use and enjoy the thing. Case law has held that the twin considerations of physical control are that the person taking physical control should be able to deal with it in the manner they determine and that no one else should be able to deal with the thing in this way.[49] After all, as Rostill explains, this is the significance of 'exclusive' control.[50] There should be a signal that makes the rest of the world alter their behaviour towards the thing that has come under a person's control. The function of this signal therefore is that the rest of the world begins to owe exclusionary duties to the person who has taken physical control of the thing. When one speaks of exclusionary conduct, the exclusion must relate to a boundary. Such boundary should be objectively ascertainable so as to imbue the exclusionary conduct with greater certainty. In relation to tangible things that can be brought within a person's grasp, the act of grasping, together with the boundaries of the physical thing itself, send a signal to the rest of the world

[49] *Powell v McFarlane* (1979) 38 P & CR 452 (Ch) 471.

[50] Rostill (n 1) 17.

that they must exclude themselves from interfering with those boundaries. For larger things that cannot be brought within one's grasp such as land, one might enclose it by a fence or hedge, which effectively alerts the rest of the world of the boundaries from which they should exclude themselves.[51] In other words, even in tangibles where the boundaries are unclear or cannot be objectively ascertained, the same act can reify the boundaries and send the exclusionary signal.

The exclusionary signalling in copyright resembles land to some extent. Interestingly, the analogy of copyright with land was first argued by Sir William Blackstone in *Tonson v Collins*.[52] Some expressions can be ephemeral and, therefore, their momentary existence may not enable an objective ascertainment of the boundaries. To enable this, by analogy with the position in land, the law goes on to require expressions to be recorded—a reification of the expression. It may be recalled that this requirement has been discussed as part of the thing-relatedness of copyright subject matter in Chapter 2, Section 3(a), that recording the work gives the work a form. The need for a thing to have a reified form is consistent with its function being to send the exclusionary signal.

It may seem that recording an expression is in itself the act of taking possession in copyright because it represents a capture. Oliar and Stern point to two methods of the first acquisition of title—first, the rule of the first committed searcher, which grants possession to the person who invested in the pursuit of a thing; and secondly, the rule of capture, which grants the right to possession to the person who captures the thing. They argue that copyright is closer to the rule of capture because of the requirement of fixation under US law, requiring the expressions to be fixed in a material form. They argue that in copyright the possession is postponed until the formation of the thing is complete.[53] Although they do refer to originality as a requirement, they do not explain how originality fits within the possession rules they describe; their focus is the timing of capture. Originality as the kernel of a relational signal cannot be ignored. As explained above, under s 3(3) of the CDPA, it is possible for a person who is not the author of a work to record the work, and it is the author and not the person recording who will acquire copyright in the authorial work. Therefore, it cannot be said that the person who records has possession simply because they captured the expression. It is important to recognise that the

[51] Where such exclusion is absent, courts have found no physical control, eg *Simpson v Fergus* (1999) 79 P & CR 398 (CA).

[52] (1760) 96 ER 180, 188.

[53] Dotan Oliar and James Y Stern, 'Right on Time: First Possession in Property and Intellectual Property' (2019) 99 BUL Rev 395, 436–37, 453–54.

exclusionary signal is the flip side of the relational signal and the two should go hand in hand.

The need for demarcating the boundary of the thing is inexorably linked to the exclusive rights. The content of the duty on the rest of the world in copyright is different from those for more rivalrous resources, but it is still possible to establish an analogy with exclusionary signalling. If the thing in question has a physical existence, the content of the duty on others is that of physical non-interference. If the thing is a work, then the content of the duty will not be the acts of exclusion from the thing itself, but rather, acts of exclusion from certain other courses of conduct, although necessarily in relation to the work. A more detailed discussion of the exclusionary duties can be found in Chapter 4. The purpose here is to show the manner in which exclusionary duties engage with the boundaries of a work.

The CDPA grants authors exclusive rights to copy, distribute, communicate, and so on,[54] against the rest of the world. This means that the content of the exclusionary duty that the rest of the world owes is to conduct themselves in such a way as to exclude themselves from exercising any of the rights reserved for the copyright owner. But the exclusionary conduct closely revolves around the work. Certain exclusionary rights engage the work itself, such as communicating or performing the work,[55] and others engage the copy of the work such as making copies and distributing copies of the work.[56] One can establish infringement only by comparing the boundaries of the work ascertained from the record of the work in these cases by comparing it with the work of the defendant or the copy of it made by the defendant. More controversial are, however, the provisions that concern 'altered copying'.[57] Here, exercising these rights might result in a form different from the form in which the prior work exists, but the rights of the copyright owner may extend to the altered form. Some may argue that the availability of altered copying takes away from the importance of the boundaries of the prior work. However, it is argued here that the form in which the author created the work takes on an even greater importance in altered copying because this is the basis for assessing the extent of alteration. Although in this sense, the initial form does not define an absolute boundary, the boundary of the altered work follows the boundary of

[54] CDPA, s 16.
[55] CDPA, ss 19 and 20 respectively.
[56] CDPA, ss 17 and 18, respectively.
[57] CDPA, s 17(3) states that in relation to artistic works, copying means reproducing a drawing, eg in the form of a sculpture and vice versa. CDPA, s 21 grants a right of adaptation—meaning turning a novel into a play and vice versa or changing the arrangement of a musical composition.

the initial work. Therefore, if altered copying is alleged, the record of the prior work draws the core boundary, against which the altered work is assessed as to whether it is captured within the penumbra of the prior work.

(b) 'Intention to Exclude' and Copyright

In the formulation of possession in the context of adverse possession and finders of goods, courts require that in addition to taking physical control of the thing, one must demonstrate an intention to exclude the rest of the world. McFarlane argues that the only way the law is able to discern intention is to look for conduct manifesting the intention.[58] Therefore, the very act of taking physical control manifests an intention to exclude the rest of the world. The conduct of excluding the rest of the world thus indicates both physical control and the intention necessary to establish possession. Outside of the first acquisition context, there may be special cases where an intention to exclude the rest of the world may have to be specifically proved. For example, one may be able to prove that one did not possess narcotic substances if one was unaware of its existence on one's person. Therefore, scholars may not be incorrect in arguing that in first acquisition, intention is normally demonstrated by the conduct of taking physical control. Likewise, in the context of manufacture, to the extent that the process of manufacture is a deliberate act, the intention to take physical control need not be separately proven.

Within the copyright context, one should be able to treat the conduct of expressing thoughts in an original manner as analogous to an intention to possess, as described in Subsections 2(a)(i) and (ii) above. To the extent that the intellectual effort itself takes place within human consciousness, it is arguable that the intention to create the work will have been satisfied.[59] Indeed, Drassinower argues that there is a striking resemblance between the idea and expression in copyright and the *animus* and *factum possidendi* in tangibles. Using the example of a case of fox hunting in *Pierson v Post*,[60] he argues that it is the deed, that is, the actual mortal wounding of the fox, which is considered

[58] McFarlane (n 1) 160.

[59] This would necessarily exclude intelligent animals creating copyright works. See Andres Guadamuz, 'Can the Monkey Selfie Case Teach Us Anything about Copyright Law?' (*WIPO Magazine*, 21 February 2018)<www.wipo.int/wipo_magazine/en/2018/01/article_0007.html> accessed 20 November 2024.

[60] 3 Cai 175 (NY 1805). The claimant here was in hot pursuit of the fox, but it was the defendant who actually killed the fox. The question was whether the claimant had done enough to take possession or the defendant.

by the court as the deciding factor for possession, rather than the unmistakable wish to capture that the person in hot pursuit of the fox might have. He posits that in the case of tangibles, the law makes a normative choice in establishing possession at a specific point between any number of possibilities from when the person forms an intention to capture (*poss*) and actually capturing the thing (*factum possidendi*). Similarly, the law makes a normative choice in establishing copyright at a specific point between the formation of the idea through to its execution as an expression. To Drassinower, 'just as one's deed is one's official proof of ownership, so is one's expression—not mere idea—one's official proof of authorship'.[61] This argument has the greatest sway in demonstrating the use of normative considerations and the spectrum of possibilities of conduct that the law recognises for the purposes of possession.

As this author has argued elsewhere,[62] Drassinower's arguments address expression, but say nothing about originality. Expressing a work is the exclusionary signal that a person sends out to the rest of the world to alter their conduct in relation to the work. The author conveys to the rest of the world that she is staking a claim to the new thing that is coming into existence by such expression. However, if the work is not original to the person, merely expressing it will not make the work theirs. While expression sends the message to the rest of the world to 'keep off', originality enables him to claim that 'the work is mine'. A person may be able to sing Beatles songs from memory, but the mere singing as an expression is inadequate to make the song the singer's own, since the song is not original to them if they are not a member of the band. For a meaningful analogy of copyright with possession, it is essential that both the originality and expression are taken into account.

In relation to entrepreneurial works, the process of creating the work is certainly a conscious act and to this extent the intention will have been satisfied. It may indeed be argued that compared to the creation of authorial works, the creation of entrepreneurial works for commercial purposes is even more an intentional act, given the resources and effort it takes. To the extent that entrepreneurial works may not have a human copyright owner but artificial persons, it may be difficult to speak of consciousness. However, by attribution of intention to the human actors in these artificial entities it would be possible to find an intention to create a work, where necessary.

[61] Abraham Drassinower, 'Capturing Ideas: Copyright and the Law of First Possession' (2006) 54 Clev St L Rev 191, 194–96, 198–99.
[62] Mysoor (n 12) 297.

(c) From Work to Copyright Work

In copyright law, the work does not exist on its own before a person acquires it. It may be recalled that the work was put forward in Chapter 2 as the analogous equivalent of a thing in copyright, which was conceptualised as the substantive content that has been expressed and recorded. The process of exertion of a certain intellectual or entrepreneurial input (depending on whether it is an authorial or an entrepreneurial work) precedes the existence of a work. For example, say P exercised certain intellectual qualities to create a symphony. This symphony did not exist on its own before P created it in his mind, unlike an apple that exists on a tree before it is plucked. The symphony so created becomes known as a copyright work—a defined expression under CDPA, s 1(2),[63] if P goes on to record it in writing or otherwise. In other words, a person puts in certain intellectual or entrepreneurial effort first, and if the result of this is an expression that is recorded in some form, then the law recognises a copyright work to have come into existence. Since the work does not exist on its own before its act of creation and acquisition, a question arises as to whether an analogy with tangible things is appropriate.

Some tangible things do exist on their own in the world even before a person acquires them. For example, shells on the seashore exist on their own before a person picks them up. But tangible things that are manufactured also do not exist in their new state before they are manufactured. For example, although flour, eggs, sugar, and so on exist as tangible things in the world, a cake in its state as a cake does not come into existence until someone exerts their labour over the ingredients to create the cake. Therefore, even in the context of the law governing tangible things it is not imperative that the thing should have an independent existence before it is acquired. So long as the act of manufacturing is recognised by the law as a legitimate means of acquiring property rights in the cake so manufactured, there should be no difficulty in recognising the cake as a thing.

By analogy, it should not pose problems that copyright law only recognises a work once it has been created by a person and becomes a copyright work by the statutory definition. For analytical clarity it still makes sense to separate the work from the copyright work. The work demonstrates the objective requirements of a thing, as explained in Chapter 2. With the act of acquisition being explained in this chapter, the work becomes a copyright work. When the term

[63] CDPA, s 1(3) also requires that certain qualifications be met for copyright to subsist in a work. These qualifications are briefly summarised in Chapter 1.

of copyright expires in a copyright work, it enters the public domain. It will retain its characteristics as a work. For example, Jane Austin's novels are out of copyright, but nevertheless these timeless classics are still regarded as literary works. From Chapter 4 onwards the thing in copyright will be referred to as 'copyright work' to signify that it not only satisfies the requirements of a thing but also that copyright has been acquired in it benefiting its owner with exclusionary rights, exclusive privileges, and powers in the work.

3. Rivalrousness, Exclusivity, and Copyright

The concept of possession is closely linked to the rivalrous nature of the thing. Indeed, in the context of digital assets, the Law Commission argues that rivalrousness is a precondition to a meaningful concept of control.[64] It must be accepted that the more rivalrous a resource is, the more powerful the exclusion.[65] It is imperative also to appreciate the true impact of the rivalrous nature of the thing on the first acquisition of title. The concept of possession has been developed such that when one person establishes their relationship with the thing as against the rest of the world, no one else can.[66] In other words, the duty placed on the rest of the world is to exclude themselves from interfering with the thing, such that only the person taking possession can do as they please with the thing. This is seen as a significant stumbling block for land law and personal property lawyers to think of possession of non-rivalrous resources. After all, Q copying P's poem does not deprive P of her poem in that P can continue to do as she pleases with the poem. On this view, P cannot have taken possession of the poem, nor could Q deprive P of its possession.

However, as explained in Chapter 2, Section 3(a)(ii), rivalrousness of a thing is a matter of degree. Property law has always recognised imperfectly rivalrous resources. Even within tangible things, some are factually rivalrous, and others are made rivalrous by the intervention of the law. It is, therefore, essential to distinguish what is a fact and what is a legal construct. Otherwise, an incorrect (and sometimes dogmatic) conclusion may be arrived at that resources that are not rivalrous can neither be the subject matter of property rights, nor can

[64] Law Commission Report (n 11) para 5.16.

[65] For a discussion on the non-rivalrousness of intellectual property and the rivalrousness of its inputs, see Henry E Smith, 'Intellectual Property as Property: Delineating Entitlements in Information' (2007) 117 Yale LJ 1742.

[66] Sarah Green and John Randall, *The Tort of Conversion* (Hart P2009) 123, where the authors use the term 'exhaustibility'.

they be acquired as such. Even if one insists that all tangible things are rivalrous and that rivalrousness is a binary concept,[67] it should be possible to analyse rivalrousness to separate the factual from the legal aspects.

There are things that by their physical nature and size make it possible for only one person to use them at any given point in time. Let us take, for example, a diamond ring. Factually, one person, P, wearing the diamond ring, excludes the rest of the world using it as a diamond ring at the same time. This aspect of factual exclusion is used by property law to formulate legal regulation. The law sees the act of wearing the ring as exercising physical control, which on its own results in factual exclusion of the rest of the world. If P was a finder of the diamond ring, P grasping the ring or wearing it when they found it makes it possible for the law to state that the title to the thing is acquired by taking possession of it, with possession here meaning taking physical control of a thing. In other words, the factual exclusion that results from the act of wearing the ring coincides with the legal exclusivity that the law seeks to confer on the wearer of the ring if they were acquiring title to it for the first time. A diamond ring, therefore, is an example of a perfectly rivalrous resource. Many resources which can be retained within human physical grasp can be regarded as rivalrous in this manner.

A fortiori, all other tangible resources which cannot be brought within human grasp in this manner are relatively less rivalrous. But there are two consequences of factual rivalrousness of these resources that the law regards as most useful. First, that others lose their ability to interact with the resource, effectively excluding them; secondly, and consequently, only one person is able to interact with the resource. If the resource is not capable of factual rivalrousness, then the law intervenes with fictions that enable these consequences. The first legal fiction is to regard as sufficient acts that seek to exert some physical control over the resource, which would otherwise not be sufficient as a factual matter. The second legal fiction is that only one person can interact with the resource at any given point in time, even though as a factual matter this may not be the case. These two fictions are most obviously at play in land law. Since these are so widely accepted in property law, one may not even realise that these are legal fictions; this is what makes scholars claim that all tangible resources are rivalrous in nature. Strictly speaking this is not correct. Without the law's intervention it would not be possible for resources like land to be rivalrous.

[67] Law Commission Report (n 11) paras 2.60, 4.34

Let us examine the first fiction in relation to land. It is true that every physical point on land is unique and can be occupied by only one person at a time. But this is not how we use land. We do not use one point on land at a time. We use plots of land as a whole. In this sense, one person's use of a plot of land does not factually exclude another person's use of the same plot of land. However, there are various ways in which a person can factually exclude the rest of the world from the plot of land, such as fencing it, growing hedges around it, building over it, and so on. Even if an impregnable fortress were to be built, it might not mean total factual exclusion, as the wearing of the ring would do in the example above. Thankfully, we do not need to build medieval-type fortresses around our land to protect it from invaders. Land law accepts as sufficient overt acts such as putting up fencing, locking gates, and so on.[68] The law recognises symbolism in these overt acts of creating a boundary. Even if the boundary does not prevent the rest of the world from interacting with the land, it sends a message to them that they should exclude themselves from the land that lies within the boundary.

As regards the second fiction, case law states in no unequivocal terms that only one person can be in physical control at any point in time.[69] This follows from the first fiction and can be described as the other side of the same coin. Although only one person can take control of a single point in space at any given point in time, multiple persons can be in control of a plot of land at the same time. It is arguable that conceptually this is what makes adverse possession possible. However, without the legal fiction that only one person can take physical control, land as a resource will not become sufficiently rivalrous for effective legal regulation. The upshot is that the law has mechanisms through which it makes resources that are not perfectly rivalrous become functionally rivalrous. Even if one accepts that intangible things are at the non-rivalrous end of the spectrum, would it not be possible also to examine what mechanisms the law has in relation to an intangible resource like a work to enable property law to operate effectively?

As argued above, in copyright, the need for a work to be recorded performs the demarcation function. Just as fences over land create boundaries from which the rest of the world must keep off, recording the expression, in copyright, enables this boundary of the work to be drawn from which the rest of the world is required to keep off. Just as the factual ability of the fence in excluding

[68] *JA Pye* (n 16) [10].

[69] ibid [41] approving the formulation in *Powell v McFarlane* (1979) 38 P & CR 452, 470–71 that physical control should be single and exclusive. Allowance is, of course, made for jointly held land.

the rest of the world is a legal fiction operating in land law, the adequacy of recording as an act capable of excluding the rest of the world is also a legal fiction in copyright law.

As regards the second fiction giving land the rivalrous quality, it is possible in copyright that the person who expresses their thoughts in an original manner may be different from the person who records those expressions. This may give rise to conflicting control over the work. Therefore, CDPA, s 3(3) requires that even if someone else records the original expression, it is the person whose original expression it is who will be the one to acquire copyright in the work. This does not prevent the person creating the record also acquiring copyright in the record, such as a record label acquiring copyright in the music they record. But they need the consent of the authors to exercise any rights in the record, acknowledging that it is the author who acquires copyright in the work. Again, just as in land, the law requires single and exclusive control, copyright also gives rise to single and exclusive ownership. While tangibility of land and intangibility of a work do make a difference, it is not inconceivable that legal constructs can and do similarly operate in these contexts.[70]

Even if rivalrousness is of great importance, it is arguable that its importance is seen more in the enforcement of property rights than in the very conceptualisation of possession. Say, for example, that P begins squatting on a part of Q's land, which is an expansive pasture. If rivalrousness means exclusivity over the land, it is attached to the property right in the land and not to the land itself. The fact that P's squatting on Q's pasture does not deprive Q of the whole of Q's pasture is not the concern of the law. If it had been, then until P squatted on all of Q's pasture there would have been no remedy, since Q has not lost all of their exclusivity. The harm caused is that Q is unable to exercise their property rights over the parts being squatted on by P, which were exclusive to Q. This is a function of rivalrousness being a matter of degree, but it demonstrates that it is not as important to the very concept of possession as some scholars make it seem.

By analogy, if P writes a poem that is original, only P has the copyright over it. Relatively less rivalrous nature of the poem means that if someone copies the poem, it does not deprive P of the poem itself. However, this is not a concern for the law, just as total exclusion of Q from their pasture was not a requirement of the law in the example above. The harm caused by copying the poem is that

[70] For an argument that it is the possession that is rivalrous and not the thing, see Peter G Watts and Kelvin FK Low, 'The Case for Cryptoassets as Property' in Sinéad Agnew and Sir Marcus Smith (eds), *Law at the Cutting Edge* (Hart 2024). 281, available at SSRN: <https://ssrn.com/abstract = 4354364> accessed 24 December 2024.

P is unable to exercise the rights that were exclusive to P over the creation of the copy of the poem, even if P is not deprived of their original expression. In case of both land and copyright, the exclusivity that arises out of rivalrousness relates to the *rights* more than it does to the *thing*, as the exclusivity of the thing is only symbolic. To the extent that possession is inexorably linked to thinghood, this suggests that rivalrousness may be of much less significance to possession than may seem to be the case at first glance.

4. Conceptual and Doctrinal Benefits

The question we must now deal with is how might identifying a concept analogous to possession in copyright change anything? There are both conceptual and doctrinal benefits that can be derived from this analysis. The following paragraphs deal with them.

(a) Taxonomical Implications

Possession underpins the binary classification of choses in possession and choses in action. Although possession itself in its technical meaning only applies to tangible things, establishing a concept analogous to possession in an intangible thing, such as a work, strikes at the root of this classification. It makes a case for the dismantling of this very classification. Even if courts and jurists feel compelled to recognise this classification for historical reasons, at the very least they will have to acknowledge that the classification is not binary. All that is not strictly a chose in possession is not automatically a chose in action. The existence of an intangible thing, as argued here, and the ability for it to be acquired for the first time in a manner other than entering into a contract should add much credence to this conclusion. This allows for intellectual property in general and copyright in particular to be classified as a separate category of its own, acknowledging that it has greater similarities with choses in possession than choses in action along the spectrum of property rights.

The Law Commission has already argued for digital assets to be the third category between choses in possession and choses in action.[71] Given that copyright predated digital assets by about three centuries, if similar arguments can be made in relation to other intellectual property rights, copyright should

[71] Law Commission Report (n 11) ch 3.

be more appropriately described as the *tertium quid*.[72] Regardless of which intangible asset comes first in the chronology, extending the taxonomy beyond choses in action and choses in possession is imperative. Once the classification is opened up to different types of intangible assets, it will be more apposite to refer to property rights as being located on a spectrum, a conceptualisation that this book strongly supports.

(b) Teleological Explanation

Thing-relatedness is a precondition for a discussion on the act of acquisition of property rights for the first time independently. In relation to copyright, all too often, judges refer to original expressions as the subject matter of copyright protection. The tendency in the EU case law, which has become part of the assimilated law in the United Kingdom, has been to grant copyright protection to all products of the human mind, without first ascertaining whether a work has come into existence.[73] Although anything 'touched by human hand' can potentially be protected by copyright under this definition,[74] scholars have argued against conflation of originality with the concept of work in the courts' approach.[75] This book makes an effort to separate the attributes of the thing in copyright from the act of acquisition of copyright. No doubt, separating the thing from its acquisition gives analytical clarity. As already argued in Chapter 2, separating the thing enables a court to develop the definitional aspects of a work independently of the manner of acquisition of the thing. This helps *numerus clausus* hold sway by shaping the normative considerations that a work should satisfy before exclusionary duties are placed on the rest of the world.

More importantly, however, it helps to focus on the normativity that underlies the act of acquisition separately from the normativity of the substantive content of the thing. This may be demonstrated more clearly in relation to

[72] Reference here can be made to the language used by Fry LJ in *Colonial Bank v Whinney* (1885) 30 Ch D 261, 285, who said that the law 'knows no tertium quid'. See also a lecture given by Professor Sarah Green, 'Time for a Tertium Quid' (University College London 25 May 2023). <www.ucl.ac.uk/laws/events/2023/may/recording-time-tertium-quid> accessed 24 November 2024.

[73] Case C-310/17 *Levola Hengelo BV v European Food Company BV*, EU:C:2018:899; Case C-683/17 *Cofemel—Sociedade de Vestuário SA v G-Star Raw CV*, EU:C:2019:721. The ruling in both these cases applies to the United Kingdom as part of the retained law under European Union (Withdrawal) Act 2018, s 6.

[74] Bernt Hugenholtz, 'Works of Literature, Science and Art' in Bernt Hugenholtz and others (eds), *100 Years of Dutch Copyright Law: Auteurswet, 1912–2012* (deLex 2012) 53.

[75] See eg Jani McCutcheon, '*Levola Hengelo BV v Smilde Foods BV*: The Hard Work of Defining a Copyright Work' (2019) 82 MLR 936.

land. In land law, trivial acts do not lead to acquisition of title. To take a simple example, grazing animals on land alone does not enable acquisition of title.[76] Practically, it does not send clear enough signals to the rest of the world. But normatively, it should not be possible for the person grazing to acquire title. The person has simply not done enough to deserve title to the land.

Under the current law, originality has a low bar, both qualitatively and quantitatively. In effect, one needs to do far too little to be eligible for copyright protection. However, the reasons why this should be the case have not been made clear. Thus, the titles of newspaper reports can be original, as can mere eleven-word extracts.[77] Equally, there are cases where a compilation of television programmes in chronological order has been held to have been the kind of labour that makes the compilation original for copyright purposes, so long as that labour was substantial.[78] More recently, putting together an iteration of a logo with a yellow circle in a blue square was held to involve sufficient skill and effort to be a copyright work.[79] Since originality is what determines the minimum input necessary for copyright protection to arise, it is imperative for the law to have justifiable grounds to set originality at a particular level.

Just as manufacture only entitles a person to a claim of ownership if the process leads to a thing that is different from its ingredients, originality can only entitle a person to a claim of copyright if the process leads to a work that is different from its ingredients. These ingredients could include thoughts, ideas, prior works, or information in the public domain. Conceptually, the greater the transformation, the stronger the justification for the acquisition of property rights. The law needs to put forward a justifiable explanation not only of the level of originality, but more fundamentally the qualities that the labour should have to qualify to be original. If the bar for originality is set too low, then copyright is not only acquired too easily, but a person's copyright also comes into conflict with another's too easily. Attributing originality conceptually to possession by analogy with tangible things could provide normative force to the argument that setting the level of originality required to trigger copyright protection low is problematic. It will help to focus on the kind of conduct that makes a work a person's own. This will mean that mere skill or mere effort will not entitle a person to copyright since these qualities do not distinguish the work of one person from that of another. Also, too small an

[76] *Powell v McFarlane* (1979) 38 P & CR 452.

[77] Case C–5/08 *Infopaq Int v Danske Dagblades Forening* [2009] ECR I–6569 (ECJ) para 45; *Newspaper Licensing Agency v Meltwater* [2011] EWCA Civ 890, [2012] Bus LR 53 [19]–[22].

[78] eg *BBC v Wireless League Gazette Publishing Co* [1926] Ch 433.

[79] *Lidl Great Britain Ltd v Tesco Stores Ltd* [2024] EWCA Civ 262 [89]–[194].

effort, such as eleven words, might not be regarded as sufficient to attract copyright. A court might, therefore, take a qualitatively and quantitatively different approach to originality. In other words, there is teleological benefit derived from disentangling the thing from its acquisition.

Balganesh has argued that the level of human agency required for the creation of a copyright work needs closer examination. He draws on the law of tort to examine the factual and legal causes of copyright being acquired by a person and argues how it is problematic that copyright is acquired automatically on the expression being recorded without further scrutiny.[80] The criteria that go into what is original certainly need a re-evaluation and re-calibration to raise the bar. This would also assist in having meaningful conversations around works generated by artificial intelligence and the extent of human agency that goes into these creations.[81]

(c) Lessons from the Evolution of the Act of First Acquisition

Historically when one looks at the act of acquisition of property rights, until intellectual property came to be conceptualised, the known modes of acquisition were only taking possession, accession, occupation and so on. With the introduction of patents and copyright, the acts of acquisition were opened up to further possibilities. This resulted in a move away from physical labour to intellectual labour around the eighteenth century. Whilst the nineteenth century witnessed the consolidation of more and more types of intellectual labour being recognised as legitimate means of acquiring property rights, the twentieth century marked another turning point. With technological innovations such as the gramophone, cinematography, and broadcasts, newer ways of disseminating authorial works were made possible. Law makers realised that without significant investments the benefits of these inventions would not be harnessed or scaled. Of course, with a great measure of lobbying by the backers of these inventions, copyright law opened the doors for acquisition of property rights also through investment of entrepreneurial resources to make new works possible.

The history of copyright demonstrates that the act of first acquisition of property rights is possible in relation to intangible things. This point is often

[80] Shyamkrishna Balganesh, 'Causing Copyright' (2017) 117 Colum L Rev 1, 47–68.

[81] See generally Daniela Simone, 'Pay No Attention to that Man Behind the Curtain!: Copyright, Authorship and Artificial Intelligence' [2023] AIPJ 120.

missed by theorists who have examined copyright as personal property. They only see rights that the statute gives rise to. They do not see that copyright is acquired in a way that has had significant impact on property law. As argued above, history has twice enabled the law to recognise acts of acquisition outside of the traditional ways of acquiring title to tangible things—once with authorial works and then with entrepreneurial works. Not paying attention to these events makes the theorisation of property rights conceptually incomplete and historically inaccurate.

(d) Doctrinal Application

Aside from shedding light on what possession is in the first acquisition context, principles such as adverse possession and finders of goods also assist in our understanding of subsequent independent acquisition of title. A concept akin to possession in copyright could help extend to copyright the ideas of subsequent independent acquisition of title through principles akin to finders of goods. If an analogy in the first acquisition context is achieved, more ambitiously, one can attempt an analogy also in relation to subsequent independent (meaning non-derivative) acquisition of title within the copyright context.

The discussion above centres on the conduct that enables a person to acquire title for the first time. The law also recognises the conduct that is essential for subsequent, but independent acquisition of title, and in particular how relativity of title is established. This is demonstrated best in the context of adverse possession of land. A person, P, may acquire title to land by, say, fencing off the land and fixing a lockable gate. P will continue to be in possession so long as they act like an owner. Another person, Q, coming along subsequently, does not have to put up a new fence or a new gate for them to acquire title. They can demonstrate taking possession in other ways, including by making use of the land like an owner would do, such as by farming the land or building over the land and so on.[82] Q acquires better title over land than anyone else, except P. As P's control over land diminishes, Q's control strengthens. What is different in adverse possession is that in time it tips over to give Q the title over the land. This is possible because the statute extinguishes P's title over land.[83]

[82] Similar to the facts in *JA Pye* (n 16) [58] (Lord Browne-Wilkinson).

[83] For unregistered land, Limitation Act 1980, s 17 extinguishes the title of the original landowner of unregistered land upon the expiry of twelve years after the accrual of a cause of action for the recovery of land. It is more difficult to extinguish title to registered land under sch 6 to the Land Registration Act 2002.

In copyright, like other personal property, there is no statutory equivalent extinguishing title, and therefore an analogy with adverse possession will not work.[84] Further, international treaties such as the Berne Convention (BC) and the WTO Agreement on Trade-Related Aspects of Intellectual Property Rights (TRIPS) mandate that the term of protection for a copyright work is not reduced from life of the author plus fifty years.[85] However, the conduct that is taken into account for establishing possession in adverse possession, such as acting like an owner, is still relevant to draw an analogy with copyright. For more rivalrous resources like land, the first person having lost possession and the second person having gained possession are both physically observable acts. For us to move beyond the physical, the conceptual structure discussed in Section 2 above reveals that physical control involves such conduct as would give out a relational and an exclusionary signal.

The application of a doctrine akin to finders of goods is best illustrated in the context of orphaned works. The Copyright and Rights in Performances (Licensing of Orphan Works) Regulations 2014 define orphan works as works the owner of which cannot be found after a diligent search. The Grover Committee has found that orphan works pose a significant challenge in relation to literary works.[86] From the discussion above, one may note that the conduct involved in acquiring title to a thing for the first time can be and is normally different from the conduct required in subsequent independent possession of the same thing, although conceptually they send across the same signals. In copyright, if P expresses their thoughts in an original manner and records the expression, P acquires copyright in the work for the first time.

As this author has argued elsewhere,[87] having acquired copyright ownership, the way P can demonstrate their possession in a copyright sense is by acting like an owner. This could include conduct such as claiming authorship when another person wishes to use the work; negotiating the possible grant of a licence; or exercising the exclusive rights such as copying, distributing, communicating, and so on in relation to the work. If P begins not to act like an owner in relation to their work, then another person, Q, can begin to act like an owner in relation to the work. Here Q's conduct does not have to involve Q engaging in the same conduct as P. It should be possible for the law to recognise

[84] *Fisher v Brooker* [2009] UKHL 41 [78], [2009] 1 WLR 1764, where Lord Neuberger stated that there is no concept equivalent to adverse possession in copyright.

[85] BC, art 7; TRIPS, art 12.

[86] The Gowers Review of Intellectual Property (December 2006) at para 4.91 estimated that about 40 per cent of all print works are orphan works.

[87] Mysoor (n 12) 299.

Q acting as an owner would in relation to the work by exercising the exclusive rights of the owner, such as making copies of the work, distributing it, communicating it, and so on. For Q to show that they have taken possession, P should have lost possession. The difficulty, however, is that the less rivalrous nature of copyright works may not make it clear when an author has given up control over their work. It is arguable that this can be overcome by factual analysis of the diligence exercised by Q in finding P, Q's efforts in negotiating for a licence, together with the conduct of P in responding or cooperating. Burrell and Hudson have argued that it is possible to apply the doctrine of abandonment to copyright works.[88] If it is possible to abandon copyright works, it may also be possible for another person to find them. If multiple users conduct themselves like an owner towards the same copyright work, the law may resolve this based on a simple 'first in time' rule. This might give a flavour of what a copyright-specific 'finders of goods doctrine' looks like.

5. Summary

This chapter addressed the following question: even if one can argue that a work is the thing in copyright, how does one make a work one's own? The chapter explored the possibility of drawing the analogy between a combination of rules of accession to a thing by manufacture and taking possession of a thing for the first time to acquire title. The biggest challenge was to separate these rules from their physical predisposition to undertake a comparison at a conceptual level with intangible things. To begin with, this chapter examined the rationale behind these rules of acquisition of title for the first time and analysed the equivalent principles in copyright law. It argued that manufacture sends the relational signal because the law grants title to the person who puts in labour and skill in creating a new thing, establishing the relationship between the person and the thing. The analogy with copyright lies in granting copyright to the person who exercises the relevant intellectual skill, labour, and judgement to create original or new work. This chapter went on to argue that taking possession sends the exclusionary signal because of the boundaries that taking physical control of a thing helps to draw, especially in relation to things such as land. The analogy with copyright lies here with the need for recording

[88] Emily Hudson and Robert Burrell, 'Abandonment, Copyright and Orphaned Works: What Does It Mean to Take the Proprietary Nature of Intellectual Property Rights Seriously' (2011) 35 Melb U L Rev 971.

the work before copyright can be acquired, which sends a message as to the boundaries from which the rest of the world should exclude themselves from interfering with.

It went on to examine how rivalrousness of a resource is a matter of degree, with some resources being factually rivalrous and others being functionally rivalrous because of certain fictions that the law recognises, especially for resources like land. It drew a comparison with copyright where the law similarly imbues a work with characteristics to make it an intangible thing that can be acquired exclusively. The chapter concluded by demonstrating the teleological and doctrinal benefits that can be reaped because of an astute understanding of the analogy of acquisition of copyright with acquisition of title to tangible things.

4
Ownership of Copyright

1. Introduction

Chapter 2 established that there is indeed a separable thing in copyright called the copyright work that has both form and content. While Chapter 3 analysed the act of acquisition of title for the first time independently, the focus of this chapter is to analyse the interest that underlies the title so acquired. It was mentioned briefly in the previous chapter that in the copyright context the interest that is acquired is copyright ownership. Scholars like Honoré have offered a non-exhaustive list of the incidents of ownership.[1] This chapter groups these constituents based on their effect on the owner and the rest of the world. This is consistent with the Hohfeldian understanding, which defines ownership as a complex aggregate of rights, powers, privileges, and immunities.[2]

It was suggested in Chapter 3 that the act of acquisition sends two important signals—the exclusionary signal and the relational signal. As the exclusionary signal is directed at the rest of the world, it mandates the particular conduct on their part, which can be characterised as an exclusionary duty. These duties mean corresponding rights held by the acquirer and one may call these exclusionary rights. The relational signal triggers within the acquirer the ability to exercise legal powers over the thing at the acquirer's discretion and the ability to exercise use privileges over the thing as the acquirer chooses. Because the focus here is not so much exclusion of the rest of the world, but rather the exclusivity that the owner enjoys, these can be referred to as exclusive powers and exclusive privileges.

The uniqueness of the rights, powers, and privileges that are acquired is that they operate against the whole world. Speaking of property rights, Worthington notes that a person's car is 'protected from thieves, vandals and joyriders merely because it is property, without [them] having to negotiate any

[1] Anthony M Honoré, 'Ownership' in AG Guest (ed), *Oxford Essays in Jurisprudence* (OUP 1961) 107, 112–24.

[2] Wesley N Hohfeld, 'Fundamental Legal Conceptions as Applied in Judicial Reasoning' (1917) 26 Yale LJ 710, 746.

Copyright as Personal Property. Poorna Mysoor, Oxford University Press. © Poorna Mysoor 2025.
DOI: 10.1093/9780191954962.003.0004

of these exclusions with the relevant parties'.[3] When a person acquires ownership, the rest of the world has a duty of non-interference, has no ability to challenge the exercise of powers, nor any right to challenge the manner of use of the thing. As we saw in Chapter 3, this is a significant reason why the act of acquisition needs to be of a kind that is determined by the law to send signals to the rest of the world, rather than by private parties through their negotiation as in a contract. One may call these rights, powers, and privileges *in rem* or those that operate against the world at large or persons generally.[4]

The exclusionary right, or the right to exclude as it is commonly called, is one of the most analysed components of ownership. There is a school of thought that regards the right to exclude as the defining feature of ownership, although scholarly opinion differs as to whether this is indeed the sole descriptor of property rights. There are also those who insist that the powers of control should be the primary determining factor of ownership. In any event, the objective here is not so much to uncover a singular descriptor of ownership as it is to understand the constituents of it. To be even more precise, this chapter seeks to analyse the difference between the rights, powers, and privileges that arise in relation to physical things, and those that arise in relation to copyright works. For the purposes of this chapter, therefore, the primary debate does not need to be resolved. It suffices for our purposes to argue that chronologically it would be sensible to analyse the exclusionary rights first, followed by powers and privileges, to offer a complete picture of the ownership. When a thing is acquired, whether it is a tangible thing or a work, it is more intuitive to think of securing the boundaries first by imposing exclusionary duties, such that the acquirer can maintain exclusivity of powers and privileges that can be exercised in relation to it. This also provides a logical flow from the discussions in Chapter 3.

Doctrinally, separating rights, powers, and privileges is also the correct way to understand copyright. Section 16(1) of the Copyright, Designs and Patents Act 1988 (CDPA) provides that the copyright owner will have the 'exclusive right to do' certain acts, which it calls 'acts restricted by copyright'. An exhaustive list of these acts is also enumerated in s 16(1), and these are to copy, to issue copies to the public, to rent, to perform in public, to communicate the work to the public, and to adapt the work. Since s 16(1) uses the expression exclusive 'right', all too often commentators take this as conveying an impression

[3] Sarah Worthington, 'Revolutions in Personal Property: Redrawing the Common Law's Conceptual Map' in Sarah Worthington, Andrew Robertson, and Graham Virgo (eds), *Revolution and Evolution in Private Law* (Hart 2018) 231.

[4] Arianna Pretto-Sakmann, *Boundaries of Personal Property: Shares and Sub-Shares* (Hart 2005) 90.

that all that the statute focuses on are rights and nothing else.[5] But it is important to understand the true meaning of exclusionary rights in this context. In his elucidation of Hohfeld, Finnis points out that a claim-right in the Hohfeldian sense 'can never be to do or omit something: it always is a claim that somebody else do or omit something'.[6] Section 16(1) is a provision that is directed at the copyright owner and not at someone else. Its use of the words 'exclusive' and 'restricted' in relation to the defined set of acts means that no one else but the copyright owner can engage in these acts. This gives copyright owners a certain power over the copyright works to do or not do as they please, and a privilege to engage in these acts at their discretion.[7] The rights in the Hohfeldian sense are provided for in s 16(2), which states that a person cannot engage in the acts restricted to the copyright owner, and, if they do, then (subject to other requirements being satisfied) the liability for infringement ensues. This provision clearly does not address the copyright owner but someone else, in Finnis's language, and therefore provides for a claim right. As such, there should be no doubt that the statute itself separately provides for rights, powers, and privileges. Furthermore, as we will see in Chapter 5, it is not merely the rights that are enforceable but also the privileges and powers associated with copyright, albeit indirectly. Therefore, it is essential to also examine privileges and powers independently from rights.

It is important to recognise that the copyright work is not only separable from the human body but is also separable from the exclusionary rights, exclusive powers, and privileges to which copyright gives rise. The consequence of this is that it is possible to conceptualise these rights, powers, and privileges as relating to and arising from the copyright work. There is a tendency among some theorists to conflate these rights with the thing in copyright, that is, the copyright work. Those who deny the existence or even the possibility of the existence of a thing in relation to copyright argue that the rights are all that copyright is made up of. The conceptualisation of copyright as a chose in action that denies the existence of a thing was dealt with in Chapter 2, Section 2. In this chapter, it would be apposite to consider those conceptualisations of copyright, which do not necessarily deny the existence of the copyright work, but choose to ignore it, misplacing the weight instead on a singular understanding of the exclusionary rights.

[5] eg Michael Bridge and others, *The Law of Personal Property* (3rd edn, Sweet & Maxwell 2022).

[6] John Finnis, 'Some Professional Fallacies about Rights' (1972) Adel L Rev 377, 380.

[7] In this sense, one can argue that copyright fits Katz's conceptualisation of ownership in empowering the copyright owner to be the sole agenda setter. See generally Larissa Katz, 'Exclusion and Exclusivity in Property Law' (2008) 58 U Toronto LJ 275. See also Section 3 for further discussion.

These theorists typically also pay little attention to the distinctive effect that the exclusive powers and privileges have on the copyright owner. Especially within the copyright context it is essential to appreciate the role of these powers and privileges in addition to the rights because each has different consequences for the copyright owner and the rest of the world. While the rights can be enforced, the privileges enable the copyright work to be used, and the power enables the copyright owner to give a licence,[8] or to grant any of the derivative interests carved out of copyright.[9] There is, therefore, a practical need to separate powers and privileges from rights. Accordingly, this chapter analyses each of these in a separate section.

Section 2 begins with an exploration of the exclusionary rights recognised by copyright and the duty imposed on the rest of the world. Theorists diverge on the content of the corresponding duty that the right to exclude imposes. While there are some theorists who agree that the exclusionary duty can be conceptualised broadly enough to accommodate those that arise in relation to intellectual property, there are others who maintain a singular immutable conceptualisation of the exclusionary duty. These theorists note not only that the thing can only be physical but also that the content of the duty can only be of physical non-interference with the thing for the corresponding right to be a property right. Clearly, this does not work for copyright because copyright does not exclude the rest of the world from copyright works themselves but only from certain actions in relation to the copyright works. Subsection 2(a) deals with the arguments of these theorists and goes on to demonstrate how within the context of land law and personal property law there are instances where the exclusionary duty does not relate to a physical thing. It goes on to show that, even in relation to physical things, the law may prohibit conduct which can be something other than total exclusion from the thing. The upshot is that the diversity of ways in which the interference is enforced in relation to tangible things can support the basis for the analogy for the kind of non-interference seen in copyright. Subsection 2(b) elaborates on the exclusionary rights recognised under the CDPA and Subsection 2(c) goes on to discuss the contours of the rights and their significance for *numerus clausus* if an interest is carved out based on these exclusive rights.

Section 3 goes on to discuss the powers that the copyright owner acquires. When the content of the right is a right to exclude the rest of the world, the law recognises the acquirer of copyright as the only person who can exercise these rights. This gives rise to a certain power in the hands of the acquirer of

[8] Chapter 6, Section 1(a) discusses how a licence can operate as a defence to infringement.
[9] Chapter 7 discusses a wide array of derivative interests.

copyright. Importantly, in exercising the powers of ownership the copyright owner can grant use privileges to others by way of licences. It examines what it means for the copyright owner to have powers of control over copyright in relation to both authorial and entrepreneurial works.

Section 4 deals with the use privileges that arise when a person acquires copyright. The proponents of the theory that copyright is a chose in action argue that since one cannot take possession of copyright, there can be no such thing as deriving benefit from the use of copyright; and the only benefit that can be derived is by suing for copyright infringement.[10] Demonstrating that copyright can be put to use tackles this argument.

2. Exclusionary Rights and Copyright

In this section, Subsection (a) focuses on the nature of exclusionary rights and the content of the corresponding duty in relation to copyright. It does this by responding to three competing arguments on the nature of copyright: as a property right in the monopoly, as a property right in the right itself, and finally arguments that copyright is not a property right because of its intangibility. The core response to these arguments is that as the nature of the thing changes from chattels to land, the law correspondingly recognises a markedly different content of the exclusionary duty. In keeping with this process of evolution, when the law goes on to recognise a certain content for the exclusionary duties in relation to copyright commensurate with the thing in copyright, it should not appear out of the ordinary. It is only an incremental extension by analogy. Having grappled with the nature of the exclusionary duty, Subsection (b) sets out the exclusionary duties under the CDPA as an example of what these entail in copyright statutes generally. This sets the stage for Subsection (c) to discuss the importance of these duties needing to have definable contours in view of possible third-party effects if the rights are assigned or licensed.

(a) The Nature of Exclusionary Rights and Corresponding Duties

Merrill is one of the strongest proponents of the school of thought that argues that the exclusionary right, or, in his words, the right to exclude, is the '*sine*

[10] See eg Carol M Rose, 'The Law Is Nine-Tenths of Possession: An Adage Turned on Its Head' in Yun-Chien Chang (ed), *Law and Economics of Possession* (CUP 2015) 60–61.

qua non of property' and that it is both a necessary and sufficient condition of property.[11] It would seem that, for him, property and ownership can be used interchangeably on the basis that there is nothing more required to establish ownership of a property interest. Merrill regards the law in relation to intellectual property as being 'even more striking in the degree to which the property right and the right to exclude go hand-in-hand', and regards intellectual property rights as 'the right to exclude others from interfering with or using the right in specified ways'.[12] There is a recognition in Merrill's work that the nature of exclusive rights can vary depending on the valued resource being addressed. Smith likens the copyright work to a thing and argues that the right to exclude operates in a similar way.[13] For these theorists, it is possible to make a natural extension of the right to exclude to intellectual property rights. However, there are theorists who believe in only one version of the right to exclude, which is exclusion from the thing itself. Their conceptualisation of copyright not only regards copyright's lack of physical thinghood as problematic but also the content of exclusionary duties that do not exclude the rest of the world from the thing itself. Of the theorists who put forward this conceptualisation, four prominent views of copyright are considered here.

(i) Copyright as a property right in the monopoly

One of the theorists who put forward this argument is Penner. He argues that a property right is only that which relates to a thing, and the right should entitle the owner to exclude the rest of the world from the thing itself. This view is held by many property theorists whose focus is tangible property rights.[14] This view of property rights is what makes Penner observe that it is an 'idiotic fiction' to recognise copyright as a property right in the expression, because this will mean that the rest of the world is excluded from the expression itself.[15] Since copyright only excludes the world from certain conduct such as copying, distributing copies, and so on, it is to him an incorrect description to say that copyright is a property right in the expression. Although he recognises that expressions do play a role, for him copyright does not relate to a thing, but relates

[11] Thomas W Merrill, 'Property and the Right to Exclude' (1998) 77 Neb L Rev 730, 740.

[12] ibid 749.

[13] Henry E Smith, 'Intellectual Property as Property: Delineating Entitlements in Information' (2007) 116 Yale LJ 1742 1755.

[14] These theorists further argue that the thing should be a physical thing. See eg Simon Douglas and Ben McFarlane, 'Defining Property Rights' in J Penner and H Smith (eds), *Philosophical Foundations of Property Law* (OUP 2013); William Swadling, 'Property—General Principles' in Andrew Burrows (ed), *English Private Law* (OUP 2013).

[15] James Penner, *The Idea of Property in Law* (OUP 2000) 118–20. Penner refers to intellectual property in general, and gives examples of patents, copyright, and trade marks. Only arguments on copyright are considered here.

only to actions. In his view, the conduct on the part of the rest of the world is something other than total exclusion, which involves specific and enumerated ways of engaging with the expression. He believes that, compared to land in relation to which the landowner has an inexhaustible number of exclusive use rights, copyright gives the copyright owner monopoly over a limited number of uses of the expression. To him, a better way to characterise copyright is as property right in the monopoly.[16]

There is much that one needs to unpack here. To begin with, although many scholars have considered whether copyright is a monopoly,[17] the term monopoly is opaque, and perhaps incorrect for the context of copyright. Penner does not explain what he means by monopoly in this context. He does not seem to use it in its technical sense, that is, a position of dominance causing a market distortion in the supply of a desired commodity.[18] By monopoly he appears to mean the ability to take certain limited actions to the exclusion of rest of the world, and, more specifically, the ability to exclude a person from a conduct rather than from a thing. For example, if the state has monopoly over criminal prosecutions, the state can exclude others from engaging in the act of prosecuting crimes. There is no 'thing' in relation to which this right operates.

This view can at best provide an incomplete picture of copyright. If copyright prohibits actions, these actions have to be in relation to something, even if it is not a physical thing (such as criminal prosecutions in the example above). The action does not take place *in vacuo*. If copyright prohibits copying, the act of copying should relate to something. And if that something is a copyright work, then how is it different from saying personal property law prohibits a person from damaging a car, for example? The act of damaging also does not take place *in vacuo* in the same way as the act of copying does not take place *in vacuo*. Furthermore, Penner only describes copyright as protecting expressions.[19] As Chapter 2, Section 3 showed, expressions only satisfy a part of the requirements of the thing that copyright protects. These expressions not only need to have the appropriate content but also to be reified such that the boundaries are determinable. This provides a coherent way in which one can understand the existence of a thing in copyright. Appreciating the thinghood of copyright also takes appropriate and sufficient consideration of the resources

[16] ibid 119–20.

[17] Michael Spence, *Intellectual Property* (OUP 2007) 14–16; Christopher M Newman, 'Using Things; Defining Property' in James Penner and Michael Otsuka (eds), *Property Theory: Legal and Political Perspectives* (CUP 2018).

[18] See David Llewelyn and Tanya Aplin, *Cornish Llewelyn & Aplin Intellectual Property* (10th edn, Sweet & Maxwell 2023) para 1-46, for a discussion on what monopoly means to intellectual property generally.

[19] Penner (n 15) 119–20.

that copyright seeks to protect—ie literary, dramatic, musical works, and so on. Ignoring the copyright work but focusing solely on the conduct mandated by the exclusionary rights misdescribes copyright.

Assuming monopoly is an acceptable description, one needs to examine the accuracy of the description of a 'property right in monopoly'.[20] If monopoly is the exclusive ability to undertake certain limited actions, as in the criminal prosecution example above, then it can be understood as a Hohfeldian privilege where the rest of the world has no right to prevent the privilege being exercised. If by property right Penner intends a similar meaning to the exclusionary right being discussed here, it places an *in rem* exclusionary duty on the rest of the world. If there is a property right in monopoly, then the rest of the world would have a duty not to interfere with the exercise of monopolistic actions on the part of the copyright owner. This would mean that the rest of the world owes a duty to the copyright owner not to interfere with the copyright owner's exercise of actions such as copying, distributing, communicating, and so on. However, this is not what copyright law requires of the rest of the world. The rest of the world owes a duty not to copy, distribute, communicate, and so on under CDPA, s 16(1), and does not owe a duty to exclude themselves from interfering with the copyright owner's exercise of these rights.

Penner acknowledges that all property rights are in one sense monopolies in that they enable a person exclusively to undertake certain actions with the thing. But the reason why copyright is a monopoly for Penner is because the number of actions that a copyright owner can undertake is limited, as opposed to, say, a landowner, whose ability to undertake actions in relation to land is open-ended. It is incorrect to conceptualise as a property right only that which enables the exercise of a wide range of use privileges. Even within tangible things, one can clearly see that a pencil has many fewer use privileges than a tract of land. This does not make the pencil any less capable of attracting property rights than land. If property right were to be conceptualised as referring not only to ownership but also to derivative interests such as easements, for example, then the number of use privileges associated with this property right is by definition highly restricted. This is because it is a requirement of easements that they relate to specific use of the land and do not extend to open-ended use.[21] Although easements are non-possessory rights, property law in general does not require an open-ended set of use privileges as a precondition to recognise a right as a property right. Therefore, describing copyright as a

[20] ibid.
[21] *Copeland v Greenhalf* [1952] Ch 488.

monopoly because it only enables a person to engage in limited number of actions would be inaccurate.

(ii) Copyright as a property right in the exclusionary rights themselves

Spence recognises that characterising intellectual property rights as monopoly is not satisfactory, as it is less clear that an intellectual property owner has an undue power over the supply of goods and services to a particular market.[22] Although Spence does speak of the rights being granted only when the intangible asset is attributed to a person, he does not regard this to mean that the rights arise in relation to the work.[23] He argues that it is inaccurate to characterise intellectual property as a property right in the intangible assets themselves. He asserts that an intellectual property right is a right that can be treated as property to 'control particular uses' of a 'specific intangible asset'.[24] In his conceptualisation, intellectual property is a property right in the legal right itself.[25]

The conceptualisation of copyright as a property right in the right itself is doctrinally problematic, not least because of its circularity. As explained above, the acquisition of copyright gives rise to exclusionary rights, exclusive powers, and exclusive privileges. From Spence's explanation, it appears that the meaning ascribed to the 'right' as the object of the property right is that of exclusive powers and privileges because he refers to the ability to control specific uses, and not to the duty of the rest of the world to exclude themselves from interference. If this is correct, a person P as a copyright owner who has the exclusive right to copy her work, has a right that the rest of the world exclude themselves from interfering with her right. According to this, liability will arise if a person Q interferes with P's exercise of their right to copy their work. However, CDPA, s 16(1) states that copyright is infringed by Q copying P's copyright work and not if Q interferes with P's exercise of her own exclusive right to copy.

Spence offers four reasons for his view. First, he asserts that if intellectual property is a property right in intangible assets, then any new valuable commercial use of the asset will have to presumptively become part of the property rights. Since new uses do not automatically become exercisable exclusively by

22 Spence (n 17) 14–15. Some scholars of personal property law also find this to be an accessible entry point into understanding intellectual property rights. For example, Bridge uses Spence to support his argument that copyright is chose in action. Bridge and others (n 5) paras 9-004, 9-005. See Chapter 2, Section 1 for Bridge's arguments.

23 Spence (n 17) 21–23.

24 ibid 12–13.

25 ibid 15–16.

the intellectual property owner, Spence argues that intellectual property cannot be a property right in the intangible assets.[26] It is indeed correct that a copyright owner is only entitled to the rights that are enumerated in the statute and nothing more. For example, until the rental and lending right was introduced under s 18A of the CDPA, it was not clear whether presumptively the copyright owners would have the ability to prohibit the lending of their works disseminated through VCDs and DVDs. If this were the parameter of a property right, no creature of statute could be the subject of a property right, because only common law can demonstrate the endless flexibility to accommodate within a property right newer uses of a thing. This parameter risks making the law of property static and monolithic. Furthermore, if the concern here is similar to Penner's—that copyright does not extend to an open-ended set of uses—then the same rejoinder given above regarding easements can be put forward here.

Secondly, Spence argues that it is the legal right itself over which the owner has 'an open-ended set of use privileges, control powers and powers of transmission'.[27] This argument makes one believe that powers and privileges can be exercised in the abstract, which is not the case. These are exercised in relation to the copyright work. If the asset to which these powers and privileges relate can be ignored in the conceptualisation of a property right, one can argue the same in relation to any tangible asset too. For example, when a person acquires ownership of a car, ownership also consists only of a property right to which all the open-ended use privileges and the powers relate, irrespective of whether it relates to a car or a pencil. If this is an inaccurate account of understanding the ownership of a car, why would it not be inaccurate for copyright works? Why would it not be acceptable to ignore the existence of the car, but acceptable to ignore the existence of the copyright work when powers and privileges are centred around it? Property theorists would regard this as inaccurate because the open-ended privileges and powers are mediated through the thing, which is the car in this example. But why are the privileges and powers not mediated through the copyright work? If the intangibility of the copyright work is the barrier, then a better way to proceed would be to understand whether the law can assist in building an intangible thing, as Chapter 2 of this book has demonstrated has done.

The third reason, and a complement to the second reason, is that there is no presumptive right to exclude the rest of the world from the enjoyment of the work (or invention) but from its use in a broadly or narrowly defined way

[26] ibid 14.
[27] ibid 15–16.

within the structure of these regimes. Like Penner's, this argument of Spence's stems from a restrictive understanding of exclusive rights as meaning exclusion from the intangible asset itself. It is possible to ignore an intangible asset in the second argument above because there is no right to exclude a person from the intangible asset. The same arguments that have been presented against Penner's arguments can be put forward here.

The fourth reason Spence offers is that the statutes regard copyright as personal property as opposed to regarding the works as personal property.[28] This argument appears misleading. The exact wording in CDPA, s 1(1) is 'copyright is a property right . . .'. Clearly there is no reference to personal property as such here. If Spence means that copyright is personal property, just as a car is personal property, the reference is to an asset and not to a property right. The copyright work is an asset, just as a car is an asset. By referring to copyright as a 'property right' the statute makes a reference to the composite of exclusionary rights, exclusive powers, and privileges, as explained above. In other words, the statute recognises this composite of rights, powers, and privileges as a property right. Further, this property right is not a right in the abstract, but indeed as the statute makes it clear, a right 'which subsists . . . in [certain] descriptions of work' enumerated in s 1(1)(a)–(c). Therefore, copyright is envisaged as a property right in the works. These works themselves are not property rights but only the subject matter, just as a car is not a property right but the subject matter to which the property rights relate. It is difficult to see why this is kind of analogy does not work for copyright in Spence's view. The disregard of the intangible thing that is the copyright work results in a conflation of the subject matter with the rights. Clearly, a reference to the ownership of a car, for example, as a 'property right' does not lead to the conclusion that there is no reference to a thing here, but only a right. It is surprising that when the same language of property rights is used in relation to a copyright work, Spence does not separate the rights from the subject matter.

(iii) Copyright as a chose in action

Closely connected with the argument that copyright is a property right in the exclusionary rights themselves is the idea that copyright is a chose in action. Among the proponents of the argument that copyright is a chose in action, Williams puts forward the strongest case. Williams insists that copyright 'is a claim on other persons' conduct; so is the benefit of an obligation'.[29] He regards

[28] ibid 13–14.

[29] T Cyprian Williams, 'Property, Things in Action and Copyright' (1895) 11 LQR 223, 232.

copyright as a forbearance on the part of the rest of the world—a duty whose corresponding right is with the copyright owner. This, in other words, is a description of copyright as merely a right and nothing else. Just as a debt is only an obligation on the part of the debtor to pay and nothing else, copyright is an obligation on the part of the rest of the world not to engage in certain conduct. Spence makes a similar argument, as noted above. Describing copyright as nothing other than a right is reductive and does not capture other very important aspects of its ontology, such as the resource being protected, the rationale behind the idea–expression dichotomy, and the reason behind the need for recording. The resources being protected are works of literature, music, art, films, sound records, and so on. Bridge et al also argue that copyright is a chose in action because the *res* is not separable from the right, but rather the rights conferred by the statute are themselves the *res*. The following paragraphs respond to the main thrust of their argument.

Bridge et al's first argument is that the work is not a *res* because 'the word "property" reflects its semantically correct root by identifying the condition of a particular resource as being "proper" to a particular person'.[30] In their view, the resource or subject matter of copyright that has been exclusively secured to the right holder is the right to reproduce the expression, and, therefore, it is that right and not the expression itself that is the *res*. To begin with, it is unclear why the semantic meaning of property is more relevant than the legal meaning ascribed to the word property. Even if one needs to look for a resource that is proper to the particular person, it is not clear why copyright work is not the resource, but the right is. The right is in relation to the copyright work and the right does not have an existence without the copyright work first having come into existence. As argued above, if intangibility of the copyright work is the stumbling block, then before dismissing the copyright work as a resource it makes sense to examine whether it has the characteristics by analogy with tangible things and if it can be acquired for the first time in a manner other than entering into a contract.

Secondly, Bridge et al argue that copyright can be correctly described as a chose in action even when the rights have not been infringed, just as it is appropriate to describe a debt repayable in the future also as a chose in action.[31] It may well be that if a debt is paid back promptly without the creditor having to initiate the action, in the hands of the creditor it is still called a chose in action. This argument misses the point that the benefit of repayment of a debt is simply

[30] Bridge and others (n 5) para 9-003.
[31] ibid para 9-006.

the receipt of the money that is owed from the debtor. The benefit, therefore, is the performance of the obligation by a particular person, that is, the debtor repaying. In the copyright context, on the contrary, if copyright is not infringed there is no dependence on any person performing a duty. The copyright work itself extends benefit to the copyright owner, should the copyright owner wish to exploit it, say by publishing it or communicating it to the public, and so on. This is similar to a person having a property right in a bicycle. If this property right is not infringed, then the benefit that the owner of the bicycle derives comes not from someone else performing their duty, but from the bicycle itself, such as riding it, lending it, and so on. As argued in Chapter 2, Section 2, this benefit comes from the inherent value of the resource being protected.

Thirdly, Bridge et al argue that there is no possibility of relativity of title in intellectual property, which they support with case law.[32] This is an extension of the argument that one cannot take possession of copyright. However, it has been demonstrated in Chapter 3 that the acquisition of copyright for the first time has a close analogy with taking possession of tangible things for the first time. It was argued therein that this indicates that there is a concept akin to possession in copyright by this analogy. It was also argued in Chapter 3, Section 4 that it is possible to develop an idea similar to adverse possession or finders of goods in copyright, both of which are based on relativity of title. There are, of course, differences in the way relativity of title operates in relation to tangible things and copyright works. It is not the argument here that tangible things and copyright works are identical in the way relativity of title operates. But with copyright, at least an analogy with relativity of title is possible, which is not the case with contractual debts.

McFarlane argues that whereas in tangible things the physical thing defines the boundaries, 'in relation to intellectual property, it is the content of the duties imposed by law which creates the "thing" protected'.[33] In other words, he supports the argument of the rights themselves being the thing. He speaks of these duties 'shifting [the] boundary of intellectual property protection'.[34] But do these duties 'define' the thing in copyright any more than the duties define the boundaries of land, for example? The number of ways in which a person may cause private nuisance to a landowner are limitless. The number of ways can change depending on the societal values and priorities. The world at large has a duty not to unduly interfere with the use and enjoyment of the land by

[32] *Farmer v Moseley (Holdings) Ltd* [2000] EWHC Patents 128 [45] (Neuberger J).
[33] Ben McFarlane and Simon Douglas, 'Property, Analogy, Variety' (2022) 42 OJLS 161, 176.
[34] ibid 175.

visual intrusion, which the commentators of tort law had believed not to be the case a few years ago. Clearly these evolving duties do not change the boundaries of land. Land remains, literally, where it was. In copyright, the core duties imposed on the rest of the world also remain defined and limited.

The Law Commission refers to s 1(1) and (3) of the CDPA to conclude that the thing in copyright does not exist outside the law. The Law Commission regards the rights as the thing and not the work or copyright work and sees this provision as indicating that the thing in copyright does not exist outside of the legal system.[35] Chapter 2 explains why the work is the thing in copyright and this chapter explains why the rights conferred by copyright statute are not the thing. While it is true that copyright as a set of rights that relate to a copyright work is a creation of statute, it does not take away from the fact that the thing in copyright is separable from the legal system. Even with things that already exist in nature, if it belongs to no one, Pollock argues that it is of 'no legal importance until something happens to bring a person into relation with it and make it the subject-matter of enforceable rights'.[36] He gives the example of 'an old iron pot thrown away and dropped at the bottom of a canal', and argues that it 'might well be no more to the law than if it were in another planet'.[37] This demonstrates that rights to tangible things all have a legal origin too. It should then not matter whether the law that recognises these property rights is common law or statutory law. Therefore, even if the Law Commission regards copyright as incapable of existence without the legal system, it is arguable that there is nothing unique to copyright about this, as no property rights arguably have existence without the legal system.

(iv) Preoccupation with the physical and exclusionary rights of copyright

A notable implication of the arguments put forward by both Penner and Spence is that, to be regarded as a property right, the exclusion should be from the thing itself. Implicit in their argument is also the view that this sort of exclusion is only possible if the thing is physical. Even if it were possible to conceive of an intangible thing, in their view it is only possible to exclude oneself from an action in relation to the intangible thing and not from the intangible thing itself. In other words, there is a certain preoccupation with the physical world in their conceptualisation of a property right. For example, one can see that a car exists in the physical world and, therefore, one can stay away from doing anything to it physically that may infringe rights in it. Similarly, with land, one

[35] Law Commission, *Digital Assets: A Consultation Paper* (Law Com No 256, 2022) paras 3.56, 3.57.
[36] Frederick Pollock, 'What Is a Thing?' (1894) 10 LQR 318, 320.
[37] ibid 320.

is excluded from crossing the boundary over to another person's land. But with a copyright work, such as a novel, the law does not require a person to stay away from the novel itself, but only requires a person to stay away from copying it, distributing it, and so on. This argument seems to emphasise the meaning of exclusion as being to prevent physical contact with the thing. If this is correct, then if there is physical contact it should follow that the property right is enforceable for such violation, and if there is no physical contact the property right is not enforceable. This sort of absolute claim requires further examination to ascertain whether it represents the correct state of the law of personal property and land law.

In an effort to distinguish themselves from other theorists,[38] Douglas and McFarlane prefer to use the language of non-interference rather than of exclusion, and a focus on the content of the duty rather than on the right. They argue that the *in rem* duty of non-interference is the defining feature of property rights, rather than the liberties or privileges enjoyed by the property owner.[39] For them, a property right is a shorthand for any property interest that imposes the *in rem* duty of non-interference, including, say, an easement.[40] Using property right in this sense helps them avoid the use of the language of ownership, which arguably does not exist in relation to land in English law.[41] They argue that the content of the *in rem* duty is to not interfere with the physical thing itself either deliberately or carelessly.[42] While this is clearly the case with chattels, in relation to land they posit that the physical interference is slightly different because of the *ad coelum* principle, which extends a freeholder's right not only to the surface of the land but also to the space above and the earth below. They give the example of *Anchor Brewhouse v Berkley House*,[43] where a crane suspended over a person's land without their permission was held actionable in trespass. In essence, their argument is that for an interference to be actionable it can only be of physical interference if it is a chattel, and of some kind of boundary crossing if it is land, even without the physical contact. They also argue that this concept is further developed by the law of nuisance.

[38] See Ben McFarlane, *The Structure of Property Law* (Hart 2008) 9 for a critique of Penner and Spence.

[39] Douglas and McFarlane (n 14) 223–24, 226.

[40] ibid 233–37.

[41] In English law, due to the doctrine of estates, it is said that there is no concept of ownership. Fee simple absolute is the closest it comes to ownership. See Kevin Grey and Susan Francis Grey, *Elements of Land Law* (6th edn, OUP 2009) paras 1.3.1 to 1.3.5. In this book, however, ownership of land is used in the same meaning as fee simple absolute, given that the discussion is at a higher level of abstraction.

[42] Douglas and McFarlane (n 14) 222–24. See also Simon Douglas, 'Kuwait Airways Corporation v Iraqi Airways Company' in Simon Douglas, Robin Hickey, and Emma Waring (eds), *Landmark Cases in Property Law* (Hart 2015) 210–11.

[43] [1987] 2 EGLR 173. See also Douglas and McFarlane (n 14) 225.

In relation to copyright, unlike Penner, the argument put forward by Douglas and McFarlane is not only that the content of the duty is different in copyright from tangible things.[44] Their argument is also a more fundamental one that copyright, and indeed any intellectual property right for that matter, does not impose duties that can coalesce around a physical thing.[45] Central to their argument is the assertion that property rights can arise only in relation to physical things. Chapter 2 discussed how copyright work does exist as a non-physical thing by analogy with physical things. But this would be insufficient without a correspondingly revised concept of property right that is commensurate with the nature of the thing that a copyright work is. Predicated on the argument that property rights can arise only in relation to physical things is the argument that the content of the duty imposed can only be that of physical non-interference. Therefore, even if it is possible for a copyright work to impose duties of non-interference in a similar way to a chattel or land, the absence of physicality means that these duties do not correspond to a property right, according to these theorists.

The arguments of theorists with a preoccupation with the physical can both be tackled as follows. In relation to copyright, it is possible to demonstrate that the duties of non-interference do not merely refer to an act of non-interference generally, but to non-interference in relation to the copyright work. In other words, while property rights in relation to tangible things coalesce around the physical thing, property rights in relation to copyright work coalesce around the copyright work. Within the context of tangible things, the law already accommodates a great deal of diversity in both the notion of the thing and the manner of interference that is actionable. Even if one were to search for a common denominator amidst this diversity, property rights in relation to tangible things do not involve a singular description of the thing, nor of the act of exclusion or non-interference. Even in relation to land and chattels it is possible to point to scenarios:

(a) where the thing is not physical;
(b) where the exclusion or interference is not physical in that it does not entail physical contact; and
(c) where the focus is not on anything physical for either of the reasons (a) or (b) above, the content of the duty by definition cannot be of physical non-interference but will need to be characterised as a much broader conduct.

[44] McFarlane and Douglas (n 33) 173–76.
[45] Douglas and McFarlane (n 14) 223–24, 240.

To the extent that the arguments above in relation to land and chattels focus on the non-physical, it is possible to extend these arguments copyright by analogy.

Let us begin with point (a) above, that is, instances where the thing is not physical. This happens in land more than with chattels because of the principle of *ad coelum*. Douglas and McFarlane acknowledge the possibility of aerial trespass without touching the physical ground. It can hardly be claimed that the thing in land means the mass of air that exists above the land. The air moves naturally over land and no one person can claim ownership of it.[46] If the effort of these theorists is to extract the essence of property rights, the extension of land into space above leaves a gaping hole (or shall we say blank space literally!) in the theory of the physicalists. To the extent that there is nothing physical above a plot of land and property rights can still extend to this space, it is possible to argue that not all property rights are (or need to be) in relation to a physical thing.

Moving on to point (b) above, that is, the modes of exclusion or interference, let us take Penner's assertion that to be a property right the corresponding duty should be to exclude oneself from the thing itself. The classic way in which this kind of duty is enforceable is in trespass.[47] It is not disputed that the right to exclude is a simple and convenient way of understanding property rights. But it risks being simplistic. It can convey the incorrect impression that property rights are enforced only by way of trespass rules, be it chattel trespass or trespass to land. While it is correct that trespass has a simple message to the rest of the world to exclude oneself from the thing itself, this is not the only kind of conduct that property law makes actionable. One should not lose sight of the tort of conversion for chattels and private nuisance for land, both of which are property torts in that they enforce property rights.[48] As will be shown below, there may be little or no overlap in actionability between trespass on one hand and these torts on the other. This means that it would paint an incomplete picture if trespass were taken to be a necessary and sufficient indicator of property rights. There are good reasons to acknowledge the role of conversion and private nuisance in informing the content of property rights and the corresponding duties to which they give rise. Property rights not only protect the physical boundaries but also protect indirectly a much broader interest, which some commentators call 'possessory interest'.[49] Correspondingly, the conduct

[46] See generally Kevin Gray, 'Property in Thin Air' (1991) 50 CLJ 252.

[47] Defined as intentional direct interference. See James Goudkamp and Donal Nolan, *Winfield and Jolowicz on Tort* (20th edn, Sweet & Maxwell 2020) para 14-02.

[48] See Chapter 5 for further discussion on property torts.

[49] Cynthia Hawes, 'Conversion by Detention' [2009] LMCLQ 188, 191.

on the part of the rest of the world cannot simply mean physical exclusion, but much broader actions.

Let us now unpack what this means first in relation to land. One must accept that the interference with land cannot always be physical, not only because of the possibility of trespass of the airspace but also because of nuisance by emanation. In recognition of this, Douglas and McFarlane argue that it is the boundary crossing that amounts to interference.[50] However, the boundaries of airspace are purely notional. Indeed, an encroachment of property rights in the airspace is possible because there is no physical boundary stopping it. If there had been a high enough wall, such as a fortress, the crane in *Anchor Brewhouse* would not have swung into the claimant's land. Physical barriers certainly block visual intrusion and arguably, to some extent, can also prevent smoke, odours, and fumes from entering a certain piece of land. Therefore, the boundary itself is notional in these cases, making physical interference also notional as opposed to real. The physical interference with land is, therefore, only tenuous.

Even if this can be regarded as sufficient physical interference, it is important to take a closer look at the very idea of boundary crossing. Let us accept that it is the space and not the molecular air that is protected. If the interference is by emanation of smoke, odours, or fumes then one can have visceral experience of it, giving it a physical dimension. However, with the decision of the Supreme Court in *Fearn v Tate Modern*,[51] it is now possible for the interference to be by visual intrusion. Of course, Douglas and McFarlane argue that in these cases there is a crossing over of the rays of light.[52] Surely, the liability in private nuisance arises because of the defendant's actions in emanating fumes, noise, or odours, and so on which enter the claimant's land. Light rays, on the contrary, do not in all cases emanate because of the defendant's actions. Depending on the source of light, the light can emanate from the claimant's own land during the night or reflect off the claimant's land during the day, which then reaches the defendant's eyes, creating the line of vision. The defendant may or may not be responsible for the emanation of light in the same way as they may be if they emanate sound or smoke. The boundary crossing may well be in the opposite direction to the cases of emanation. Any insistence on the idea of boundary crossing of this kind risks being a hollow dogmatic attachment, rather than a principled deduction from the case law (and indeed the laws of physics!). These cases prevent the common denominator of property rights being

[50] Douglas and McFarlane (n 14) 225.
[51] [2023] UKSC 4.
[52] Douglas and McFarlane (n 14) 232.

physical interference. If there is still an insistence on the physical connection, one can again only argue for a tenuous connection.

Let us move on to chattels. Writing on the law of conversion, Douglas has analysed numerous ways in which a person can interfere with a chattel for the interference to amount to conversion. He deduces that for conduct to amount to an interference 'the defendant's conduct must have had *some* effect on the claimant's chattel'.[53] The chattel may or may not be damaged. Indeed, Douglas demonstrates that physical contact is not a strict requirement for an interference with a chattel to be actionable in conversion. He puts forward many instances where this would be the case:[54] first, where the defendant orders his servant to make physical contact with the chattel without the defendant himself making contact;[55] secondly, where the defendant prevents access to the chattel on his land completely, even if the defendant has never himself made any physical contact with the chattel;[56] and thirdly, where the defendant impairs completely the use of the chattel by the claimant without making physical contact with the chattel.[57] These are examples where the defendant has physically excluded himself from the thing itself and yet has been held liable in the tort of conversion, showing that the content of non-interference is something different. Therefore, even within the context of chattels, it is not an absolute rule, nor the common denominator in all cases that the defendant excludes themselves physically from the thing itself. This makes it possible for the idea of exclusion to mean something more distant from the immediate physical exclusion. It can be an exclusionary activity that has a reference to the thing but does not involve the thing itself. This suggests that even if the act of interference has a distant connection with the physical, there may still be a liability for conversion.

With the benefit of the discussion thus far, let us now turn to point (c) above, that is, the content of the *in rem* duty corresponding to the property right. The content of the duty is discerned from the kinds of interferences that the courts would be willing to enforce. This should include not only trespass but also conversion and private nuisance. In relation to chattels, a person is liable for conversion if they intentionally interfere with a thing so as to exclude the

[53] Simon Douglas, *Liability for Wrongful Interferences with Chattels* (Hart 2011) 65 (emphasis supplied).

[54] ibid 66–67.

[55] *Lewis Trust v Bambers Stores Ltd* [1982] FSR 281 (Ch D).

[56] *Oakley v Lyster* [1931] 1 KB 148 (CA); *England v Cowley* (1873) LR 8 Ex 126 (Exch) 128.

[57] *Douglas Valley Finance Co v S Hughes (Hirers) Ltd* [1969] 1 QB 738. In essence, Douglas's argument is that in the tort of conversion, if the law does not insist on the defendant making a physical contact with the chattel, the effect should be that the claimant is excluded from the use of the chattel. Douglas, *Liability for Wrongful Interferences* (n 53) 67–68, 74.

lawful owner completely from controlling the thing.[58] As pointed out above, Douglas has demonstrated that the interference does not have to be physical so long as the exclusion of the lawful owner is complete. This means that the content of the duty is not merely one of refraining from interfering physically with the thing. It is also one of refraining from interfering with the thing in such a way that it excludes the lawful owner completely from controlling the thing, even if this does not involve physical contact.

In relation to land, a person is liable for private nuisance if they intentionally and unduely interfere with the claimant's use and enjoyment of the land.[59] This means that the content of the duty is again not one of refraining from interfering physically with the land. It is instead refraining from interfering in such a way that it unduly interferes with the use and enjoyment of the land, even if the interference does not involve physical contact. For example, if a person P emanates smoke on her land and it happens to cross over to her neighbour Q's land, there is physical interference with P's land according to the definition of land accepted above. But no liability arises for P's emanation of the smoke until Q can show that the smoke interferes substantially and unduly with Q's use and enjoyment of her land. What does this say about the content of the duty imposed on P? It is not simply to exclude herself from physically interfering with Q's land. It is to not interfere with it in such a way that it unduly interferes with Q's use and enjoyment of her land. If the only content of property rights was for P to physically exclude herself from interfering, then P would not be able to make use of her own land in ways that emanate anything from her own land. Perhaps having a barbecue in her garden once in a while during summer is not such a use that would affect the use and enjoyment of Q's land. But if Q's property right over her land meant that P had to exclude herself physically from interfering with Q's land, P would not even be able to make reasonable use of her own land. Clearly, the law of nuisance tells us otherwise.

When the duty is assessed in this light, one clearly sees a dilution of the absolutist argument that all property rights in relation to tangible things give rise to a duty of physical non-interference. Instead, it shows that the focus of the duty is not squarely on the physical, but instead on other interests the claimant has in the thing. In conversion this is the interest of the claimant to control the chattel, and in private nuisance it is the interest of the claimant to use and enjoy the land. Implicit in this argument is the notion that the ability to control the chattel is exclusive to the claimant, which is why the claimant can challenge it

[58] Douglas, *Liability for Wrongful Interferences* (n 53); See generally Sarah Green and John Randall, *The Tort of Conversion* (Hart 2009).

[59] Goudkamp and Nolan (n 47) para 15-03.

when they are deprived of the control in an action for conversion. Similarly, the ability to use and enjoy the land is exclusive to the claimant and therefore, when the claimant is unable to derive this benefit, they can challenge it in an action for private nuisance. If this is the case, it opens up the possibility that what the law requires is an interference with the exclusivity that the claimant can exercise over the chattel or land, and not the chattel or land itself. Removed from the chattel or land, this exclusionary duty can be described more as an *action* that requires non-interference with certain interests, rather than physical exclusion from the *thing*.

It is now opportune to assess how this discussion may help our understanding of the exclusionary rights in copyright, particularly because, in their analysis, Douglas and McFarlane exclude all rights that do not relate to physical things from qualifying as property rights.[60] In light of the discussion above, each of the claims of Douglas and McFarlane can be qualified in a way that moves the understanding of property rights further away from the physical. This is summarised in Table 4.1.

Table 4.1 Qualifying the notion of property rights as rights to physical things

Perception of theorists with a predisposition to the physical	**Qualification required to account for non-physical aspects within land and personal property law**	**What does this mean for copyright law?**
All property rights relate to a physical thing (only property rights are those that relate to a physical thing)	In certain situations, there is no physical thing; for example, aerial trespass	Law can and does work with non-physical thing by extension of notional boundary
Content of *in rem* duty is not to interfere with the physical thing itself, deliberately or carelessly	- Interference need not always involve physical contact in conversion - Even if there is interference, it may only be tenuous and distant from the physical thing, and not immediate and direct, as in private nuisance - Interference may be broadly directed towards exclusivity of the thing and not with the thing itself, as in conversion and private nuisance	- To be enforceable, interference does not always have to be with the physical thing itself - Interference can also be with exclusivity of the property owner - Conduct of interference does not always have to be of physical exclusion; it can be of other conduct that interferes with the exclusivity of the property owner

[60] Douglas and McFarlane (n 14) 223–24, 226.

If these qualifications are accepted, then it is not difficult to see how this opens up a coherent understanding of copyright. A property right can relate to a non-physical thing such as a copyright work. With the conclusion we have drawn above in relation to the reduced importance of physical contact in the torts of conversion and private nuisance, no sensible argument can be made that when considering copyright, somehow the only interpretation of the interference is that of physical non-interference. The right to exclude in copyright does not have to mean exclusion from the copyright work itself, as Penner claims. As in the case of chattels, it can mean an exclusionary activity that has a reference to the copyright work, such as copying of the work or distributing copies of the work, but it does not have to mean that one must stay away from the copyright work itself. In doing so, the content of the duty is directed towards actions that take away the exclusivity of the copyright owner in engaging in acts such as copying, distributing, and so on.

In reality, in the context of tangible things there is already a wide appreciation of the word 'interference'. Converting a bracelet does not involve the same act as converting a ship. The malleability of the law is even more evident when we move on to consider land, especially in relation to the number of ways in which the airspace above land can be interfered with. Implicit in this discussion is an acknowledgement that there is no singular way in which the law makes the interference enforceable even within personal property law. When tangible property law accommodates such diversity of interpretation of interference, it is not easy to appreciate why the diversity cannot be extended when the thing is not physical. A closer examination reveals that exclusionary rights or the corresponding duties they impose cannot be considered in isolation. These must be considered in relation to the content of the subject matter they attach to.[61] The conceptual understanding of exclusionary rights must be calibrated depending on the content of the subject matter. For certain subject matter, the exclusion is not from the subject matter itself, but from certain actions in relation to the subject matter. If the subject matter has physical existence, then the exclusionary conduct can be of physical non-interference of either an immediate or tenuous kind, having at the same time an impact on the non-performance of certain actions. If the subject matter is intangible, then the exclusionary conduct will necessarily be of non-performance of certain actions. The nature of exclusive rights, in other words, is inexorably linked to the nature of the subject matter.

[61] See Chapter 2, Section 3(a) for a discussion on the substantive content of the thing.

Among those who have specifically written about copyright theory, Breaky uses Hohfeldian analysis to explain copyright as a property right. He provides four different explanations of property right, namely, right to exclude, exclusivity of performing an activity, prohibiting others from an activity, and power of disposition.[62] He argues that copyright cannot be explained by way of a singular theory, but leans in favour of exclusivity of performing an activity and prohibiting others from the activity as a more apposite description of copyright.[63] The arguments presented in this book support those of Breaky. The difference is that this book draws out the trajectory of the development of the exclusionary duties from tangible things to intangible things. While doing so, it points out areas in land law and personal property law where the understanding of property right may be more consistent with the way copyright is understood. In other words, this book argues that the divergent understanding of property rights is not mutually exclusive even as one moves from tangible things to intangible things.

In summary, the exclusionary rights in copyright impose duties that have different content from those that relate to tangible things. On the surface it appears that copyright only imposes duties that are directed towards actions such as exclusion from copying, distributing, and so on, and that it has nothing to do with the thing itself, that is, the copyright work. However, on a closer examination one can see that there are significant differences in the content of the duties imposed in relation to different tangible things, demonstrated by the variety of subject matter and the differences between the torts of conversion and private nuisance. This makes one conclude that the duties imposed by property rights that relate to tangible things are not simply of physical non-interference with the thing itself but relate to an exclusionary action directed towards an interest in the things. This enables building bridges of analogy with copyright. Just as copyright imposes duties of exclusion that relate to certain actions in relation to the copyright work, property rights to tangible things impose duties of exclusion in relation to the interest in those tangible things.

(b) Restricted Acts and Exclusionary Rights

Having established that the content of exclusionary rights in copyright bears a close resemblance to the exclusionary rights to tangible things, this subsection

[62] Hugh Breaky, 'Properties of Copyright' in Helena Howe and Jonathan Griffiths (eds), *Concepts of Property in Intellectual Property* (CUP 2013) 147–51.
[63] ibid 154–58.

moves on to explain the exclusionary duties that the statute imposes. The CDPA enumerates the acts that are restricted to the copyright owner. These can be divided into three categories. First, the restricted acts that concern only the record are the rights to public performance and communication to the public. These rights apply to both authorial works (excluding artistic works for public performance) and entrepreneurial works alike. Sections 19 and 20 of the CDPA respectively refer to the acts of public performance and communication to the public of the copyright work. Secondly, the restricted acts that concern the copy of the work are rights to make copies, issue copies to the public, and rent and lend copies of the work, as set forth under CDPA, ss 17, 18, and 18A. Again, these rights apply to both authorial and entrepreneurial works. Thirdly, the restricted acts that concern the content of the subject matter are the rights against non-literal copying. This applies only to authorial works. Accordingly, in the United Kingdom, CDPA, s 17(2) prohibits reproduction of an authorial work in any material form, meaning copying a work in any significant or relevant way, which can include taking the content. For entrepreneurial works, the CDPA only protects the record and its copy, whereas for authorial works, the record, the copy and the content are protected.

The implication of these acts being restricted to the copyright owner are that only the copyright owner has the ability to engage in these acts and the rest of the world has a duty not to engage in these acts without the copyright owner's licence. These are two sides of the same coin. The former refers to the copyright owner's own abilities and the latter refers to the rest of the world. In other words, the same restricted act describes the powers and privileges on one hand, and rights on the other. This is different from property rights in tangible things like land, for example. The law does not enumerate the acts that the landowner can engage in. It follows that the law also does not enumerate the acts that the rest of the world is prevented from engaging in. This is pointed out by many commentators to characterise copyright as a monopoly. Arguments as to why this characterisation is incorrect are addressed in Subsection 2(a)(i) above. However, instead of taking away from the characterisation of copyright as a property right, the defined enumeration of these restricted acts reinforces another deep-rooted aspect of property rights, namely *numerus clausus*. This is discussed in the subsection below.

(c) Exclusionary Rights and *Numerus Clausus* in Copyright

The exclusionary rights impose corresponding duties on the rest of the world without their consent. As argued in Chapter 1, Section 5, it is opportune to consider the impact of exclusionary rights on *numerus clausus*. There are serious implications of not appreciating the nature of exclusionary rights. If the exclusionary rights are thought of only as monopolies and not as *in rem* rights that impose *in rem* duties, then we may not pay much attention to interpreting it astutely. If we understand exclusionary rights to mean choses in action, then the picture can be bleaker in that there may not even be an appreciation of the *in rem* nature of the duties imposed. This is why Subsection 2(a) above discussed at length the precise manner in which the exclusionary rights of copyright fit within the property discourse, such that due attention is given to the impact of these exclusionary rights on *numerus clausus*. In addition to being understood in the context of ownership, the exclusionary rights have significance also in relation to the derivative interests. Since it is possible to partially assign copyright, as will be discussed in Chapter 7, Section 2(a)(i), it is all the more important to ensure that the trespassory liability of the partial assignee is enforceable. If the right assigned is itself ill-defined, then the rest of the world will not be able to discern the act, the doing of which will attract liability for copyright infringement.

As explained in Subsection (b) above, the acts from which the rest of the world should exclude themselves are enumerated in the CDPA, and indeed any copyright statute of any other jurisdiction. Unlike the law governing tangible things, copyright statutes declare to the rest of the world the specific conduct from which they should exclude themselves. These exclusionary rights also form a closed list in that if a person engages in conduct that is not enumerated in the copyright statute, it will not amount to copyright infringement. Copyright statutes across the globe have seen expansion of the exclusionary rights through legislative action, some more significant than others.

An example from recent history is the rental and lending right. These rights were included as part of the copyright statutes when VCRs and DVDs were a significant means of disseminating cinematographic films. Before this right was introduced into the CDPA in 1996, it was still possible to regard this manner of dissemination as issuing copies of the work to the public. With the recognition of this right separately, it is now possible to assign this right partially, such that it is clear to the assignee what right they have acquired and what duties they can expect the rest of the world to owe to them.

The role of the courts in interpreting the exclusionary rights is also an important factor in maintaining certainty. Historically, translating a work without its author's consent, for example, had not been regarded as an infringement of a copyright work, until courts began to accept that the exclusionary right of the author went beyond the recorded form, all the way to the content.[64] This shows that courts are required to exercise caution before imposing new exclusionary duties in relation to the copyright work. However, courts have not exercised similar degree of caution, not only in keeping the boundaries of these rights separate but also defining these rights within the natural meaning of the statutory provisions. While this book does not seek to dwell on this doctrinal issue in detail, a summary is given below.

Of the rights recognised by copyright, the right of communication to the public is one of the most vulnerable to challenge for its doubtful boundaries.[65] Section 20 of the CDPA provides an inclusive definition of what amounts to communication to the public. It includes broadcasts and making the work available to the public by electronic transmission in such a way that 'members of the public may access it from a place and at a time individually chosen by them'. The case law of the Court of Justice of the European Union (CJEU), which is now part of assimilated law, has introduced meanings which are far removed from the meaning that can be discerned from the words used. One strand of the cases involves the interpretation of the word 'public'. In a series of cases, the CJEU has held that communication to the public should be directed towards a 'new public'.[66] The way this interpretation operates is, for example, that a copyright owner P, making a blog P authored freely accessible on the internet involves P exercising their right of communication to the public. If Q hyperlinks to P's blog, which has already been lawfully communicated to the public by P, this will not amount to infringement by Q because Q did not communicate to a new public. However, suppose P never posted the blog on the internet, but someone did so without P's consent. The very fact that the blog remains on the internet makes the blog an infringement of P's copyright. If Q hyperlinks to this content, then even though Q has communicated to a new public, Q's actions will only infringe P's right of communication to the public if Q 'did not know or could not reasonably have known' that the content was infringing.[67] But if Q is motivated by profit, then there is a rebuttable presumption that Q infringed the right of communication to the public. Here each of the concepts of new public, knowledge, and profit motive is alien to the language of the right of communication to the public.

[64] Brad Sherman and Lionel Bently, *The Making of Modern Intellectual Property Law* (CUP 1999) 55.

[65] See generally Poorna Mysoor, 'Unpacking the Right of Communication to the Public: A Closer Look at International and EU Copyright Law' [2013] IPQ 166.

[66] Important among this series is Case C–466/12 *Svensson v Retriever Sverige AB*, EU:C:2014:76, para 24.

[67] Case C–160/15 *GS Media BV v Sanoma Media Netherlands BV*, EU:C:2016:644, paras 47–48.

Commentators do not see this as a *numerus clausus* problem, although they do realise that this interpretation by the CJEU is untenable conceptually, doctrinally, and logically.[68] It is a *numerus clausus* problem because this kind of interpretation only increases the uncertainties as to the boundaries of the exclusionary duties. The rest of the world will be at a loss to ascertain the conduct that helps them avoid infringement. It is acknowledged that one cannot expect the bare bones of the statute to stand the test of time and the march of technological innovation. But any interpretation of the exclusionary right should have connection with the language of the provision at the very least and follow incremental expansion, bearing in mind Lord Wilberforce's *Ainsworth* criteria.[69] However, the CJEU's interpretation of the right of communication to the public fails to make it definable, identifiable by third parties, and capable of assumption by third parties, and risks losing stability of its interpretation.

3. Exclusive Powers and Copyright

In this section, the discussion will centre around why it is important to focus separately on the powers that arise with the acquisition of copyright, and how the powers could be separated from rights and privileges. One may begin with the legal power that a person exerts to acquire a thing, as elaborated in Chapter 3. For example, with land it may be in fencing the boundaries; with a jewel it may be grasping it in the hand. These myriad ways of taking 'possession' are recognised by law as giving title to the thing to the acquirer. A part of this title is the continuation of this legal power to decide at the acquirer's discretion what happens to the thing. If it is land, the acquirer gets to make decisions such as whether it will be tilled, built over, or a derivative interest such as a charge or an easement granted over it, and so on. If it is a chattel like a jewel, the acquirer can decide whether to pledge it or sell it, and so on. In the same way, an authorial work comes into existence when a person exercises their power of original expression, which is reified, and an entrepreneurial work comes into existence when a person exercises the power of creating a work that is not a copy of an existing work. This manner of acquiring copyright is recognised by

[68] eg Bently and others provide a detailed flow chart to make sense of the myriad criteria inserted by the CJEU. Lionel Bently and others, *Intellectual Property Law* (6th edn, OUP 2022) 185–86.
[69] *National Provincial Bank v Ainsworth* [1965] AC 1175, 1247–48.

the CDPA.[70] Once copyright is acquired, the same power continues with the copyright owner, to decide what happens to the work—whether it will be used for the owner's own benefit, licensed or some other derivative interest granted, or assigned in totality to someone else.

Let us now distinguish the legal power from the exclusionary right. The power is inward facing in that it enables the owner to exercise control over the thing. The right is outward facing in that it places duties on the rest of the world. This means that rights have the prima facie ability to alter the conduct of the rest of the world, with the possible consequence of legal enforcement if there were to be any infractions. In this sense, legal powers do not alter the conduct on the part of the rest of the world in the same way as rights do, although the power holder wields this ability exercisable at their discretion. The consequence for the rest of the world is that they cannot challenge the existence or exercise of the power by the owner. In other words, there is a disability on the part of the rest of the world. For example, if P, a landowner, decides to plant a rose garden on their land, the rest of the world cannot challenge this. If a member of the public, Q, comes into this garden to pluck flowers without P's permission, then this breaches P's exclusionary right, for which P can seek legal redress against Q in trespass. In the same way, the author of a novel, P, deciding in their discretion to self-publish their novel on a web-based platform, cannot be challenged by the rest of the world. But if a member of the public, Q, copies substantial parts of this novel, then P will have a right of action against Q for the breach of their exclusionary right to make copies of the work.

In their discretion, the owner exercising the power can change the legal relations with a person they choose at their discretion. The usual manner in which this happens is that the exercise of power by the owner results in a change from duty owed by the person to a privilege. The exercise of this power is what legitimises licences. A licence is a privilege which negates a duty that was in existence before. The power to negate the duty and when and how to do it, and in favour of whom to do it, is the power that the copyright owner wields. This is what Worthington posits as the owners of property having the ability to determine who will not have the benefit of their property in the future.[71] For example, P's ownership of land means that the rest of the world including Q owe exclusionary duties. P can decide in their discretion that they will allow Q to park their car on P's land. Q will then no longer owe a duty but will have a privilege to use P's land for this purpose. P could grant a licence or an easement in

[70] CDPA, s 1(1)(a) for authorial works and ss 5A(2), 5B(4), 6(6), and 8(2) for entrepreneurial works.
[71] Worthington (n 3) 231.

favour of Q at their own discretion. Similarly, in copyright with the exercise of power, licences and indeed any other interest in copyright can be granted.

Katz argues forcefully that the right to exclude is at best a weak description of ownership, if it is a description at all. She argues that if the rest of the world is excluded, by default it means that the owner is the one to exercise the powers and the privileges, and that this says nothing at all about the nature of the ownership interest. She argues instead for the primacy of the role of the owner as the sole 'agenda setter' as being the true descriptor of ownership. She argues for focusing not on the exclusion of the rest of the world, but on the exclusivity of the property owner.[72] This conceptualisation also has the support of other theorists such as Balganesh, who argues that Katz's arguments as to exclusivity are a fitting way to explain the ownership of the relatively less rivalrous resources that copyright protects.[73]

Analytically, however, there may be a lumping effect if we are to conclude that, upon completing the process of acquisition for the first time, what the person acquires is an interest that gives him the ability to be the sole agenda setter for that resource. This will mean that at once the person will acquire powers, privileges, and rights in the resource. While Katz's argument to avoid conflation between exclusion and exclusivity is acknowledged, exclusivity should also not result in conflating the concept of ownership. Doctrinally it may be more difficult to unpack this to understand the content of each of the powers, privileges, and rights. Intuitively it seems to make more sense to think of securing the boundaries first and then begin to exercise powers over the resource within. Katz's argument—that once the boundary is secured, the only one left is the owner—is correct. But this is the very effect desired at the point of acquisition. If the rest of the world does not keep off, the owner cannot claim the resource as theirs. The twin messages of 'keep off' and 'this is mine' are but two sides of the same coin. Focusing on one to the neglect of the other will only reveal a part of the picture. At the same point, this means that the right to exclude is a necessary but insufficient requirement for ownership. In this sense, neither of these theories needs to be mutually exclusive. Some theorists may refer to this as the integrated theory, where exclusion and use are both given equal significance.[74]

[72] Katz (n 7) 277–78.

[73] Shyamkrishna Balganesh, 'Alienability and Copyright Law' in Helena Howe and Jonathan Griffiths (eds), *Concepts of Property in Intellectual Property Law* (CUP 2013) 161, 178; Newman, 'Using Things' (n 17) 72, 76.

[74] See eg Adam Mossoff, 'What is Property? Putting the Pieces Back Together' (2003) 45 Ariz L Rev 371.

It is also interesting to note that much of the lobbying behind gaining property status for entrepreneurial works such as sound recordings, films and broadcasts was because this power of control over the finished product was the end game. Entrepreneurial works can come into existence as a record of authorial works such as literary, dramatic, or musical works, or as works that record content not protectable by copyright, such as a sporting spectacle. In either situation it made sense for them to lobby for independent ownership of the record they create. As publishers of authorial works, they still need to obtain a licence from the authors before their works can be incorporated in the entrepreneurial works. But the owner of the entrepreneurial work still has the power to bring independent legal action if there is an infringement of the recorded part of the entrepreneurial work, and generally to deal with the record as an owner would do.

The real power of the owners of entrepreneurial works is demonstrated by their ability to turn content into copyright works which would otherwise not be. For example, sporting spectacles and public events such as coronations or funerary processions are not eligible for copyright protection on their own because there no originality attaches to the way these events unfold. But if these events are captured in a record, the record becomes the entrepreneurial work, and the owner can exercise ownership powers over this record. A notable exception is a broadcast, which is not a record but only a transmission of signals that may only exist ephemerally. Yet, as discussed in Chapter 2, history tells us that broadcasts became copyright works because broadcasters of sporting events lobbied the government for protection of their investment in creating these broadcasts. Having ownership powers meant that these broadcasters could legitimately prevent the rest of the world from replaying their broadcasts without their licence and exploit their broadcasts in any manner the broadcaster pleases.

In the CDPA, the provision that manifests the copyright owner's powers is s 16(1), which enumerates acts that the copyright owner has an 'exclusive right' to do. This provision is addressed to the copyright owner and has the effect that only the copyright owner can engage in these acts and no one else. This provision, therefore, leaves it to the discretion of the copyright owner to do as they please with the copyright work. They can engage in any, all, or none of the acts at their discretion, or grant it to someone else to exercise. This is what it means to act like an owner in the copyright context.

The exclusivity that a copyright owner enjoys is not factual exclusivity that the owner of, say, a diamond ring can enjoy. Balganesh argues that the only way in which copyright can maintain this exclusivity is by going to law.[75] In other words, this is the assertion that copyright is non-rivalrous and a chose in action; the only benefit that the copyright owner derives is of exclusivity, and that the copyright owner will have to go to court to realise it. A cross-reference may be made here to the arguments presented in Chapter 2, Section 3(c)(ii), in response to Balganesh's assertions. Further arguments on the non-rivalrous nature of a copyright work are addressed also in Chapter 3, Section 2(a)(ii) in relation to a concept akin to possession. In summary, it may be argued that in relation to land, despite being a tangible thing, factual exclusivity cannot be enjoyed. Although self-help is available, it is highly limited by law. Land does not enjoy factual rivalrousness but only functional rivalrousness because the law imbues land with rivalrous characteristics. Just as land law enables exclusivity and possession in land, in the same way copyright law can enable copyright works to demonstrate exclusivity and possession by analogy.

In exercise of their power when they do engage in any of these acts or authorise others to do so, it amounts to the exercise of the privilege. This leads us to the section below, which elaborates on the privileges.

4. Exclusive Privileges and Copyright

The proponents of the argument that copyright is a chose in action insist that copyright demonstrates no use interest and that the only action one can take in relation to it is to initiate an action if the benefit is withheld unlawfully. For example, Rose denies that one can act like an owner in relation to copyright because, for her, this means 'little more than the holder's efforts to keep others from using this very abstract right'.[76] This statement is incorrect at many levels as it is evident here that copyright is very far from this notion. To begin with, copyright is not simply an abstract right. Chapter 2 demonstrated that copyright does relate to a thing and Chapter 3 established that copyright can be acquired for the first time in a manner that does not involve entering into a contract. Indeed, it was argued that acquisition of copyright is more akin to acquiring title by taking possession. One of the reasons for acquiring copyright is the ability to use and enjoy the work and exploit the licensing opportunities.

This is consistent with the view held by theorists who regard the right to exclude as a means to facilitate the end of enabling the use of the resource in question. Smith posits that the right to exclude from a designated thing protects our

[75] Balganesh (n 73) 178–79.

[76] Rose (n 10) 61. She refers to intellectual property generally.

interests in the use of things.[77] Newman regards a person's freedom to use their property as they please as a sort of affirmatively vested entitlement inherent in the very possession of property.[78] Although Penner regards copyright as a property right in the monopoly, Penner's exclusion thesis defines a property right as 'a right to exclude others from things which is grounded by the interest we have in the use of things'.[79] This is also consistent with the doctrinal consequences of taking possession of a tangible thing, which is to enable a person to exercise the use privileges in relation to the thing. With land as much as with chattels the converse is also true—being able to use a thing is how a person demonstrates that they are acting like the owner.[80]

Commentators on copyright law typically characterise the exclusionary rights as negative rights—rights that entitle the copyright owner to require that others do not do something, rather than placing a positive duty on them to do something.[81] Unlike patent law or trade mark law, which imposes a duty on the state to register the respective right if the relevant conditions are met, copyright comes into existence automatically without the need for registration. This makes copyright appear to consist only of negative rights. This may give the impression that copyright exclusive rights are somehow hollow or that tangible property rights are somehow more substantive. This may bolster the view that copyright only imposes duties of exclusion on the rest of the world, and that there is nothing substantive within copyright to give rise to a use interest.[82]

However, the truth is that all property rights are negative. Indeed, if it was not negative it may not be property right at all, according to certain scholars who regard the right to exclude as the core of property rights.[83] But if one argues that the negative rights in copyright mean that copyright only speaks of what the rest of the world cannot do, and not what the copyright owner is positively able to do, this is incorrect. Section 16(1) of the CDPA clearly states that the copyright owner has the right to engage in certain conduct in relation to the copyright work.[84] This is a positive action the copyright owner can take in

[77] Henry E Smith, 'Intellectual Property as Property: Delineating Entitlements in Information' (2007) 117 Yale LJ 1742, 1747, 1179.
[78] Christopher M Newman, 'Vested Use-Privileges in Property and Copyright' (2017) 30 Harv J L & Tech 75, 76.
[79] Penner (15) 71.
[80] *JA Pye v Graham* [2003] 1 AC 419.
[81] David Llewelyn and Tanya Aplin, *Cornish, Llewelyn, Aplin Intellectual Property: Patents, Copyrights, Trademarks & Allied Rights* (10th edn, Sweet & Maxwell 2023) para 1-04.
[82] Bridge and others (n 5); Williams (n 29).
[83] eg Merrill (n 11).
[84] For other jurisdictions, see eg Australian Copyright Act 1968, s 31(1), which states 'copyright, in relation to a work, is the exclusive right: . . .'.

relation to the copyright work, or what one may call a liberty that the copyright owner has to do something if he so chooses. Engaging in these positive actions amounts to using and enjoying copyright.

It should surprise no one that entire industries are set up based on the ability of copyright being put to use. For example, the entertainment industry licensing music, lyrics, dramatic works such as screen plays, artistic works, and so on. Clearly the copyright owner can themselves use the privileges in relation to their work—such as a sculptor making a limited number of copies of the sculpture or a musician self-publishing their music on an online platform. Or the copyright owner can authorise someone else to exercise one or more of the use privileges. For example, this author has authorised Oxford University Press to make copies of her work and to distribute them. It is important to recognise these as use privileges. In the Hohfeldian sense, the rest of the world has no right to engage in any of these activities. The exclusive privileges, therefore, do mean that a copyright work can be put to use.

There are certain important consequences that follow from the conclusion that copyright ownership gives rise to use interest. First, the chose in action conception can be decidedly shown to be an inaccurate conceptualisation of copyright. The benefit to a copyright owner is far beyond going to the court if the rights are infringed. Secondly, as will be seen in Chapter 7, licences, both exclusive and non-exclusive, are an important derivative interest that arises from copyright, and one that is commonly granted by copyright owners in return for licence fees. Thirdly, the ability to grant a copyright licence makes it possible for courts to grant licence fee damages for copyright infringement. As this author has argued elsewhere,[85] the underlying reason for courts to treat intellectual property infringement cases as being similar to property torts is because intellectual property can be put to use by granting licences in the same way as tangible things can be. Courts can use this as the substantive basis to award damages based on the hypothetical licence fee that the property owner would have charged to permit the infringing activity.

5. Summary

This chapter examined what it is that a person acquires when they acquire copyright ownership. It argued that, principally, the ownership interest has

[85] Poorna Mysoor, 'Licence Fee Damages and the Nature of IP Rights' [2025] Harv J L & Tech (forthcoming).

three components: exclusionary rights, exclusive powers, and exclusive privileges. This chapter dealt with each of these in turn, addressing misunderstandings as to their conceptualisation in copyright.

With exclusionary rights that copyright recognises, the perception is that the duties they impose relate to an action rather than to a thing; and even if it can be shown that these duties relate to an intangible thing like a copyright work, the content of the duty cannot mean exclusion from the copyright work itself, but only from an action. Section 2 addressed this argument by showing that property rights in relation to tangible things also impose duties that do not always relate to a physical thing, nor to the exclusion from the physical thing itself. It based these arguments on the conclusions from torts such as conversion and private nuisance. Having established that the content of the exclusionary duties in copyright is not so divergent from the duties imposed in relation to tangible things, it explained what the exclusionary duties in copyright entail. It went on to point to the interpretation of some of these exclusionary duties adopted by the CJEU that could become problematic from a *numerus clausus* perspective. Section 3 analysed the exclusive powers of the copyright owner and why these powers are significant. Section 4 examined the exclusive privileges of copyright in order to establish, much against the general perception, that copyright works can indeed be put to use.

5
Copyright Enforcement and Remedies

1. Introduction

A hallmark of any claim right in the Hohfeldian sense is that if the right is infringed, the right can be enforced, leading to legal consequences sounding in remedies. While enforcement entails a cause of action being taken to the court, the practical end entails the grant of a remedy if the claimant were to prevail. Excluding rights barred by limitation, in general, rights and remedies go together. The most classical form of enforcement of property rights was *vindicatio*, which was a proprietary action tracing its roots to Roman Law.[1] *Vindicatio* could be asserted when a person was dispossessed of a thing. The remedy enabled the claimant to take back the thing itself. For *vindicatio* to be available, the thing needed be tangible. In English common law, if a person is dispossessed of land, a proceeding for repossession can put the claimant back in possession of the land. However, if a person is dispossessed of a chattel, in most cases an action does not lie in *vindicatio* to put the owner back in possession of the chattel.[2] *Vindicatio* is, therefore, available for land, but not for chattels in English common law. However, Pretto-Sakmann argues that the availability or not of *vindicatio* is not an indication that a right is a property right.[3] This means that there should be other ways of enforcing property rights.

How are property rights enforced then? Complete dispossession is not the only kind of grievance a property owner can have. Property owners may also suffer lesser injury, such as a scratched car or misdrawn boundary. Broadly speaking, according to Winfield, if the right is held against persons generally, tortious liability will ensue for the breach of the corresponding duty.[4] Among the rights, privileges, and powers, it is the right that depends on another person's conduct for its existence. To illustrate, P as a freeholder of a land can

[1] Arianna Pretto-Sakmann, *Boundaries of Personal Property: Shares and Sub-Shares* (Hart 2005) 7.
[2] Simon Douglas, *Liability for Wrongful Interferences with Chattels* (Hart 2011) 9, 64. Sarah Green and John Randall, *The Tort of Conversion* (Hart 2009) 54–55.
[3] Pretto-Sakmann (n 1) 98.
[4] James Goudkamp and Donal Nolan, *Winfield and Jolowicz on Tort* (20th edn, Sweet & Maxwell 2020) para 1-003.

Copyright as Personal Property. Poorna Mysoor, Oxford University Press.
DOI: 10.1093/9780191954962.003.0005

mandate the rest of the world not to infringe the boundaries of their land. If Q builds over part of P's land then P can enforce this through the tort of trespass, seeking an injunctive remedy or damages. Enforcing P's right means another person, Q, being mandated to conduct themselves in a particular way. Privilege, on the contrary, gives no right to others to question the exercise of the privilege. It does not depend on someone doing something but instead asserts others' inability to do or not do anything. P's ability to grow pink roses in their garden simply points to the inability of the rest of the world to stop P from growing pink roses. The rest of the world has no right to challenge P growing pink roses, and P has no duty to the rest of the world not to grow pink roses. In this sense, the domain of the privilege is with the holder. The same is true for legal power. P can decide at their discretion whether to grow or not grow anything on their land, and the rest of the world has no ability to compel P otherwise. Therefore, when one speaks of enforcement, this discussion makes us believe that only rights can truly be enforced.

But there is more going on in property torts. What is enforceable in private nuisance is the undue interference with the use and enjoyment of land by one person because of the conduct of another person. In our example above, if P's neighbour Q emits smoke to such an extent that all of P's rose plants die, Q may be liable to P if P is able to establish that the interference was undue. Here, the tort of private nuisance indirectly enforces P's privilege to use their land in a particular way. Connected to this privilege, P's power to use the land in particular ways may also be enforced. But it is important to note that any crossing of smoke into P's land will be actionable only when it amounts to an undue interference with P's use of the land. In this assessment, there is some room for reasonableness. Liability does not arise until the interference is shown to be undue. While trespass involves direct interference with land, private nuisance involves indirect interference and, therefore, it is softened by the assessment of reasonableness. The tort of conversion also has a similar relationship with trespass to goods, in that trespass to goods enforces the right of non-interference, while conversion enforces the possessory interest in the chattel requiring more substantial interferences. Conversion is only established when a person intentionally interferes with a chattel so as to exclude its owner from the chattel altogether or impairs the owner's use totally.[5]

The above discussion reveals that when a property right relates to land, the causes of action are torts of trespass or private nuisance, and when the property right relates to chattels, the most common causes of action are in trespass

[5] Douglas (n 2) 67.

to goods and conversion, in addition to negligence (collectively, 'property torts'). The evolution of property torts indicates the varied interests that the property torts are capable of protecting and enforcing. How are rights to intangible assets enforced then? As assets that are not land (and therefore personal property), could an interference with these assets be enforced by trespass or conversion?

A majority of the House of Lords in *OBG v Allan* held that it was not possible for choses in action to be a subject of conversion.[6] The specific assets in question were certain debts. The House of Lords also rejected the alternative argument that economic torts of inducing breach of contract had been established. Green and Randall have forcefully argued against this position, foregrounding the possibility of intangible assets being the subject matter of conversion. They also rightly assert the impossibility of copyright being a subject matter of conversion.[7] Copyright does not need to be amenable to conversion because copyright infringement is enforceable under the statute. But the question is, what kind of tort is copyright infringement?

Most judges and commentators agree that copyright infringement is a tort that relates to breach of property rights.[8] However, there are others who characterise copyright infringement as an economic tort, a term given to a slew of disparate torts including malicious falsehood, inducing breach of contract, and the like. They regard copyright infringement (and infringement of other intellectual property) to be 'contiguous' with 'core economic torts'.[9] It may well be that these torts arise from similar policy concerns because these torts 'limit the liberty of competition'.[10] The focus of economic torts being primarily on protecting economic interests might explain why torts of intellectual property infringement are considered together with economic torts in the discussions on damages. Commentators recognise the diversity of economic torts and acknowledge that nothing much turns on the classification of economic torts as they do not have much in common.[11]

[6] [2007] UKHL 21.

[7] Green and Randall (n 2), 107, 112–15, 118ff. See also Sarah Green, 'To Have and to Hold? Conversion and Intangible Property' (2008) 71 MLR 114.

[8] Gwilym Harbottle and others, *Copinger and Skone James on Copyright* (19th edn, Sweet & Maxwell 2025) para 6-11; *Weatherby & Sons v International Horse Agency & Exchange Ltd* [1910] 2 Ch. 297, 305; *Hawkes & Son (London) Ltd v Paramount Film Service Ltd* [1934] Ch 593.

[9] Andrew Tettenborn and others, *Clerk & Lindsell on Torts* (24th edn, Sweet & Maxwell 2024) para 23-02.

[10] Lord Wilberforce described patent infringement as an economic tort in *General Tire Co v Firestone Tyre Co Ltd* (1975) 1 WLR 819 while discussing the compensatory nature of damages to be awarded. James Edelman states that the torts of intellectual property infringement are 'allied' to torts such as injurious falsehood. James Edelman and others, *McGregor on Damages* (22nd edn, Sweet & Maxwell 2024) para 49-38.

[11] Edelman and others (n 10) ch 49 entitled 'Economic Torts and Intellectual Property'.

This chapter argues that it helps to analyse copyright infringement by analogy with property torts and not as an economic tort. It posits that property torts provide the required anchoring to help reassess the fault requirement in copyright infringement. Being classified as an economic tort offers no guidance as to how one may examine copyright infringement. Instead, it might reinforce the incorrect conclusion that copyright is a chose in action, a conceptualisation to which this book takes strong objection as already discussed in the previous chapters. It is admitted that there are obvious differences between the property torts and copyright infringement. However, an examination of this kind still merits attention because the manner in which the fault element plays a role in property torts reveals a delicate balance that the courts try to achieve between competing interests. The legitimacy of property torts is linked to whether the fault element is appropriately calibrated. The foregoing chapters of this book have sought to demonstrate the various ways in which copyright is a property right. If these arguments are to hold water, then similar considerations of fault must inform the legitimacy of copyright infringement.

Property torts have varying requirements of fault depending on whether the interference is direct or indirect, and whether the interference is voluntary or involuntary. There is much academic debate on what strict liability means and whether a tort can both require a fault element and attract strict liability. This book is not the place to resolve this debate.[12] Doctrinally, in English law the fault element in the property torts is reasonably well established. Trespass to land is a tort where the interference with land is both voluntary and direct. This attracts the strictest liability of all property torts in that it is actionable even without the claimant having to show any damage.[13] One may have a similar view on trespass to goods, although there is academic disagreement as to whether trespass to goods requires direct interference or only voluntary interference.[14] In private nuisance, however, where the interference is voluntary but indirect, liability arises only if there is an undue interference with the use and enjoyment of the land.[15] The claimant must show damage, although if the interference is substantial, damage may be presumed.[16] Green and Randall

[12] For an excellent discussion on this topic, see John Goldberg and Benjamin Zipursky, 'The Strict Liability in Fault and the Fault in Strict Liability' (2016) 85 Fordham L Rev 743.

[13] Goudkamp and Nolan (n 4) 14-001, 14-003, 14-010.

[14] Douglas argues that in its modern version trespass to goods does not require direct interference. See Douglas (n 2) 64–75. However, Green and Randall define trespass to goods as direct interference (n 2) 47.

[15] Goudkamp and Nolan (n 4) 15-010, 15-011. See also *Miller v Jackson* [1977] QB 966, 980 (Lord Denning MR).

[16] Goudkamp and Nolan (n 4) 15-057.

have argued that conversion is comparable to private nuisance in that the liability only arises if the interference is substantial.[17] Commentators have argued by analogy with torts of trespass to the person that if the interference either with land or with goods is involuntary, regardless of whether it is direct or indirect the law should impose only negligence liability.[18]

There is only one tort of copyright infringement enshrined in the statute which, over the years, has come to bear a closer resemblance to trespass to land or chattels, making it a strict liability tort.[19] The innocence or not of the infringer does not matter for liability for copyright infringement to arise. Whether the interference is direct or indirect, voluntary or involuntary, the liability arises without any considerations of reasonableness softening it. There is no liability in negligence for involuntary interferences. Since copyright infringement does not give rise to physical damage, any damage by this account can only be regarded as a pure economic loss. This prevents finding of liability in negligence for copyright, despite a distinct possibility of the act of copyright infringement being entirely unintentional. The singular tort of copyright infringement subsumes all types of infringement but attracts the same level of strict liability as trespass does, making copyright infringement unnecessarily harsh. If copyright infringement was analysed as being more analogous to property torts with the same range of fault requirements for different kinds of interferences, it would be possible for liability for copyright infringement to arise in a fairer and nuanced way.

Making copyright infringement a more balanced tort has implications beyond coherence of the law. Rarely can one say that a copyright work is truly independent of its environment. There are bound to be influences both of other protected works and unprotectable material that remain in the public domain. The harshness of copyright infringement could stifle creation of new works. One must, therefore, ask whether there is any justification for the liability for copyright infringement to arise so readily. One may point to some softening that takes place in the grant of remedies. One may also argue that the existence of numerous defences to copyright infringement (which will be examined in Chapter 6) softens the liability *ex post*, as an external matter. However, if the regime governing tangible property rights is paradigmatic, it is surprising that the flexibility and cushioning that is seen in these torts is absent from copyright infringement.

[17] Green and Randall (n 2) 60–62.
[18] Goudkamp and Nolan (n 4) 18-009; Douglas (n 2) chs 8 and 9.
[19] Patrick Goold, *IP Accidents: Negligence Liability in Intellectual Property* (CUP 2022) 21-23.

Once copyright infringement is established, the copyright owner can avail of the same remedies that are available for the infringement of any other property right.[20] In this sense, remedies make no distinction between violation of intangible property rights and of tangible property rights. Indeed, it is arguable that certain powerful remedies that are granted more sparingly in property torts are granted more readily for copyright infringement. One such remedy is the award of negotiating damages, which are based on the hypothetical licence fee that the copyright owner would have charged the infringer to regularise the infringement. The other is disgorgement of profits, more commonly known as account of profits, where the copyright owner can seek a court order for the infringer to account for all the profits made and pay it to the copyright owner. In some cases, this may go beyond putting the claimant back in a place where the tort did not occur. Strict rules for liability coupled with powerful remedies could make both property lawyers and tort lawyers question the legitimacy of copyright infringement.

In this chapter, Section 2 examines the tort of copyright infringement and demonstrates that it is unnecessarily harsh on the alleged infringers. It begins in Subsection 2(a) by comparing copyright infringement with trespass. A direct boundary crossing being at the heart of trespass, this subsection shows how it is only the literal infringement of copyright that bears a close analogy to the tort of trespass to land. Since non-literal infringement is also actionable under copyright infringement, Subsection 2(b) moves on to establish a closer analogy of non-literal infringement with private nuisance. It analyses the different ways in which the liability in private nuisance balances various interests. It compares it with the singular approach to copyright infringement, which takes no account of competing interests and shows how it fails to balance these interests, demonstrating that copyright infringement is a stricter liability tort than property torts. Since copyright infringement makes actionable not only conscious but also sub-conscious and unconscious copying, Subsection 2(c) examines whether this amounts to an involuntary infringement of copyright. It considers the general consensus among judges and commentators that an involuntary interference with property rights should attract only negligence liability and explores how negligence liability can be incorporated into copyright infringement.

Section 3 discusses the remedies for infringement. It begins by showing how innocent infringers are treated by the courts and how this has become a primary method of balancing competing interests. However, it goes on to show

[20] CDPA, s 96(2).

how even innocent infringers could be slapped with powerful remedies such as accounting for profit and negotiating damages.

2. Copyright Infringement by Aanalogy with Property Torts

Due to the lack of convincing arguments as to how copyright is a property right, and the prevalence of the view that copyright is a chose in action, copyright infringement has not been examined by analogy with property torts. In the context of US law, scholars have highlighted the harshness of copyright infringement as a tort, suggesting solutions that support liability based on foreseeability,[21] or in negligence.[22] Much less attention is given to whether a closer analogy with property torts itself can demonstrate that copyright infringement is harsher even in comparison with property torts. Furthermore, copyright infringement being a tort of statutory origin alienates it further from property torts that have a common law origin. Yet, it seems counterintuitive that the enforcement of property rights in tangible things has a softer approach to infringement than property rights in intangible things such as copyright. Building on the previous chapters as to how copyright is a property right with closer analogies to land and chattels than hitherto acknowledged, this section seeks to establish the analogy between property torts and copyright infringement to help guide a principled way to reform the latter.

Section 16(2) and (3) of the CDPA provide the ingredients of copyright infringement, which can be paraphrased as follows:

(i) The exercise by the defendant of a right restricted to the copyright owner;
(ii) The defendant's work being 'derived' from the claimant's work;[23] and
(iii) The exercise by the defendant of the restricted act in relation to the whole of the claimant's work or a substantial part of it directly or indirectly.

It appears from s 16(2) that the absence of the licence of the copyright owner is also a component of copyright infringement. However, a claimant who complains of infringement is not required to produce positive proof of the

[21] Shyamkrishna Balganesh, 'Foreseeability and Copyright Incentives' (2009) 122 Harv L Rev 1569, where Balganesh presents foreseeability as a general theme in common law drawn from the tort law of negligence, contract law, family law, property law, and patent law.

[22] Goold (n 19). To the extent that Goold refers to negligence liability within property torts, his work is discussed in Subsection 2(c) below.

[23] Lionel Bently and others, *Intellectual Property Law* (6th edn, OUP 2022) 194.

negative—that they did not grant a licence. The claimant only needs to show prima facie that they did not grant a licence to the defendant. The burden of showing the existence of a licence is upon the defendant. Therefore, it is better analysed as a defence.[24]

Regarding (i) above, Chapter 4, Section 2(b) of this book provided the discussion on the content of the rights. It will not be reinforced here. It suffices to state here that the statute provides an exhaustive list of the rights, the infringement of which leads to liability. These rights, however, can be infringed in numerous ways. For example, if P has written a novel in English, Q infringes P's copyright if Q translates the novel to Spanish without P's consent or if Q makes a stage play based on the novel without P's consent. The right infringed in both cases is the same—the right to make an adaptation.[25] The facts leading to infringement differ. Therefore, the components of the right should be established together with the facts that support the exercise of the right. This would be the same for interference with tangible things, although the number of ways in which interference can take place is more extensive. The discussion below will compare copyright infringement with different property torts, in relation to components (ii) and (iii), with only a cursory reference to (i) above.

(a) Copyright Infringement and Trespass

Trespass to land occurs when the claimant's boundary is infringed. The boundary is not restricted to the surface of the land but extends to the air column above and the earth beneath. Not all interferences are enforceable. First, the interference must be voluntary. Commentators have described this variously as an intentional interference or deliberate interference, knowing or conscious interference. While the knowledge that one is crossing over to the claimant's land is not required, the act of walking or being on the claimant's land should be voluntary. This has been described as a wilful muscular contraction.[26] For our discussion here, the interference should be a conscious act of the defendant and not because the defendant has been pushed onto the claimant's land or was carried over by others. If no defences are available, it gives rise to a liability in trespass. Other characteristics of trespass are that even the most trivial and minor crossing into the claimant's boundary is

[24] See Chapter 6, Section 2(a) for an analysis of licence as a defence.
[25] CDPA, s 16(1)(e).
[26] Douglas (n 2) 69 citing Oliver Holmes, *The Common Law* (Dover 1991) 54.

enforceable. Furthermore, trespass is a tort against an interference with possession. This means that the person bringing an action in trespass must have possession or an immediate right to possession. Trespass is actionable per se, which means that there is no need for the claimant to show that they have suffered any damage. The following table summarises the comparisons being made, and the following paragraphs analyse each of the elements in relation to copyright infringement by analogy.

Following Table 5.1, let us begin with the interference. What amounts to an interference in copyright infringement by analogy? The CDPA uses no language that speaks expressly of interference. However, implied in the language of the CDPA is the requirement that the defendant's work be derived from the claimant's work. Section 16(2) states that copyright in a work is infringed when a person does 'any of the acts restricted by the copyright'. Section 16(1) defines the acts restricted by copyright as rights that only the copyright owner can exercise. When a defendant is alleged to have exercised any of these rights, the allegation cannot exist in a vacuum. The rights must have been exercised in relation to a work, and it is this work which needs to be derived from the claimant's copyright work. For example, if P engages in communicating a work to the public, P will only be liable for copyright infringement to Q if the work P communicated is Q's copyright work itself or if P utilised Q's work in creating the work that P communicated to the public. Although derivation is required in all cases of infringement it is easier to understand this with the rights that engage with copies because it is inherent in the meaning of the word 'copy' that it should be a likeness of something else.[27] Therefore, if P engages in the act of issuing copies to the public, P will only be liable to Q if the work that they distribute was created by utilising Q's work. Accordingly, if in both instances P can show that the work they distributed was not derived from Q, but was created independently by P, then no liability for copyright infringement ensues.

A deeper examination reveals that the need for derivation can be further analysed into two components: first, the defendant must have had access to the claimant's copyright work. Let us pause here and see if the need for access might also be implicit in the tort of trespass to land. A person cannot commit trespass to land if they do not have access to another person's land. The same applies to trespass to goods. Since access is such an obvious requirement of trespass, in most cases it may not require to be proved separately. In copyright, however, this can be divided further into two parts—that the work was accessible to the defendant and that the defendant in fact accessed it. Depending on

[27] See Chapter 4, Section 2(b) for a discussion on different rights under the CDPA.

Table 5.1 Comparison of copyright infringement with trespass

<table>
<tr><th>Trespass to land</th><th colspan="2">Interference with land</th><th>Voluntary</th><th>Direct</th><th>A tort against possession</th><th>Minor infractions actionable</th><th>A tort actionable per se</th></tr>
<tr><td>Copyright infringement</td><td colspan="2">Derived from claimant's work</td><td rowspan="3">Conscious</td><td rowspan="3">Literal</td><td rowspan="3">A tort that protects original parts (authorial works) or parts created with substantial investment (entrepreneurial works)</td><td rowspan="3">Whole or substantial part of the work, but substantial part interpreted to mean any part</td><td rowspan="3">A tort actionable per se</td></tr>
<tr><td rowspan="2"></td><td>Claimant's work being accessible</td><td rowspan="2">Exercise exclusive rights</td></tr>
<tr><td>Defendant accessing claimant's work</td></tr>
</table>

the nature of the work infringed both these aspects can be a matter of physical observation. For example, in *Designers Guild v Russell Williams*, the claimant's design had been displayed in a trade fair and the design had been marketed widely, making it accessible to the defendant, and a senior representative of the defendant indeed attended the trade fair.[28] With many works such as musical works, despite their ubiquity online, normally all that can be proved is that the claimant's work was accessible, but not definitively that it was accessed by the defendant. In *Sheeran v Chokri*,[29] all that could be shown was that Chokri's song was accessible online, but not that Sheeran indeed accessed it. Infringement was not found in this case, but it could be dangerous to equate the accessibility of the work with proof of access by the defendant.

Secondly, the defendant should have exercised one or more of the claimant's exclusive rights in relation to the claimant's copyright work in a way that some commentators regard as misappropriation.[30] In other words, there should be some kind of taking of the claimant's work by the defendant. In trespass to land, the defendant needs to have exercised a right which only the landowner is entitled to exercise, even if it simply means physically crossing over the claimant's boundary. Much in the same manner, having access to the claimant's work, the defendant needs to have exercised one or more of the exclusive rights in relation to the claimant's work. Clearly, an interference in the context of trespass to land can be physically observed with the boundary crossing. Because of the intangible nature of the copyright work, the interference will have to be understood differently. In copyright, a person, P, interferes with a copyright work of Q's if P has exercised one or more rights exclusive to Q. What happens in trespass at a conceptual level is not very different to this. If the right to walk over one's land is one of the many rights that an owner of land has, then another person X exercising that right over the land that belongs to Y amounts to interference with Y's land. While Q's right is directed at the copyright work, Y's right is directed towards land as the subject matter. While land has physical boundaries, copyright work has a conceptual boundary artificially created by law. Chapter 2, Section 3(c) of this book speaks of the requirement of form in relation to a work, which is fulfilled by creating a record of it. It was discussed there that this meets the requirement of defining the boundary of a copyright work. Once a work has acquired a form, if a person exercises one of the rights, then one can argue that there has been an interference with the work. Continuing

[28] [2000] 1 WLR 2416, 2427.
[29] [2022] EWHC 827 (Ch) [78]–[84].
[30] David Llewelyn and Tanya Aplin, *Cornish, Llewelyn and Aplin Intellectual Property: Patents, Copyrights, Trademarks & Allied Rights* (10th edn, Sweet & Maxwell 2023) para 12.05.

with the same example above, if Q writes a poem by typing it onto their computer, the poem as a literary work will have acquired a form. If P takes Q's poem and posts it online, Q will have interfered with P's work by exercising the right of communication to the public.

In trespass to land, the interference needs to be voluntary. Even if the trespasser does not know that they are trespassing, they should know and want to engage in the relevant activity on another's land—such as walking over the land. Voluntariness in the copyright context translates to the defendant's act of deriving their work from the claimant's from being a conscious act. Since direct evidence of the defendant's act being conscious may not always be available, courts normally regard this as a matter of inference.

The next requirement in trespass to land is that the interference must be direct. An unauthorised walking over another's land is a direct interference with their land. What amounts to a direct interference can be understood based on what is an indirect interference. An example of indirect interference is if the branches of a tree from a person's land encroach over another's land. To the extent that the landowner has no control over the direction in which the tree branches grow, the interference with their neighbour's land is indirect. Such indirect interference is not actionable under trespass, although it may be actionable in private nuisance (which is discussed later in this chapter). What kind of infringement is a direct interference with a copyright work? Interestingly, s 16(3)(b) expressly recognises that the infringement can be direct or indirect. What this means is, in the example above, that if P took the poem from Q in the same form as Q had recorded their expression, one can regard this a direct interference with Q's work. This may also be called literal or verbatim interference. Here, in abstract terms, P goes into the expressive space that had been demarcated by Q when they recorded their expression. The same happens also in relation to entrepreneurial works other than broadcasts, since an entrepreneurial work comes into existence because of a record made of it—be it in the form of a sound recording or a film.

It is important to appreciate that literal infringement is the only kind of infringement that can truly be regarded as a direct interference in the trespassory sense. It is only in the context of literal infringement that the inference of the act of derivation being conscious can be regarded as well founded. In other words, if the defendant accessed the claimant's work, the defendant's act of exercising the right being a conscious act will be a reasonable inference if it is in relation to the claimant's work itself or a literal equivalent of it. This is so even if the defendant is unaware that they are exercising a right in relation to the claimant's work. For example, if P creates a collage using old photographs taken by Q believing the copyright term in the photographs to have expired, it still amounts to infringement of Q's copyright. It may also be possible for a court to come to the conclusion that the defendant consciously derived their work from the claimant's if it can be shown that the claimant's work was accessible, even if it cannot be shown that the defendant did in fact access it. If P publishes their poem on their blog and subsequently Q creates a poster showing P's poem verbatim, even if it cannot be shown that Q in fact visited P's blog to copy it, a court will infer that Q infringed P's copyright. Therefore, if the defendant exercises rights in relation to a work that is identical to the claimant's work, courts draw an inference that the defendant's actions were conscious. This is on the basis that the chances of the verbatim recreation of a work by another person independently are very low and that a mere coincidence would be unlikely to explain this satisfactorily.

Trespass is a tort against possession in that only a person in possession can sue for trespass. How does this correspond with copyright infringement? A person infringes copyright only if they take a part of the work that is original. For example, if a sculptor, P, creates a sculpture on a square base, another person, Q, creating a work that has a square base will not infringe P's copyright in her work, although the square base is an integral part of P's work. Even if copying the square base is encompassed within the boundary of P's work, the square base is not original to P's work. Square bases for sculpture are commonplace and may also be a functional feature. On this basis, it may even be arguable that Q did not derive the base of their sculpture from P's work. A work can consist of original and unoriginal parts, and the fact that copyright infringement arises only when the original part is taken means that not every part of the work enclosed within the form is protected. It was discussed in Chapter 3 that a person acquires copyright in an authorial work by expressing a work in an original manner and recording it, and in an entrepreneurial work by creating a record that did not exist before. It was also argued that this corresponds by analogy to acquiring title to a thing by taking possession of it. To the extent that trespass is an interference with possession of land, copyright infringement is an interference with the original expressions in a work. If what is taken is mere ideas or concepts underlying the work, or other non-original parts such as parts that are attributable to the public domain, then it does not amount to infringement. It is worth being reminded here that it helps to raise the bar for originality because the lower the bar for originality, the more readily the liability for infringement arises.

Trespass can occur if any part of boundary is crossed. In theory, trespass is actionable even for minor transgressions. Under CDPA, s 16(3)(a) copyright infringement is actionable only when the whole or a substantial part of a work is taken. This makes copyright infringement seem like a kinder tort for not making a person liable for trivial infringements. Unfortunately, the express words of the statute are deceptive, as their meaning lies in their interpretation by the courts. One needs a careful examination of what a 'work' is in this context, what amounts to 'substantial', and what is a 'part' of the work under s 16(3)(a) to ascertain the true position. It also helps to separate authorial works from entrepreneurial works.

Let us begin by understanding what a work is. While discussing thinghood, Chapter 2 discussed what a work is. The question for us here is at what point in time does a work become an entity protectable on its own? No one doubts that this monograph is a literary work. Does each chapter of this monograph constitute a separate work or each section or subsection? How much further can one go in defining a work? Laddie J was quite vocal against breaking a work into very small pieces and holding it to be a work. To him, copyright is not 'a package of copyright works' consisting of copyright not only in the whole but also in 'an infinite number of subdivisions of it'.[31] Bently describes a work as having a 'discrete, natural, or non-artificial shape'.[32] As he points out, a consequence of regarding smaller units as a work is that a copyright owner can argue that the whole of the work has been taken even when it is only a small part that is taken. It renders meaningless not only the notion of wholeness of the work but also the substantiality of a part of the work if the smallest units could be regarded as complete works in themselves.

Therefore, when a defendant is alleged to have taken the whole of a work, it should mean the natural whole of the work such as the whole book, the whole song, the whole sculpture, and so on for authorial works; and the whole of the sound recording, film, or the programme broadcast that will be a work. If the defendant has exercised rights in relation to the whole of the claimant's work, then it follows that the defendant's work and the claimant's work are identical. In our example above, the poem written by Q is a work with its own natural boundaries. If P posts online the poem as recorded by Q, then P will have exercised the right of communication to the public in relation to the whole of Q's work. Naturally, the poem P uploaded will be identical to Q's poem. As a result, no further questions need to be asked as to the derivation of P's poem. A court can infer that P's poem being identical to Q's in its entirety could not be due to

[31] *Hyperion Records v Warner Music* (unreported, Chancery Division of High Court, 17 May 1991) in Bently and others (n 23) 218–19.

[32] Bently and others (n 23) 219.

a mere coincidence. This leads to the conclusion that P has derived his work directly, and most likely voluntarily from Q's work. The analysis will not be different if Q created an entrepreneurial work such as a sound recording, and P uploaded it online.

Moving on to the word 'substantial', the UK courts had historically followed a multi-factor approach to deciding what amounts to a substantial part, which was a qualitative and quantitative test. However, there has been a shift in the courts' appreciation of what is substantial from that which is essential or important to that which simply is not *de minimis*. This trend has been legitimised by the harmonisation of EU copyright law in this regard. The CJEU held in *Infopaq International v Danske* that parts of a work should not be treated differently from the whole of the work.[33] Notoriously in *Infopaq*, eleven-word summaries of news articles were held to be capable of being works in their own right if they were original.[34] Accordingly, copyright is infringed if the part taken is itself original, without the part having to be substantial. In this approach, neither the parameters of a work nor the assessment of substantiality are required. So long as the part taken is not *de minimis*, all that matters is to assess whether the part taken is original. Since UK courts had applied *Infopaq* before Brexit, it has now become part of laws that are assimilated, unless a higher court decides to diverge from this case law.[35]

This leaves the question of entrepreneurial works and the assessment of 'substantial part'. Copyright in entrepreneurial works is acquired by creating a work that is not a copy of a pre-existing work but is new. One may argue that copyright in entrepreneurial works is infringed only when the part of the work that is new is taken. In practice, in an entrepreneurial work an assessment of what is substantial normally subsumes the question of what a 'part' is. A court might consider aspects such as the amount of investment that has gone into the part and the importance of the part to the rest of the work to assess whether a part is substantial.[36] This assessment will likely subsume the question as to whether the part is also new. For example, if P has filmed a live cricket match and Q makes copies of clippings where the batter has hit sixes, then it may amount to the taking of a substantial part. The investment made in filming a live sporting match captures both the requirement of the record having to be

[33] Case C–5/08 *Infopaq International v Danske*, EU:C:2009:465, [2009] ECDR 16, para 38.
[34] ibid paras 48–51.
[35] European Union (Withdrawal) Act 2018, s 6(5). See *Pasternak v Prescott* [2022] EWHC 2695 for a recent decision that applies the *Infopaq* test of infringement in the United Kingdom.
[36] Bently and others (n 23) 217.

new and substantial. However, like authorial works, taking even small parts might be sufficient, so long as it is more than *de minimis*.

Trespass is actionable per se, as is copyright infringement. It is clear from CDPA, s 16 that the claimant is not required to show any damage in terms of any economic loss that the exercise of the right by the defendant has caused them. The mere showing of the defendant exercising a right in relation to the whole or a substantial part of the claimant's work is sufficient. The claimant does not need to have derived, or even have the potential to derive, any commercial gain from their work. Nor does the claimant need to show that the exercise of a right by the defendant has tarnished the claimant's work, reduced its value, or somehow made the claimant commercially worse off. If the claimant has not suffered any loss, it will only be reflected in the remedy but not in the finding of the liability.

Given the drastic consequences that ensue from the tort of copyright infringement being actionable per se, the interpretation of substantiality should not be diluted to mean any part, however insignificant. This undermines the statute. As already argued, the act of infringement being conscious is a matter of inference if accessibility can be shown in relation to verbatim infringement. The inference of derivation drawn would be justifiable only if the part taken is the whole or a substantial part. If copyright infringement can extend to a very small part being taken by the defendant, copyright infringement will be found more readily. This is particularly serious for musical works where the number of notes is limited; the shorter the piece, the more likely that literal infringement can be found. Therefore, even within the context of verbatim copying, taking of a substantial part is essential, even if, as a matter of analogy with trespass, insignificant encroachment can also be trespass.

The above discussion reveals that it is only literal infringement that can truly be regarded as being inspired by the tort of trespass. It is arguable that copyright infringement is closer in analogy to trespass to land than the statutory language lets us believe. All the attributes of trespass, including that of attracting the strictest liability of all property torts, are ascribed to copyright infringement because of this analogy. However, copyright is infringed not only because of literal interference with the claimant's work but also non-literal interference. If it is possible to demonstrate that non-literal interference amounts to an indirect interference, then an analogy with private nuisance will be possible. This has obvious benefits in that private nuisance as a property tort is characterised by a different level of fault requirement than trespass and the balancing of competing interests. If an analogy of copyright infringement with private nuisance is taken to its logical end, it would be possible to separate the strands of infringement that should not attract the kind of strict liability that an analogy with trespass would attract. This takes us to Subsection (b) below.

(b) Copyright Infringement and Private Nuisance

Clearly, copyright infringement does not arise only based on a literal interference. Non-literal interference is one of the most powerful ways in which copyright owners can enforce their rights. It is argued here that non-literal copying corresponds to private nuisance in being an indirect interference, but almost all of the balancing mechanism that exists in relation to private nuisance is absent in copyright infringement. Let us examine this with the help of Table 5.2.

Table 5.2 Comparison of copyright infringement with private nuisance

<table>
<tr><th>Private Nuisance</th><th>Indirect</th><th colspan="2">Interference with use and enjoyment of land</th><th>Voluntary</th><th>Balancing act and reasonable user</th><th>Foreseeability and damage</th></tr>
<tr><td rowspan="3">Copyright infringement</td><td rowspan="3">Non-literal</td><td colspan="2">Derived from claimant's work?</td><td rowspan="3">Conscious?</td><td rowspan="3">Whole or substantial part, where substantial is interpreted as any part</td><td rowspan="3">No special damage needs to be shown</td></tr>
<tr><td>Claimant's work being accessible</td><td>Exercise exclusive rights?</td></tr>
<tr><td>Defendant accessing claimant's work</td><td></td></tr>
</table>

Following Table 5.2, let us begin with the indirectness of the interference. The difference between trespass and private nuisance is that in nuisance the interference is indirect, in that it does not require a direct and immediate entry of the defendant onto the claimant's land.[37] Unlike in trespass, the interference here can be caused by physical encroachment, the spread of noxious substances, and so on. What might amount to an indirect interference in copyright infringement? Again, interestingly, s 16(3)(b) states that copyright infringement can take place directly or indirectly. We saw above that the most direct and immediate interference with the claimant's work happens when the

[37] Tettenborn and others (n 9) para 19-02.

defendant takes the claimant's work as a whole or a part. There is a crossover by the defendant into the claimant's expression actually recorded. But this is not the only way in which copyright infringement takes place. It is possible to infringe copyright also by taking not the expression in its recorded form, but non-literal elements that make up the expression.

Two points need clarification at the outset. First, non-literal infringement is only possible in relation to authorial works because of deeper protection offered by the law. For authorial works the protection extends beyond the recorded expression in its literal form to a deeper level of comparison. One cannot speak of a non-literal part of an entrepreneurial work because the protection extends only to the taking of surface aspects of the work and not the deeper elements. As explained in Chapter 3, these works will have come into existence because of the investment made in creating them and not because of expressing the work in an original manner. It is not the content of the work that is protected, but the record. In this sense, it may be less problematic for entrepreneurial works to be only amenable to trespassory liability. Secondly, commentators ascribe a different meaning to indirect infringement. In their view, an indirect infringement takes place when a person copies not from the original work, but from a copy of the work or a different version of the work—say from a photograph of a sculpture.[38] But in the analysis here, non-literal infringement is regarded as a more appropriate comparison to indirect infringement because it is not an occupation of the very expressive space taken up by the claimant, but something deeper than what is expressed in the claimant's work.

Let us examine what it means to go deeper than the surface of the work to find the non-literal components. What these components are differs based on the nature of the work. If the work is a literary work such as a novel, non-literal components can include the plot and the scenes.[39] For musical works, it can include the melody,[40] rhythm, arrangement, and so on. For dramatic works it can be the scenes or the screenplay.[41] For an artistic work such as a photograph, it can be the angle, lighting, perspective, and framing.[42] But courts are required always to exercise caution to ensure that in digging deeper for non-literal elements, protection is not extended to ideas underlying the work. As

[38] Llewelyn and Aplin (n 30) para 12-05.
[39] *Harman Pictures v Osborne* [1967] 1 WLR 723, 728.
[40] *Sheeran v Chokri* [2022] EWHC 827 [34] (Ch).
[41] *Brighton v Jones* [2005] FSR (16) 288.
[42] *Krisarts SA v Briarfine* [1977] FSR 557, 562.

stated in Chapter 2, Section 4(c), ideas cannot be the content of the subject matter for protection by copyright because these are the building blocks of culture and the raw material for other works to be created. In other words, non-literal aspects also need to be original for copyright protection to be extended. To take an example from popular culture, Dan Brown's novel *The Da Vinci Code* did not infringe Baigent and Leigh's copyright in *The Holy Blood and the Holy Grail* because what was taken was not the plot or the storyline, but facts and ideas that supported Jesus Christ having descendants, at a high level of abstraction.[43]

In private nuisance, since the interference is indirect, the rest of the requirements of the tort differ completely from trespass. The tort of private nuisance will not be made out simply because there is some kind of encroachment or emanation from the defendant on to the claimant's land. A mere crossing of the boundary is not sufficient, as already argued in Chapter 4, Section 2(c). Only the kind of emanation that unduly interferes with the claimant's use and enjoyment of the land is relevant for liability to arise in private nuisance. In other words, once the defendant's manner of interference is determined, the enquiry shifts focus to an examination of the claimant's situation in ascertaining whether the claimant's use or enjoyment of the land is affected. However, with copyright infringement, even where the taking is of non-literal elements, the ingredients of the tort do not change from cases where the taking is of literal elements. The enquiry does not shift the focus to the claimant's situation to ascertain whether the defendant's taking has affected the claimant's use of the work in any way. This means that it is sufficient that the defendant derived the non-literal parts of their work from the claimant's work, which is demonstrated by showing the same elements of access and exercise of rights, as stated in Table 5.2. The inference of voluntariness becomes especially precarious under these circumstances.

Again, direct evidence of the defendant's derivation may not be forthcoming. In many cases, all that can be shown is that the claimant's work was accessible, and not that the defendant accessed the claimant's work. It was seen above that when the taking is literal, courts soften the need to show the defendant's access to the claimant's work. They draw an inference that there must have been access because it is not plausible for it to be a coincidence that two persons create works that are identical. The inference here without strict proof might not lead to significantly unjust results, though it may be indicative of rough

[43] *Baigent v Random House Group Ltd* [2007] EWCA Civ 247, [2008] EMLR 7 [34].

justice. However, if the comparison is of non-literal elements, drawing an inference based on similarities that the defendant must have derived their work from the claimant's work might lead to unjust results.[44] While the chances of two persons creating identical expression are low, the chances that two persons create works based on the same theme independently are not necessarily low. Even if it cannot be shown that the defendant did access the claimant's work, courts sometimes go by the defendant's familiarity with the claimant's work, which seems to be a lower threshold than complete access.[45]

Moving on to the next requirement, like trespass private nuisance also requires voluntary interference on the defendant's part. Examined in the context of copyright infringement this should mean that the non-literal taking by the defendant must be a conscious act. This is a matter of inference also in non-literal infringement, in the same way as derivation is a matter of inference. This means that if it is shown only that the claimant's work was accessible, even if it cannot be shown that the defendant indeed accessed it but only that he was familiar with it, based on the non-literal similarities, conscious derivation is inferred. With such important elements being a matter of inference, copyright infringement as a whole will become a matter of inference, more like patent infringement where objective similarity is all that is required.

In private nuisance the interference with the use or enjoyment of the land should not only be voluntary but also significant and undue.[46] An important feature distinguishing private nuisance from trespass is that the court conducts a balancing act between competing interests.[47] To determine what amounts to a substantial interference, the frequency, duration, intensity, and so on of the interference are considered.[48] Many aspects go into this balancing, including whether the claimant and defendant are making common and ordinary use of land.[49] In private nuisance typically issues arise between neighbours, both of whom want to use the same resource (land) but in different ways. The competing interests of these land users are assessed based on what may be considered common and ordinary. In copyright infringement, on the contrary, there is no assessment of substantial interference although s 16(3)(a) refers to 'a substantial part'. As explained in Subsection 2(a) above, courts have

[44] There are cases that have followed this logic. See generally *LB (Plastics) v Swish Products* [1979] FSR 145.
[45] *Mitchell v BBC* [2011] EWPCC 42 [121].
[46] *Miller v Jackson* [1977] QB 966, 980 (Lord Denning MR).
[47] *Southwark LBC v Tanner* [2001] 1 AC 1, 21 (Lord Millett).
[48] See generally *Coventry v Lawrence* [2014] UKSC 13, [2014] AC 822.
[49] *Fearn v Tate Modern* [2023] UKSC 4.

interpreted 'substantial part' to mean any part, which can be a very small part. Interestingly, the factors that went into establishing substantiality in the law before *Infopaq*, namely the importance of the part taken by the defendant to the claimant's work and to the audience of the work, are comparable to the factors taken into account in private nuisance to establish the claimant's diminution in the enjoyment of the land. Furthermore, there is nothing comparable in copyright infringement to the assessment of what is common and ordinary that is carried out in private nuisance. Indeed, none of the factors affecting the defendant is considered for finding liability for copyright infringement.[50] A court does not have to carry out any balancing act between the considerations of the claimant and the defendant in copyright infringement.

The final element for discussion is the need for damage and foreseeability. The liability in private nuisance does not arise unless the claimant shows certain damage. The damage does not have to be physical, though in case of nuisance by physical encroachment damage may be presumed. Noxious substances, noise, and so on which lead to a loss of amenity can also be a recognisable form of damage. Where the interference with the use and enjoyment is substantial, a court might infer the damage.[51] Furthermore, the law also requires that only the type of damage that is foreseeable by the defendant is actionable in private nuisance.[52] In copyright infringement, on the contrary, there is no need to show any damage whatsoever. The claimant needs to have suffered no loss or damage at all and the liability for copyright infringement will still arise. The fact that the claimant had not commercialised the work may affect remedies (such as quantum of damages), but it will not affect liability. Further, even if it was completely unforeseeable to a defendant that their actions might infringe someone else's copyright, the liability for copyright infringement arises nevertheless.

The worryingly unfair result brought about by copyright infringement bringing all these elements together can be illustrated using an example. Suppose P had written a novel with a unique plot and had self-published it in the United Kingdom decades ago, circulating only 500 physical copies. Q writes a book whose plot is substantially similar to P's. P needs to show that Q derived their work from P's book. For this, the best case scenario is for P to show that Q had a copy of the book, that Q read the book and had retained its

[50] At the stage of granting remedies, some consideration may be given to the defendant's inability to foresee the loss that was caused to the claimant. For further discussion, see Section 2 of this chapter.

[51] Tettenborn and others (n 9)) paras 19-25, 19-26.

[52] *Cambridge Water v Eastern Counties Leather* [1994] 2 AC 264, 300.

content in their mind when Q wrote their book, which will amount to Q exercising P's right to make a copy of their own book. If it cannot be shown in the first place that Q did not have a copy of P's book, then one can conclude that on balance of probabilities Q did not derive their work from P's, and therefore that there has been no copyright infringement. But suppose P's novel went on to become very popular and was also released as an eBook with extracts of it covered in popular media. Then, even if Q did not have a copy of P's book, based on the similarities not with a substantial part but even a small part of P's plot, a court may draw an inference that Q 'must have' consciously derived their plot from P's. This will lead to a liability for copyright infringement without any regard to whether it could have been foreseen by Q that P's copyright might be infringed. This demonstrates how access to the claimant's work being an inference makes derivation and consciousness of the act also an inference, making the liability for copyright infringement stand on precarious grounds, leading to unjust outcomes.

The discussion thus far focused only on one of the property torts, namely private nuisance. Nothing has been said of the tort of conversion. In conversion, whether the interference is direct or indirect, so long as it leads to a deprivation of the use or enjoyment of the chattel, then the liability will arise. One may cite this in support of the argument that property torts do not always have softening elements for indirect infringement, or the requirement of reasonableness. Indeed, commentators in the United States regard conversion as the true comparison for copyright infringement and justify the imposition of strict liability.[53] There are equally other commentators who argue that conversion is an incorrect analogy for copyright infringement because conversion applies to rivalrous resources, which, they argue, makes it a misfit for copyright works which are relatively less rivalrous.[54] Conversion in English law requires complete deprivation or substantial impairment of use of chattels, which necessarily presupposes the existence of more perfectly rivalrous resources such as chattels. But instead of focusing on the deprivation in the hands of the claimant, if we focus on the substantiality of interference on the part of the defendant, then it becomes clear that conversion is more comparable to private nuisance than to trespass. Table 5.3 provides the comparison of the tort of conversion with torts of private nuisance and copyright infringement.

[53] eg David Nimmer, *Nimmer on Copyright* (Matthew Bender 2020) para 13-08[B](i).

[54] eg Dane S Ciolino and Erin A Donelon, 'Questioning Strict Liability in Copyright' (2002) 54 Rutgers L Rev 351.

Table 5.3 Comparison of copyright infringement with private nuisance and conversion

<table>
<tr><th>Private Nuisance</th><th>Indirect</th><th colspan="2">Interference with use and enjoyment of land</th><th>Voluntary</th><th>Balancing act and reasonable user</th><th>Foreseeability and damage</th></tr>
<tr><td>Conversion</td><td>Direct or indirect</td><td colspan="2">Interference with use of the chattel</td><td>Voluntary</td><td>Total deprivation of the chattel or total impairment of use</td><td>No damage needs to be shown</td></tr>
<tr><td rowspan="3">Copyright infringement</td><td rowspan="3">Non-literal</td><td colspan="2">Derived from claimant's work</td><td rowspan="3">Conscious?</td><td rowspan="3">Whole or substantial part, where substantial is interpreted as any part</td><td rowspan="3">No special damage needs to be shown</td></tr>
<tr><td>Claimant's work being accessible</td><td rowspan="2">Exercise exclusive rights?</td></tr>
<tr><td>Defendant accessing claimant's work</td></tr>
</table>

Green and Randall argue that 'nuisance is to real property what Conversion is to personal property'.[55] They argue citing cases drawn from nuisance and comparing them with conversion that close analogies can be drawn in relation not only to the nature of interference but also the degree and extent of the interference.[56] Douglas also argues that conversion requires a complete deprivation of use or enjoyment of the chattel, and that only very significant interferences can be regarded as meeting this threshold. He further argues that even in the cases of impairment of use, unless the impairment is complete, no action for conversion arises.[57] Even if the other requirements are strict in conversion, as indicated in Table 5.3, conversion requires complete or substantial deprivation of the claimant's use of the chattel. In copyright infringement, one could similarly have pointed to the requirement of 'substantial part' in CDPA, s 16(3)(a) that copyright infringement arises only when the whole or a substantial part of the work is taken. However, as argued above, with *Infopaq* and its application by the courts in the United Kingdom, the law is that liability for copyright infringement arises if any part of the work is taken, if such part is original.

[55] Green and Randall (n 2) 60.
[56] ibid 60–65.
[57] Douglas (n 2) 64, 67–68.

In summary, property torts in relation to land have strict requirements when the interference is direct and voluntary, but the requirements change dramatically when the interference is indirect. From enforcing even minor infractions in trespass, the assessment becomes far more nuanced and layered based on reasonableness and balancing competing interests in private nuisance. From being actionable per se in trespass, the assessment becomes one of foreseeability and of damage in nuisance. But copyright infringement is one immutable tort with a close resemblance to trespass, and with ingredients that stay the same whether the interference is literal or non-literal. Apart from being actionable per se and enforcing infringement even for minor infringements, copyright infringement pays no heed to reasonableness or balancing of any kind. While a claimant in private nuisance and conversion is required to show a substantial interference on the part of the defendant, in copyright infringement the claimant is only required to show that a part is taken so long as it is on its own capable of demonstrating originality. The tort of private nuisance incorporates into the analysis aspects that influence the defendant's conduct, such as whether the defendant's use of their own land is common and ordinary. Copyright infringement takes no account of any circumstance relating to the defendant. This makes copyright infringement unjustifiably harsh on the defendants.

Private nuisance recognises the inevitability of everyone having to share the use of land—a resource that is limited and valuable. From its approach to liability, it would seem that private nuisance acknowledges that everyone's use of land is legitimate unless shown to be a substantial and undue interference with the use and enjoyment of land by someone else. Similarly, copyright should proceed on the acknowledgement that the aggregate of copyright works makes up the knowledge base of humanity. Sharing in it is a legitimate interest of everyone. In addition to the obvious free speech concerns, there is no denying that knowledge grows knowledge. The approach to copyright infringement should be similar to private nuisance. Unless a claimant shows that the non-literal interference with their copyright work is substantial and unreasonable, liability for copyright infringement should not arise.

We do not need to look too far to understand what amounts to a 'substantial' interference. As already argued, in the days before *Infopaq*, courts had developed a multifactorial, qualitative, and quantitative test. This incorporated elements such as the importance of the part taken to the claimant's work, substantiality in terms of both quality and quantity, the importance of the part taken to the audience, functional importance, and whether the part taken can itself be protected as a copyright work.[58] In addition to the substantiality test, courts should conduct a balancing exercise between the use of the claimant's work made by the defendant in the context of the defendant's work and any loss that this causes claimant, similar to the balancing of common and ordinary use in private nuisance cases. In addition, some consideration should be given to the damage caused to the claimant and the defendant's foreseeability of such damage being caused. If the claimant has not commercialised their work at all and the taking does not harm the claimant's economic interests, consideration could be given to this in deciding whether liability should arise. These additional requirements can mark the distinction between the liability rules for literal infringement and non-literal infringement along similar lines as between trespass and private nuisance.

Finally, in non-literal copying, whether the defendant did access the claimant's work should not be a matter of inference from general accessibility of the claimant's work and the defendant's general familiarity. Even if, for literal copying, this is a safer inference to draw on the balance of probabilities that two persons cannot have created identical works, for non-literal copying it is not safe at all. Courts should not settle for the defendant's general familiarity with the claimant's work as a substitute for having to show that the defendant did access the claimant's work. Together with the substantiality, the balancing of competing interests, and the need for damage that is foreseeable as explained above, non-literal infringement can be transformed into a robust and justifiable tort.

Once non-literal infringement is distinguished in this way, then the cases where the claimant's work is shown to be accessible, but the defendant's access to it cannot be shown, it will be difficult to conclude that the defendant's actions are conscious. This may mean that the defendant's actions are subconscious or unconscious. Apart from the difficulty of proving what goes on in the subconscious or unconscious mind, this edges towards involuntary exercise of rights. In chattels and in land, courts and commentators insist that for involuntary interference the liability should only be in negligence. However, there is no liability for negligently infringing copyright. This takes us to Subsection 2(c) below.

[58] *Designers' Guild v Russell Williams* [2000] 1 WLR 2416.

(c) Copyright Infringement and Liability in Negligence

It may help to begin the examination with a recent case from popular culture, *Sheeran v Chokri*.[59] Here, a pop star, Sami Chokri, alleged that the well-known singer and songwriter Ed Sheeran had taken eight notes from Chokri's song and incorporated it into Sheeran's song. Chokri argued that Sheeran consciously copied, and if the court was not persuaded, in the alternative he argued that Sheeran subconsciously copied his song. The court was indeed not convinced that Sheeran consciously copied the song because of the issues around access. The court sensibly held that while the possibility of access could be shown with Chokri's songs being available on the internet, it could not be shown that Sheeran had actually heard it. Therefore, the court went on to consider whether there had been subconscious copying.[60]

Subconscious copying has also been described as unconscious copying or unintentional copying.[61] In *Sheeran*'s case above, Chokri needed to show the following. Sheeran may have heard Chokri's song and may have filed it at the back of his mind. When Sheeran got down to create a song, he might have copied Chokri's tune without his conscious mind realising that he was doing so. If Chokri managed to show this on balance of probabilities, the law would conclude that Sheeran's work is derived from Chokri's work. As indicated in Subsections (a) and (b) above, a work is derived from another work if one can show access to the prior work and the exercise of one or more rights in relation to it. The case law on subconscious copying maintains that it is a factual inference based on many factors, such as the degree of familiarity (proved or inferred) with the claimant's work, the character of the work that makes it particularly memorable, the chances of these characteristics being coincidental, other influences on the alleged infringer, objective similarity between the two works, and the quality of the alleged infringer's own evidence.[62] It could not be shown that Sheeran had any familiarity with Chokri's work at all, and the part alleged to be copied was not regarded as particularly memorable.

Although this does show that a conclusion on subconscious copying is not lightly arrived at, that it is a possibility at all as one of the ways of infringing copyright is troubling. If an analogy were to be drawn with trespass, this would amount to an unconscious trespass. A person commits trespass when the act of walking, that is, the exercise of the right to walk over a person's land, is

[59] [2022] EWHC 827 (Ch).
[60] ibid [7], [9], [35]–[37], [81]–[82].
[61] *John Richardson Computers v Flanders* [1993] FSR 497, 548.
[62] *Francis Day & Hunter v Bron* [1963] Ch 587, 614–15.

voluntary, even if the person is unaware that the land belongs to someone else. The exercise of the right will be voluntary when it is a conscious act—walking while knowing that one is walking. The same cannot be said of subconscious copying. One is not exercising the right of copying while being conscious of copying. Indeed, the conscious part of the mind is engaged in creating the work. If the conscious mind can have no control over the influence of the subconscious mind, then any alleged act of copying should be regarded as involuntary. Nevertheless, the liability for copyright infringement arises in exactly the same way as it does for conscious copying.

One may argue that, in reality, it is difficult to say where conscious copying ends and subconscious copying begins, because direct evidence of derivation in many cases will not be available and therefore it becomes simply a matter of inference.[63] Even for conscious copying, the greater the similarity between the defendant's work and the claimant's work, the greater the likelihood of access being presumed.[64] The basis for this is that the chances of the high level of similarities being a coincidence are very low.[65] Therefore, for conscious copying the level of objective similarity should be high enough to make the inference well-founded. The problem is that when this inference is not possible, the legal enquiry for copyright infringement does not stop there by arriving at a conclusion of no infringement. It goes into the domain of subconscious copying.

How do land law and personal property law respond to involuntary interferences? Before we consider land and chattels, it might make sense to consider trespass to the person where a clearer statement of law has been pronounced. In *Letang v Cooper*, the defendant ran his car over the claimant's legs injuring her. The claimant brought a case for battery, an intentional tort of trespass to the person. Lord Denning held that if the defendant[66]

> does not inflict injury intentionally, but only unintentionally, the plaintiff has no cause of action today in trespass. His only cause of action is in negligence, and then only on proof of want of reasonable care . . . If negligent and causing damage, it is the tort of negligence . . . If it were trespass, it would be actionable without proof of damage[.]

[63] *IPC Media Ltd v Highbury Leisure* [2005] FSR 20, 434, 443.

[64] *LB (Plastics) v Swish Products* [1979] FSR 848, 857–58.

[65] *Designers' Guild v Russell Williams* [2000] 1 WLR 2416, where the House of Lords affirmed the finding of derivation based on numerous similarities. *Mitchell v BBC* [2011] EWPCC 42 held against derivation based on fewer similarities.

[66] [1965] 1 QB 232, 239–40.

While all three Lords Justices were unanimous in finding negligence, it was less clear if they all agreed that the existence of damage was an essential ingredient of negligence in this context.[67] *League against Cruel Sports v Scott*[68] provided an opportunity for the courts to apply this in the context of trespass to land. Here, the defendants' animals strayed onto the claimant's land, whereupon the claimant sued in trespass to land. Park J held that a person will be 'liable in trespass to the owner of such land if, owing to the negligence in his control of the pack, hounds entered or crossed that land'.[69] He held the defendant liable since he had not taken reasonable care. It was clear that the defendant did not voluntarily or directly enter the claimant's land, and no damage had been caused by such entry. Yet the defendant was held to have negligently trespassed the land. This decision has attracted much criticism for not following the principle enunciated by Lord Denning in the context of trespass to the person, by analogy to land. Coherence of the law demands that only voluntary interference be actionable under trespass and involuntary interferences be only actionable if fault by way of negligence and damage can be shown.[70]

Douglas has forcefully argued in relation to personal property that where the interference is intentional, it should lead to strict liability and where the interference is unintentional, the liability should be fault based.[71] He explains that strict liability is compatible with the requirement of intention in a tort, where all that is meant is that property torts require voluntary action.[72] He further argues that unintentional or involuntary interferences should only attract liability in negligence, by analogy with *Letang v Cooper*. Douglas has provided philosophical justifications on this division of liability between voluntary and involuntary interferences. These arguments should hold good by analogy also with copyright, but there are stumbling blocks.

In English law negligence liability arises when a person owes a duty of care. To ensure that courts do not have to 'reinvent the wheel', as it were, common law has identified certain cases where the existence of a duty is presumed. Where a defendant engages in a positive act which leads to a physical injury, then a duty of care is presumed to arise. Any loss that is not physical will be

[67] Danckwerts LJ agreed with Lord Denning, [1965] 1 QB 232, 242. Diplock LJ did not expressly agree with this.

[68] [1986] QB 240.

[69] [1986] QB 240, 249.

[70] Goudkamp and Nolan (n 4) paras 14-002, 14-003.

[71] Douglas (n 2) ch 7.

[72] Douglas (n 2) 73–74. He also agrees with Oliphant on this point. See Ken Oliphant, 'The Structure of the Intentional Torts' in Jason Neyers (ed), *Emerging Issues in Tort Law* (Hart 2007) 514. Green and Randall are sceptical of intention as a requirement, although they accept that a voluntary act is required for the tort of conversion. Green and Randall (n 2) 70.

recoverable only if it is a loss that is a foreseeable consequence of a physical injury. This is how the lost earnings of an injured person or the value of repairs to a damaged car are recoverable in negligence. However, if there is no physical injury, any loss that is incurred will be regarded as a purely economic loss. If a fact situation presents a purely economic loss, then a duty of care cannot be presumed, but will arise under more limited and exceptional circumstances famously carved out in *Hedley Byrne v Heller*,[73] applying only to situations of assumption of responsibility in cases akin to contract. Therefore, a negligence action does not lie for causing pure economic loss unless the cause of action falls within the exception created by common law. Since the injury in copyright infringement is not a physical injury and is not consequent upon physical injury, nor is it covered by *Hedley Byrne* exception, it would be regarded as a pure economic loss.

There are many critics of this rule, and some common law jurisdictions have done away with it. A discussion as to whether it is advisable to do away with this rule altogether for all circumstances beyond copyright infringement is not within the scope of this book. Such sweeping change in order to accommodate copyright infringement may be a disproportionate response. One alternative is not to limit property damage to physical damage, but extend it also to damage to intangible things such as copyright works. If this is seen as a step too far for common law courts, another alternative is for the courts to hold that copyright infringement, being a statutory tort, is a new exception to pure economic loss. Courts might be hesitant to read negligence into copyright infringement, stating that if Parliament wanted to impose negligence requirements within copyright infringement, they would have stated this. However, the statute does not say anything about subconscious copying either, but the courts went ahead to formulate this on their own. If courts can put forward subconscious copying as a possibility, they can also put forward negligence as an appropriate fault element to be read into copyright infringement.

Courts have on occasion been asked to consider negligence liability for an involuntary infringement. The best example of this can be seen in *Paterson Zochonis Ltd v Merfarken Packaging Ltd*.[74] In this case, the defendants were printers who were asked by the competitors of the claimants to print certain labels. The copyright in the design of the labels was owned by the claimants. Upon having the labels printed the competitors used the labels to pass off their own goods as those of the claimants. The claimants sued the defendants on

[73] [1964] AC 465, 529.
[74] [1983] FSR 273.

the ground that the defendants failed to exercise reasonable care to ensure that their labels were not used to pass off goods. Goff LJ considered whether a duty of care should not be found in this case because the claimant would only have suffered a pure economic loss. He noted that courts hesitate to impose a duty of care in situations where doing so may impose liability on an indeterminate set of persons to an indeterminate degree. He further noted that no such feature can be found in the case at hand and went on to consider whether the printers did owe a duty of care to the claimants.[75] On the facts, Goff LJ found that it would be too onerous to impose such a duty on an unsuspecting printer to make enquiries each time an order is received. He therefore agreed with the court below that the action deserved to be struck out.[76] From the tenor of the judgment it does not appear that the court was rejecting the existence of the duty of care. Instead, it seems more apposite to conclude that the defendant had not breached his duty because he could not have ascertained that the print order given was for copying someone else's copyright work.

This case was referred to by the House of Lords in *CBS Music v Amstrad*,[77] a case on accessory liability. The question was whether sellers of tape recorders owed a duty of care to copyright owners not to enable copyright infringement by those who bought the instrument. The House of Lords held that there was no such duty of care, but not because the duty led to pure economic loss. It was because, under the Copyright Act 1956, Amstrad owed a duty not to infringe copyright and not to authorise an infringement of copyright; but they 'did not owe a duty to prevent or discourage or warn against infringement'.[78] These cases show that courts are not averse to an argument circumventing pure economic loss in order to apply negligence liability to copyright infringement cases. This means that copyright infringement can be recognised as an additional exception to the rule that there is no duty of care if there is only a pure economic loss.

It should, therefore, be possible to extend negligence liability for subconscious copying. Currently, with subconscious copying, the conclusion is not only based on access and objective similarities but also the memorable nature of the claimant's work and so on. If these are proved, then the evidential burden shifts to the alleged infringer. Here, it can be a difficult onus to discharge, because the alleged infringer will have to show that it is impossible to ever have come across the claimant's work.[79] Musical works and artistic works such as

[75] ibid 299–301.
[76] ibid 300–02.
[77] [1988] 1 AC 1013.
[78] ibid 1060 (Lord Templeman).
[79] Bently and others (n 23) 215–16.

photographs are most in danger of being held to be subconscious derivations.[80] Dissemination of music and art online makes them significantly more accessible than they might have been in the previous century. The ubiquity and the ease of access make it impossible for a defendant to argue that they had never come across the claimant's work. If the inference cannot be rebutted by the claimant, a defendant may be held liable for copyright infringement of the claimant's work in situations where any derivation may be unconscious, and involuntary to this extent.

Therefore, subconscious copying should only attract liability in negligence. If the facts only show that the claimant's work is accessible and at best that the defendant may have been generally familiar with it, then no inference of conscious derivation should be drawn. Courts should be careful not to substitute objective similarities with the need to show that the defendant accessed the claimant's work. Any objective similarities should extend to a substantial part of the claimant's work and not to any part in the *Infopaq* sense, so that liability is not sought to be established for trivial infringements. In these circumstances, liability should only arise if the defendant did not take reasonable care to ensure that they steered clear of the claimant's work. Well-established industries such as the music industry, publishing industry, film, art, and so on can formulate best practices that could help demonstrate the standard of care to be taken to avoid infringing other works. Only if these standards are breached should a court hold that the defendant's actions caused the infringement. As in all cases of negligence, the initial burden of proof of establishing a prima facie case of negligent infringement should lie with the claimant. A comparison of how copyright infringement can incorporate a variety of fault elements instead of being one singular tort is depicted in Table 5.4.

It is not the first time that negligence liability for copyright infringement is being proposed. Goold has forcefully argued in favour of introducing negligence liability for what he calls 'IP accidents', that is, where infringement occurs because of lack of care more than because of intentional infringement.[81] But he casts his argument much more broadly than what this book proposes. In addition to subconscious copying, for which he gives wide-ranging empirical evidence drawn from the United States, he speaks of two other categories of accidents.[82] First, if a person reasonably believe that the licence extends to the act they are engaged in, but ends up infringing copyright, Goold argues that the

[80] *Sheeran v Chokri* [2022] EWHC 827 (Ch) demonstrates a recent case of subconscious copying in the music industry.
[81] Goold (n 19) ch 2.
[82] ibid 16–18.

Table 5.4 Incorporating different fault elements into copyright infringement

<table>
<tr><td rowspan="8">Copyright infringement</td><td rowspan="3">Literal (akin to trespass)</td><td colspan="2">Derived from claimant’s work</td><td rowspan="3">Conscious (can be inferred)</td><td rowspan="3">Whole or substantial part of the work that is original (authorial works) or created with substantial investment (entrepreneurial works)</td><td rowspan="3">A tort actionable per se</td></tr>
<tr><td>Claimant’s work being accessible</td><td rowspan="2">Exercise exclusive rights</td></tr>
<tr><td>Defendant accessing claimant’s work (can be inferred)</td></tr>
<tr><td rowspan="3">Non-literal (akin to private nuisance)</td><td colspan="2">Derived from claimant’s work</td><td rowspan="3">Conscious (cannot be an inference)</td><td rowspan="3">Whole or substantial part, and balancing use made by claimant and defendant</td><td rowspan="3">Damage and foreseeability required</td></tr>
<tr><td>Claimant’s work being accessible</td><td rowspan="2">Exercise exclusive rights</td></tr>
<tr><td>Defendant accessing claimant’s work (cannot be an inference)</td></tr>
<tr><td rowspan="2">Non-literal (liability in negligence)</td><td colspan="2">Derived from claimant’s work</td><td rowspan="2">Subconscious or unconscious</td><td>Whole or substantial part</td><td rowspan="2">Damage and foreseeability required</td></tr>
<tr><td>Claimant’s work being accessible</td><td>Exercise exclusive rights</td><td>Standard of care set by courts or industry best practices</td></tr>
</table>

liability should only arise if reasonable care cannot be shown. However, this can be dealt with better under the defence of implied licence if it can be shown that the copyright owner's conduct was such that a reasonable person would believe that licence had been granted, as discussed in Chapter 6, Section 2(a). Secondly, where a person is aware of the existence of copyright but is unaware whether the term has expired or not, Goold also argues for extending negligence liability. To the extent that copying is a conscious act it will be difficult to regard this as anything other than a clear case of copyright infringement. If a comparison is to be drawn with property torts, this is a situation where a person walks over another person's land without knowing that the land belongs to someone else. To the extent that walking is direct and voluntary, a liability for trespass arises. Ordinarily this would not be subject to negligence liability because the walking over the land is deliberate, even if the person does not have the knowledge that they are walking over someone else's land. Extending negligence liability in this situation will result in a total overhaul of the copyright infringement doctrine, which is what Goold proposes.[83] This book also argues for the reform of the copyright infringement doctrine, but only for it to reflect more closely the liability regimes and the fault requirement of property torts.

The consequences of the liability for copyright infringement arising too readily are that the copyright owner has a panoply of powerful remedies to choose from. Although there are provisions such as CDPA, s 97, which states that if the infringer was unaware of the existence of copyright, they will only be liable in damages and that no injunction can be issued against them. It begs the question of the extent to which this might be helpful. This is discussed in Section 3 below.

3. Proprietary Remedies for Copyright Infringement

Remedies represent the practical end of a legal right. They help actualise in real world terms what it means to set right the infraction of a right. Once the copyright infringement is established, the copyright owner has a slew of remedies that they can access. Remedies for copyright infringement do differ from those available for property torts that relate to land. If a person is dispossessed of land, they can be restored to the possession of that very land by way of specific enforcement; but if an exclusive right of copyright is infringed, one cannot

[83] ibid 122–26.

meaningfully argue for restoration of the right. Instead, one can seek damages for infringement. This, however, is not unique to copyright. Scholars have shown that English common law does not recognise *vindicatio* for chattels.[84] Therefore, despite being dispossessed of the thing, in conversion the claimant cannot seek to get back the very thing; instead, they can only claim damages. Other commonly awarded remedies are injunctions. Since copyright recognises exclusionary conduct on the part of the rest of the world, it is explicable that injunctions would be available to restore exclusivity to the copyright owner. Injunctions are a common remedy against trespass to land and private nuisance more than for trespass to goods and conversion.

The above differences aside, the remedies for copyright infringement are co-extensive with remedies for the commission of property torts. Section 96(2) of the CDPA states that in an action for infringement of copyright all such relief would be available to the claimant 'as is available in respect of the infringement of any other property right'. The reason why this is problematic should be immediately apparent here. As already discussed in Section 2, while the CDPA attracts stricter liability for copyright infringement than for property torts, all the remedies that would be available against property torts are also available against copyright infringement. This makes the consequences of copyright infringement doubly harsh. This is particularly so when one considers the possibility that there are certain remedies that are harsher but could be more readily available for intellectual property infringement cases. These are the award of negotiating damages and disgorgement damages. These remedies, therefore, deserve to be examined briefly as to why this might be the case.

(a) Negotiating Damages

Before dealing with negotiating damages, it helps to understand some of the general principles of the award of damages. Since by the remedial stage the liability for infringement will have been found, courts have held that damages are to be awarded liberally against the infringer, but the objective is only to compensate the claimant and not to punish the defendant.[85] Although damage does not need to be specifically proved for the liability to arise, it must be proved for the award of damages. For minor infringements, therefore, there may be

[84] Douglas (n 2) 9, 64; see also Pretto-Sakmann (n 1) 98.

[85] *Gerber Garment Technology Inc v Lectra Systems Ltd* [1997] RPC 443, 452. See also Harbottle and others (n 8) para 24-297.

only nominal damages awarded. The burden of proving damage is upon the person claiming infringement. The infringement must have been a cause of the damage, even if not the only cause. While foreseeability plays no role in establishing liability, once liability is established only damage that is a foreseeable consequence of the infringement is recoverable (ie not too remote).[86]

If the claimant shows damage that was foreseeable, courts adopt one of the following three approaches to awarding damages.[87] First, they may calculate the actual damage suffered by the claimant. This is indicated by lost sales. This typically happens when the claimant is a manufacturer of articles that incorporate copyright works. Damages are calculated based on the volume of sales diverted because of infringement. This approach is more common in patent cases.[88] More frequent for copyright cases is the second approach, where the court tries to ascertain the licence fee that the defendant should have paid to exercise the right lawfully. Here, the licence fee is calculated based on the normal rate charged by the claimant in other instances. This presupposes that the claimant has other licensees from whom they receive a licence fee, such that a similar basis is applied to the calculation of damages.[89] If this approach cannot be adopted, there is a third and more controversial method of calculating damages. This goes by various names such as negotiating damages or licence fee damages.[90]

Negotiating damages are based on the hypothetical licence fee that the claimant could have charged the defendant to carry on the infringing activity lawfully. It differs from the second approach in that here there is no actual basis for the calculation of the licence fee. These damages may be available even where the claimant does not have an established market for their work because the court hypothesises a negotiation between the claimant and the defendant. Sometimes a court may decide to order damages based on trade practices, expert opinion, or any evidence showing the value of the right.[91] However, in relation to chattels, Lord Shaw has admitted that this approach to awarding compensation is to a large extent 'the exercise of a sound imagination and the practice of a broad axe'.[92] This decision and this approach have been applied also to copyright cases.[93] Having established general principles that require

[86] *SDL Hair Ltd v Next Row Ltd* [2014] EWHC 2084 (IPEC) [31].
[87] *General Tire Co v Firestone Tyre Co Ltd* [1975] 1 WLR 819, 824–27.
[88] *Ultraframe (UK) Ltd v Eurocell Building Plastics Ltd* [2006] EWHC 1344 (Pat).
[89] eg see *Stovin-Bradford v Volpoint Ltd* [1971] Ch 1007, 1016, 1020.
[90] In land law, these are also called Wrotham Park damages after the case on restrictive covenants, *Wrotham Park Estate Co Ltd v Parkside Homes Ltd* [1974] 1 WLR 798.
[91] Harbottle and others (n 8) 24-302.
[92] *Watson, Laidlaw, & Co. v Pott, Cassels, & Williamson* 1914 SC (HL) 18, 29–30.
[93] eg *SPE International Ltd v Professional Preparation Contractors (UK) Ltd* [2002] EWHC 881 (Ch) [86]–[87].

damage, causation, and foreseeability of such damage, to proceed to base the calculation of damages on something entirely hypothetical gives this area a surprising twist. Courts have tried to make the calculation on this basis as objective as possible, but aspects of conjecture remain, brought alive in the words of Lord Shaw.

In general, remedies do not help draw the finer line of distinction between property right to tangible things and copyright, or indeed between property rights and obligations. Remedies that are regarded as proprietary, such as injunctions, are available for breaches of personal rights in contracts; and remedies that are regarded personal, such as grant of damages, are widely available for the violations of property rights.[94] It is arguable that negotiating damages are the kind of remedies that are only available when property rights are infringed, whether property rights related to tangible things or intellectual property, because only property rights can be put to use (and therefore, licensed).[95] However, negotiating damages are more attractive in copyright cases because licensing rights in exchange for a fee or royalties is much more important as a method of deriving economic value in copyright than any other property right. Ordinarily the availability of this approach to calculation of damages might have given less cause for concern if copyright infringement had been a well-balanced tort that gave appropriate consideration for indirect and involuntary infringement. But, as argued in Section 2 above, this is not the case. A strict liability tort coupled with powerful remedies risks making this aspect of copyright law unjust for indirect and involuntary infringements.

(b) Account of Profits

If copyright infringement is proved, the copyright owner can elect either between damages on any of the grounds discussed in Subsection (a) above or being awarded an account of profits. A claimant normally chooses an account of profits when the profit made by the infringer is higher than the loss incurred by the copyright owner. However, a court will not refuse account of profits

[94] Sarah Worthington, 'Revolutions in Personal Property: Redrawing the Common Law's Conceptual Map' in Sarah Worthington, Andrew Robertson, and Graham Virgo (eds), *Revolution and Evolution in Private Law* (Hart 2018) 232–33, where she forcefully argues that remedies do not help make a distinction between property and obligation.

[95] *One Step v Morris Garner* [2019] AC 649 [95(1)], [95(2)]. See generally Poorna Mysoor, 'Licence Fee Damages and the Nature of IP Right' (2025) Harv J Law and Tech (forthcoming), exploring common criteria that may unite intangible property rights enabling them to seek an award of negotiating damages when infringed.

simply because damages would have been an adequate remedy. Account of profits is an equitable remedy and, therefore, its award is discretionary, unlike damages to which a claimant will be entitled if he establishes damage. The basis on which account of profits is awarded is that the claimant condones the infringement and accepts the profits made by the infringement; whereas in damages the claimant does not accept infringement and therefore is compensated for the infringement of the right. Account of profits is a restitutionary remedy, meaning that the focus is to deprive the defendant of the profits made by the wrong, rather than to compensate the claimant for having suffered the wrong. Claimants normally apply also for an injunction to stop the defendant from carrying on the infringing activity and disgorge the profits made by him that are due to the infringing activity.[96]

One of the unsettled controversies in relation to the award of account of profits is whether it is available even when the infringement is innocent. As stated above, s 97(1) of the CDPA states that if a person did not know that a work was protected by copyright at the time of infringement, then no order for damages can be made against them. However, this is without prejudice to any other remedy being available. Since an account of profits is not damages it is possible for this remedy to be granted in case of innocent infringement. Nevertheless, in *Wienerworld Ltd v Vision Video Ltd*,[97] it was held that there is no reason why account of profits should not be available when the infringement is innocent if the infringer has made a profit from the infringement. The court referred to the Copyright Act 1956, the predecessor of the CDPA, which had specifically provided under s 17(2) that where the infringement is innocent, damages are denied, but a court may order an account of profits. Although s 97(1) of the CDPA does not specifically mention account of profits, it was held that the CDPA had not changed the law on this point.[98] On the contrary, *Glaxosmithkline UK Ltd v Wyatt Holdings LLC*, a patent case, states that account of profits should only be available when there is unconscionable conduct on the part of the defendant. If the infringement is innocent, it automatically means that the defendant's conduct will not be unconscionable.[99] It is arguable that patent cases are different because s 62(1) of the Patents Act

[96] Bently argues that historically an account of profits could not be awarded if the injunction had been refused. He points to this as an unresolved controversy. Lionel Bently, 'Accounting for Profits Gained by Infringement of Copyright: Where Does it End?' (1991) 13(1) EIPR 5, 6–8. See also Lionel Bently, 'Account of Profits for Infringement of Copyright. Potton v Yorkclose and Others' (1990) 12(3) EIPR 106.

[97] [1998] FSR 832.

[98] ibid 835–38.

[99] [2017] EWHC 91 (Pat) [23]–[26].

1977 specifically denies damages and account of profits to a claimant where the infringement is innocent. However, given the origin of account of profits as an equitable remedy, it provides better justification for this award to be based on unconscionable conduct.

There are many other difficulties with account of profits. Since it is an alternative to damages, it is not clear how the rules that apply to damages in relation to causation and remoteness apply to account of profits. Also, there are issues around apportionment of profits when the part infringed forms a minor part of the defendant's work.[100] While the remedy is powerful, it is rendered unpredictable because of these unsettled issues. With all these challenges, if account of profits is available for infringement that is indirect or involuntary, as argued in Subsections 2(b) and (c) above, then it would mean that an unbalanced liability regime will be bolstered by a powerful remedy. The consequences can be drastic. The award of account of profits raises important issues on the non-compensatory nature of this remedy. Since copyright infringement is a tort, albeit a statutory tort, the aim should be to put back a victim of tort in a place where the tort had not happened. But disgorgement could leave the victim of tort better off than before the tort. There is much debate as to whether this remedy is an appropriate one for the commission of property torts. The same questions should be raised about this remedy being available for copyright infringement.

These two remedies show the power of property rights and the reason why thorough consideration must go into the enforcement mechanism of property torts. It is unfortunate that courts are readily willing to accept the analogy of property remedies for copyright without accepting an analogy with property torts in their enforcement mechanisms. Simply pointing to the availability of a large number of defences under the CDPA will not in itself be sufficient to justify why copyright infringement should attract stricter liability than property torts.

4. Summary

This chapter argued that copyright infringement is analysed better by analogy with property torts than with economic torts. This is not only because copyright as a property right bears much closer analogy with those of land and chattels but also because of the manner in which property torts can guide the fault

[100] Bently, 'Where Does it End' (n 96) 10–13.

requirement for copyright infringement. This would help the singular tort of copyright infringement where the liability arises regardless of whether infringement is voluntary or not, direct or not, to deal with the liability in a more nuanced way.

In drawing the comparison, it argued that the strictest liability akin to trespass should only arise in relation to literal infringement in copyright. Trespass being a tort that enforces direct and voluntary crossing of the boundary, a true analogy for this is restricted to verbatim copyright infringement. The chapter argued that inference as to derivation of the defendant's work from the claimant's is justifiable only if the substantiality test from the case law as it existed before *Infopaq* is resurrected. It went on to argue that all instances of non-literal infringement should only attract liability akin to private nuisance, because the indirect interference with land is comparable to non-literal infringement of copyright. It went on to argue that derivation for non-literal copying should not be a matter of inference, insisting on bringing back the substantiality test as it applied before *Infopaq*, and posited additionally that the court should engage in the balancing of competing interests and the consideration of reasonableness that dominates the discussion in private nuisance. It finally considered situations where derivation is not adequately proved and argued that this amounts to an involuntary or subconscious infringement. Just as it has been argued that involuntary interference should only attract negligence liability for property torts, for copyright infringement there should similarly only be a negligence liability. To conclude, the chapter considered certain powerful remedies for copyright infringement, such as negotiating damages and account of profits, which are arguably only available for infringement of property rights. It argued that the availability of these remedies makes it particularly harsh for those held liable for indirect and involuntary infringement, if copyright infringement is not reformed along the lines argued here.

6

Defences and Limits on Uses

1. Introduction

Defences gnaw at everything that is exclusive about property rights—the rights, powers, and privileges. When a defence is made out, despite the ingredients of a property tort being established, no liability for the infringement of the property right arises. Defences differ from denials in that the justification for defences comes from factors extraneous to the elements of the claimant's action, whereas denials are simply assertions that one or more components of a tort are not made out.[1] The extraneous factors are justifications, some of which could be rooted in policy considerations. In this sense defences are an *ex post* re-balancing of competing interests. On the face of it, it appears that, on one hand, the law sets up a liability regime to enforce the infractions of the exclusive rights, powers, and privileges; but on the other, takes them away through defences. In general, therefore, the fewer the number of defences, the sharper the liability regime. As such, the number of defences to infringement and the considerations that underlie their applicability in a legal system should be closely monitored, especially for property torts. The existence of too many or too loosely framed defences can make property rights illusory.

Copyright statutes in most jurisdictions including the United Kingdom set forth a number of defences to infringement. Chapter III of the Copyright, Designs and Patents Act 1988 (CDPA) lists most of these defences. These defences address specific policy considerations, most notably free speech and expression. They are based on the realisation that a particularly sharp liability regime can be counter-productive to the creation of new works, which depend not merely on the facts and ideas in the public domain but also from copyright works of others. Like all valuable resources, the exploitation of copyright takes place within the context of the interests of the public at large in using the copyright works and creating new works. The fundamental values of free speech and expression are at stake if the rights of the owners are not balanced

[1] James Goudkamp, *Tort Law Defences* (Hart 2013) 2, 5–7.

Copyright as Personal Property. Poorna Mysoor, Oxford University Press. © Poorna Mysoor 2025.
DOI: 10.1093/9780191954962.003.0006

with those of other users and creators. Therefore, much reliance is placed on defences as the primary means to achieve the required balance. Of particular significance are fair dealing defences that exclude liability for infringement for news reporting, criticism, review, and so on, as long as such dealing with the copyright work is fair.[2] What amounts to 'fair' in dealing with the protected work when these defences are raised is a multi-factor test laid down by the courts. Other important defences include those that enable access to copyright works for the purposes of education,[3] libraries,[4] producing copyright works in different formats for differently abled persons,[5] reproducing works that have become 'orphaned',[6] and so on.

The number and the nature of defences of copyright infringement are often put forward by the property theorist to argue that copyright is unlike a property right.[7] These defences impact copyright to no lesser degree than defences to property torts[8] impact property rights to land or chattels. It does not seem apposite to single out the defences to copyright infringement and insist on their impact on copyright in robbing it of its nature as a property right. Smith explains this by what he calls exclusion strategy and governance strategy. By exclusion strategy he means a mechanism whereby an interference with a physical thing can be enforced by way of trespass. It is a simple on-off mechanism without much argument or granularity. Governance strategy on the other hand takes into account finer considerations to decide whether liability should arise, as is the case in private nuisance. Smith argues that one can see both these strategies also being adopted in intellectual property law.[9] Agreeing with Smith, Van Houweling goes further to argue that the exclusion and governance strategies are along a continuum.[10] The difference between approaches to copyright infringement and property torts is that while in private nuisance reasonableness is built into the ingredients of the property tort itself thereby informing the enforcement debate, in copyright these considerations are externalised and brought within the purview of defences. Smith compares the

[2] CDPA, ss 30 and 30A.
[3] CDPA, ss 32–36A.
[4] CDPA, ss 37–44A.
[5] CDPA, ss 31A–31F.
[6] CDPA, s 44B.
[7] Ben McFarlane and Simon Douglas, 'Property, Analogy and Variety' (2022) 42 OJLS 161, 175–76.
[8] Chapter 5 refers to trespass to land and chattels, private nuisance, conversion, and negligent damage to tangible property collectively as property torts.
[9] Henry E Smith, 'Intellectual Property as Property' (2007) 117 Yale LJ 1742, 1782–86.
[10] Molly Shaffer Van Houweling, 'The New Private Law and Intellectual Property: Calibrating Copyright on the Common Law Continuum' in Andrew Gold and others (eds), *The Oxford Handbook of the New Private Law* (OUP 2020) 413.

balancing act in private nuisance with that of fair use in US copyright law.[11] While fair use is a particularly open-ended defence found in US copyright law, but not found in the CDPA, the balancing act carried out in fair dealing defences under the CDPA is similarly comparable to the balancing act in private nuisance.

Of course, in the context of copyright, the nature of the work makes an enormous difference to the nature and number of defences to copyright infringement. Copyright works being relatively less rivalrous in nature make them capable of being used by multiple users at the same time. Interestingly, the nature of the thing, that is, whether it is land or chattels, also influences the defences to property torts. A statute might provide a defence against private nuisance by permitting the emission of noise and dust, for example.[12] But this statute will be meaningless if applied to a bicycle. Therefore, even within tangible property law there is no one-size-fits-all solution to defences. Equally, there are defences to property torts that do not exist in copyright—prescription as a defence to private nuisance being one of them. While adverse possession is not regarded as a defence to trespass (because it is more commonly used as a counterclaim in proceedings for possession or a standalone claim), it is also a doctrine that does not find a place in copyright.[13] Accordingly, different policy considerations underlie defences to torts that relate to land from those that relate to chattels, and from property torts to copyright. With copyright, there is a much larger spread of considerations, but commensurate with the nature of the work.

Copyright statutes also place certain limits on the copyright owner's ability to exploit their works, albeit much more indirectly than in patent law.[14] In general, copyright owners are free to exploit their works in the manner they choose. However, given the difficulty in managing the negotiation and grant of licences and monitoring the licence fee payments, copyright owners have formed themselves into collecting societies. There are different societies for authors of different types of authorial works, and also different societies based on the rights they manage.[15] Users of copyright works need to approach the

[11] Smith (n 9) 1771.

[12] Railways Act 1993, s 122(3)(a)(i) recognises a defence to private nuisance when acting in furtherance of the statutory authority within this enactment.

[13] Although this book argues in Chapter 3 that adverse possession should be extended to copyright by analogy.

[14] Compulsory licences are more commonly debated in relation to patents than in relation to copyright works. See Section 3 of this chapter for further discussion.

[15] eg the Performing Rights Society manages music and lyrics of works and the playing of these works by way of, say, a sound system, or as broadcast or streamed. See <www.prsformusic.com/> accessed 21 September 2024. The Authors Licensing and Collecting Society manages rights such as for

relevant society for a licence to use the works they manage. For example, a news aggregator that compiles news in the form of newsletters for its clients will require a licence from the Newspaper Licensing Association. The CDPA has an indirect jurisdiction to regulate the licences issued by these collecting societies.[16] Copyright statutes also rely on these limitations on the exploitation of copyright to balance competing interests, in addition to the defences.

Limitation on use is not unique to copyright. In addition to defences that extinguish liability, both land law and personal property law place limits on the use of the thing. No one has the absolute despotic dominion over the thing which Blackstone spoke about in the eighteenth century. Readily discernible examples include certain kinds of land use being subject to planning laws and chattels like cars being subject to fitness certification for their use on public roads under the road traffic legislation. These laws are formulated with the recognition that the exercise of privileges over things takes place within the larger context of society. In other words, it is an acknowledgement of the need to balance public good against private rights. These are not available as defences, nor are they enforceable by a member of the public, but they are enforceable by the state as a regulatory matter against non-compliance. Nevertheless, these limits take away from the privileges and powers of the owner.

This chapter seeks to establish that the number and nature of defences to copyright infringement do not undermine the nature of copyright as a property right. It argues that the nature of defences to property torts is not significantly different from those of copyright infringement; to the extent that the defences are different, these differences are attributable to the difference in the nature and importance of the thing itself, be it land, chattels, or copyright works. Accordingly, Subsection 2(a) begins with the defence that is common to both property torts and copyright infringement, namely licence. It examines the extent to which this reinforces copyright infringement as a property tort. Subsection 2(b) moves on to defences in both copyright and property torts that are informed by extraneous public policy considerations. In the copyright context, it takes the example of fair dealing defences and in the property tort context, it examines the defence of the authority of the law as a comparison. It argues that property torts are not as immune to defences influenced by policy as property theorists seem to think. Subsection 2(c) goes on to consider a defence that is only found in copyright and not in property torts and is normally

photocopying, digital reproduction, and so on of literary works. See <www.alcs.co.uk/> accessed 21 September 2024.

[16] CDPA, ch VII.

referred to as the public interest defence. Although broadly worded, it points to the narrow use made of this defence in practice. It also discusses the possibility of putting forward arguments based on human rights to defend against any infraction of freedom of expression. Finally, Subsection 2(d) discusses the defences to property torts that are not recognised in copyright and explores whether there are any lessons for copyright in this regard.

Section 3 proceeds to deal with the most significant limits on the use and exploitation of copyright. These include exceptional use of compulsory licences, the limits placed by competition law, and so on. By analogy it demonstrates a similar role played by planning and building laws for land and other regulatory regimes for chattels ordinarily noticeable in everyday lives. This seeks to demonstrate that even if it is not often acknowledged, land law and personal property law do place many restrictions on the use and exploitation of the thing on its owner.

2. Defences to Copyright Infringement and Property Torts

One may argue that copyright is so different from property rights in land or chattels that this kind of comparison is pointless. The argument here is not that the defences to property torts are identical to those for copyright infringement. It is rather that there may be more that is common between these torts than may have been acknowledged in the past. There may be lessons for copyright to examine the considerations that go into some of the defences to property torts. With this in the background, this section begins with the defence that is common to both property rights in tangible things and copyright, namely, licence.

(a) Licence

Although copyright statutes incorporate licence as part of the statutory provision defining infringement, the claimant only needs to show prima facie that they did not license the defendant's actions. The existence of licence must be proved by the defendant in the same way as in trespass and in nuisance. This is because licence is a defence that arises by the very nature of property rights as *in rem* rights, whether they relate to tangible things or to copyright works. This means that if P, for example, has a property right, it places a corresponding duty of non-interference on the rest of the world, which includes

Q, R, S, and so on. Licences arise when these duties are transformed into privileges by the exercise of a legal power. Hohfeld defines a licence as nothing but operative facts that lead to a privilege.[17] The operative facts embody the exercise of the relevant powers which transform the duty owed by a person, say Q, into a privilege, resulting in a licence in Q's favour. Once Q has a licence, Q no longer owes a duty of non-interference but will be able to exercise the licence within the scope defined by P. In essence, Q has a permission to exercise a particular privilege, which, if not for the licence, would amount to infringement.[18] Regardless of whether the property rights are in relation to land, chattels. or copyright works, this is the common mechanism through which licences arise.

A licence cannot come into existence without a power being exercised to transform the duty into a privilege. This author has argued elsewhere that there are broadly three sources of power that can give rise to licences.[19] One may analyse licences that arise based on each of these sources and examine what distinguishes them. A licence can be express or implied, bare or contractual, depending on whether consideration was given in exchange for the licence.

(i) Property owner's power to consent

As we saw in Chapter 4, when a person acquires a property right, together with the exclusive rights, the owner of the right also acquires powers and privileges. In exercise of their powers, P might decide to themselves enjoy the use privileges, or give one or more privileges to someone else to exercise, say Q. Q will then have a licence, the basis of which is P's consent. P's invitation for Q to attend a dinner at P's house, P's handing their bicycle to Q to ride, and P granting permission to Q for P's novel to be published are all examples of licences which are based on P's power to consent.

A consensually granted express contractual licence tends to be transactional in nature, voluntarily entered into between the parties. However, it may still serve as a defence if the licensee is alleged to have gone beyond the scope of the licence, but on proper construction it can be shown that the licensee's actions were covered by the licence. Determining the scope of the licence will be a matter of interpreting the terms of the licence. However, often in the disputes relating to land, the person claiming infringement is a successor in title to the licensor, and therefore the central issue in these cases is whether a licence is a property interest binding on successors in title. In land law and personal

[17] Wesley N Hohfeld, 'Some Fundamental Legal Conceptions as Applied in Judicial Reasoning' (1913) 23 Yale LJ 16, 20.

[18] *Thomas v Sorrell* [1673] EWHC (KB) J85.

[19] Poorna Mysoor, *Implied Licences in Copyright Law* (OUP 2021) 30–38.

property law, licences are regarded as personal and not as property interests. In copyright, however, the statute has modified the nature of licences in this regard. This aspect of licences is better analysed as derivative interests which are consensually, and most often expressly, created by the copyright owner in favour of another person. Chapter 7, Section 3(b) provides further discussion.

In addition to express licences, implied licences can be put forward as a defence to the infringement of a property right. While implied bare licences arise informally by the conduct of the copyright owner and the surrounding circumstances, implied contractual licences normally mean that the term being implied into the contract is a licence to exercise some privilege in relation to the thing. However, determining the scope of implied licences can be challenging. This author has proposed frameworks for implying copyright licences based on the consent of the copyright owner.[20] These frameworks can equally work for licences in relation to property rights in tangible things, specifically land.

This author has argued that when consent is the basis for implying a bare licence, the process of consenting can be divided into three parts: a positive act providing access to the thing, a neutral act of staying back while the thing is used, and the surrounding circumstances including the knowledge thereof that determine the scope of the licence. An example in copyright is *Banks v CBS Songs Ltd.*[21] Here, the claimant wrote lyrics of a song on a piece of paper and gave it to her friend who had asked for her help with this. This amounted to the positive act. She stood back while the friend took the lyrics, which is the neutral act. But the friend assigned the copyright in it to the defendant, holding himself out to be the copyright owner. The issue was whether the defendant's use was an infringement. What was within the claimant's knowledge was only that the friend was himself going to sing in the band. The circumstances did not indicate that by handing the paper on which lyrics were written she was assigning the copyright in it. Rather it was only an implied licence to compose music to the lyrics and sing it with the band. Accordingly, the defendant having another singer perform the song was held to be an infringement.

In relation to land, implied licences based on consent can be similarly analysed. Take, for example, *Robson v Hallett*,[22] where it has been held that if a person living in a house with a garden leaves the gate unlocked, he gives an implied licence to whoever comes to his door for lawful purposes to be on

20 ibid ch 3.
21 [1996] EMLR 440.
22 [1967] 2 QB 939, 953–54 (Diplock LJ).

the land for that purpose. Providing access up to the front door is a positive act, and standing back when a person enters the premises is the neutral act. The scope of an implied licence will be determined by the lawful purpose for which entry is gained, which in this case was a police investigation. Implied bare licences arise informally and bring much flexibility to our everyday lives. Consider the everyday example of being invited to a friend's house for dinner, or entering a supermarket during opening hours, and so on.

Copyright licences that are implied into a contract normally arise when a person commissions a copyright work. An example of this can be seen in *Ray v Classic FM*.[23] Here, the defendant had commissioned the claimant, a musicologist, to catalogue their entire collection of classical music records. The claimant created the catalogue, which was an original database in which copyright subsisted and handed it to the defendants. But the contract between the claimant and the defendant had said nothing about copyright. The defendant used the catalogue outside the United Kingdom. The claimant sued the defendant for copyright infringement claiming that the defendant had no right to use the catalogue in this manner. The defendant put forward a defence that the copyright in the catalogue had been impliedly assigned to them. But in the alternative, they claimed that they had at least the benefit of an implied licence whose scope was wide enough to leave them free to use the catalogue as they chose. The court held that the defendant did indeed have the benefit of a copyright licence implied into the commissioning contract, but based on the overall bargain, the amount paid, and so on, the scope of the licence was confined to the United Kingdom. Contractual licences in land arise all the time, whether express or implied. When a person books a hotel room, pays for parking, or pays for the cinema, contractual licences to be on the respective premises arise. If this licence is not expressly stated in the contract, similar considerations go into implying a contractual licence in relation to land.

Further discussion on the technicalities of licences is beyond the scope of this book. It suffices to state that licences that are based on consent of the copyright owner operate in a similar way to a defence to property torts as much as copyright infringement. Indeed, on one account, it may be argued that consent-based copyright licences are as old as copyright itself. The Statute of Anne states that if a bookseller, printer, or other person prints, reprints, or imports or causes to be printed, reprinted, or imported, any such Book or Books 'without the consent of the proprietor or proprietors thereof . . . and obtained

[23] [1998] FSR 622.

in writing signed in the presence of two or more credible witnesses' during the term limited by this Act, then he is liable under the Act.[24]

(ii) Power of customary practices to permit use

The power to permit the use of a thing may arise from a custom kept alive in the practices of a group of persons. The practices can extend to a locality if it is a land-related custom, say, a right to dry fishing nets on the owner's land,[25] or a practice that extends to a type of work in a specific industry, such as academic articles submitted to journals in the publishing industry.[26] When a licence is implied based on a custom, it is not the property owner exercising powers at their own discretion, but rather being compelled by the existence of a custom to permit a privilege to be exercised in relation to the property right. The most important issue here is therefore whether the custom has come into existence.

Since a custom does not require a judge to rule in favour of its existence, it is essential to examine what kind of conduct brings a custom into existence. Although there may be much less reliance on customs in modern times, the criteria that are important for its existence are certainty, notoriety, reasonableness, not to be contrary to law, and recognised as binding. These criteria are based on cases that arose in commercial law.[27] Objectively, the same criteria should apply whether the custom relates to the use of land or to the use of copyright.

A custom within the newspaper industry was at the heart of the litigation in *Barnier v News Group*.[28] Here the claimant was a photojournalist whose photograph was published by the first newspaper who had an express licence from him. The defendant newspaper copied the photograph published in the first newspaper and published it in their own newspaper later on. The claimant sued the defendant for copyright infringement. The defendant claimed a custom in the newspaper industry that permitted them to publish the photographs already published in other newspapers and seek a licence from their author later on. The court held that such a custom cannot exist because it would

[24] Statute of Anne, London (1710) in Lionel Bently and Martin Kretschmer (eds), *Primary Sources on Copyright (1450–1900)* <www.copyrighthistory.org> accessed 23 September 2024.

[25] *Mercer v Denne* [1904] 2 Ch 534. Other examples include the right to draw water from a spring on another person's land (*Race v Ward* (1855) E & B 702) and the right to use another person's land for recreation (*Hall v Nottingham* (1875) 1 Ex D 1). See Andrew Tettenborn and others, *Clerk & Lindsell on Torts* (24th edn, Sweet & Maxwell 2024) paras 18-46, 18-47.

[26] It is customary for the journal editor to send copies of the article submitted to the editorial board for discussion or to reviewers for review.

[27] See generally *Cunliffe-Owen v Teacher and Greenwood* [1967] 1 WLR 1421; *Con-Stan Industries v Norwich Winterthur* (1986) 64 ALR 481.

[28] [1997] FSR 812.

be unreasonable for newspapers to publish photographs first and leave it for the relevant author to trace the published photos and claim compensation. While in relation to land the importance of customs may be reduced, in copyright, the publishing industry, art industry, and software industry all have customary practices, and occasionally courts do ascertain whether the custom at issue does really exist.[29]

(iii) Power of the state to permit use based on public policy

More controversially, a public policy that may have been embodied in the statute or common law can also be the basis for implying a licence. When a licence is implied at law, again, it is not the property owner who exercises their powers at their discretion. They are compelled by the existence of a law to give the licence. Any term implied at law diminishes the property owner's powers. However, it is common in contract law for terms to be implied at law based on statutes. A ready example in relation to physical things is contracts for the sale of goods into which warranties of fitness for purpose and sufficient quality are implied under the Sale of Goods Act 1979, s 14. Another example is the implied covenant for human habitation under s 9A of the Landlord Tenant Act 1985. The existence of a contracting party who has given consideration in exchange for the goods or premises justifies this kind of interference with both the powers of the property owner and their freedom to contract.

If the parties are not in a contractual relationship, then a bare licence implied at law takes the form of immunity from being sued for infringement more than as a permission to exercise the privilege. For example, if a person is permitted by law to go on their neighbour's land to prevent the spread of fire,[30] then this rule offers immunity from the liability for trespass. Similarly, if the law states that a teacher is allowed in an educational establishment to reproduce content protected by copyright for the purposes of teaching, then the teacher's doing of this act gives them immunity from copyright infringement. One need not call it a licence at all because it will simply be a rule of law mandating the property owner to permit certain use of the relevant thing. This is what all defences do—they make a person immune from the liability for infringement. Therefore, these are considered separately under Subsection 2(b) below discussing statutory fair dealing defences within the CDPA, and Subsection 2(c) below discussing the defence of public interest drawn from common law, other statutes, and human rights.

[29] Mysoor, *Implied Licences* (n 19) 155–67.
[30] *Cope v Sharpe* [1912] 1 KB 496.

(b) Defences of Fair Dealing

Of all the defences to copyright infringement this subsection discusses only fair dealing defences because the flexibility inherent in these defences and the underlying policy considerations make them the most controversial. Scholars point to these defences as marking a significant divergence of copyright from property rights in land and chattels. They point to fewer and narrower defences to the violation of property rights that are not driven by policy considerations, making them normatively more appropriately characterised as property rights.[31] The purpose of this subsection is to demonstrate that the approach to establishing a fair dealing defence is comparable to the balancing act that a court carries out in private nuisance cases. The difference, of course, is one of timing—whether it is *ex ante* or *ex post*.

While Subsection 2(a) above dealt with a defence inherent in the nature of property rights as being *in rem*, the fair dealing defences are driven by the nature of copyright works as a relatively less rivalrous resource and policy considerations. If copyright works were rivalrous in nature like bicycles, one person using the thing would have effectively prevented the rest of the world from using the thing at the same time. With the relatively less rivalrousness nature of copyright works, multiple users can make use of copyright works at the same time. Rather than seeing the lack of perfect rivalrousness as a weakness of copyright, it should be seen as a strength, especially in the light of copyright works being capable of furthering certain policy objectives, such as the promotion of free speech and expression, learning, and education. In furtherance of these policies, the CDPA identifies certain key uses in relation to which the defence is available, but only so long as the user's dealing with the work is fair. Dealing here simply means use of the work. These key uses are specifically defined and are exhaustive, unlike the fair use defence in the United States, which is open-ended.[32] The key uses that are permitted so long as the use is fair under UK law are:[33] research or private study;[34] criticism or review;[35] quotation;[36] reporting current events;[37] parody, caricature, or pastiche,[38] and illustrations

[31] McFarlane and Douglas (n 7) 176.

[32] The fair use defence is enshrined in the US Copyright Act under 17 USC §107.

[33] Bently and others helpfully summarise the acts permitted that are subject to the fair dealing defence. See Lionel Bently and others, *Intellectual Property Law* (6th edn, OUP 2022) 245–46.

[34] CDPA, s 29(1) and (1C).

[35] CDPA, s 30(1).

[36] CDPA, s 30(1ZA).

[37] CDPA, s 30(2).

[38] CDPA, s 30A(1).

for instruction.[39] The conditions to be satisfied for each of these defences are specifically laid down in the CDPA. Of relevance to us here is how a court arrives at the conclusion of what makes the dealing fair.

It is worth reminding ourselves from our discussion in Chapter 5 that the only considerations that go into finding liability for copyright infringement are whether the defendant took a part of the claimant's work that is original. No factors relating to the defendant that underlie the taking are considered, although this author has argued in Chapter 5, Section 2(b) that, for non-literal copying, factors relevant to the defendant's use should also be considered. But the law as it stands currently makes it even more crucial that the factors that go into determining fairness in the fair dealing defence balance the one-sided approach to infringement. Clearly, an assessment of fairness needs to begin with ascertaining the part taken by the defendant qualitatively and quantitatively. But beyond this, certain factors relating to the defendant's actions come into play. Let us examine them.

First, a court conducts a deeper examination of the use that the defendant makes of the work to ensure that one or more of the six purposes indicated above are satisfied. For example, if the defence of criticism is put forward by the defendant, the context of the rest of the defendant's work should contain a critical engagement or an analysis of the claimant's text. If the defence of quotation is claimed, the rest of the text should provide a context to the quote. Secondly, how the defendant obtained the claimant's work matters. If it was obtained by lawful means, such as from a library or from a book that the defendant purchased, then this factor will be considered. Thirdly, the motive of the defendant, such as whether it is honest and not merely for financial gain will be considered. A non-commercial motive of the defendant will go a long way in supporting fairness of the use. These factors are balanced against whether the part taken by the defendant has harmful consequences on the market for the claimant's work and whether the defendant has acknowledged the claimant for the part taken.[40]

The above considerations should be viewed in the context of the argument that fair dealing defences in copyright are not comparable to any defence to a property tort. Douglas and McFarlane assert that the fair dealing defences result in 'boundary shifting' of copyright.[41] This is because they see copyright as nothing more than the right itself—a chose in action. The boundary of this

[39] CDPA, s 32.
[40] For a doctrinal exposition of how fairness is determined, see Bently and others (n 33) 245–51.
[41] McFarlane and Douglas (n 7) 175–76.

right is simply the extent to which the right can be exercised. The foregoing chapters maintain that copyright is more than the mere rights. It is vital to appreciate the thinghood of copyright for a more contextual understanding of the fair dealing defences. The availability of the thing in copyright, that is, the copyright work, is central to free speech, access to information and knowledge, and for the functioning of a free society. Any impact on the exclusionary rights should be viewed from this perspective.

For comparison, one needs to consider the factors that go into the assessment of whether a defendant's actions affect unduely the use and enjoyment of the land by the claimant. Among them, *Fearn v Tate* highlights the importance of the defendant's use of the land being common and ordinary.[42] It is arguable that engaging with a work for criticism, review, parody, news reporting, and so on are common and ordinary uses of copyright works. In private nuisance a court considers the defendant's actions in the context of the character of the locality and planning permission that changes the land use patterns. This is comparable to a court considering the part taken by the defendant in the context of the market for the claimant's work in general to determine if there might be any harmful consequences. The utility of the defendant's conduct and the public interest angle associated with it is comparable to the public interest that underlies each of the six fair dealing defences. Malice of the defendant in private nuisance is comparable to the motive of the defendant in copyright infringement. Conceptually, therefore, the balancing act that takes place in establishing a fair dealing defence is similar to the balancing act that takes place in establishing private nuisance.

The question then is whether it makes a difference whether the balancing act takes place before liability is imposed or after. On one view, it is arguable that the timing does not make a difference as far as the characterisation of the rights as property rights is concerned. On another view, it is arguable that by insisting on a balancing exercise before liability is imposed, private nuisance indeed takes a much more contextual stance on property rights than an absolute one. This is because if a defendant is successful in establishing reasonableness, the liability itself does not arise. In copyright infringement, on the contrary, the absence of balancing act occurring before the liability is imposed makes the property right more absolute than contextual. Even the reasonableness assessment that takes place after liability is imposed in copyright infringement is not open-ended as it is in private nuisance but relates to the six specific uses enumerated above. As such, it is incorrect to point to fair dealing defences to conclude that this takes away from copyright being a property right. On the

[42] [2023] UKSC 4 [27]–[35] (Lord Leggatt).

contrary, within the existing doctrine copyright infringement and defences to infringement only make copyright a stronger property right.

It may be clarified that the argument above is consistent with the stance taken in Chapter 5 of this book that non-literal copyright infringement should resemble private nuisance. Despite taking into account competing interests, the balancing act in private nuisance does not dilute the nature of property rights in land. Indeed, one can see a certain deliberate distinction being made in the approach to private nuisance from trespass when one views the trajectory of common law in developing the ingredients of these torts. Surely, no suggestion can be made that the development of private nuisance makes land less of a subject matter for property rights. In the same way, introducing the balancing exercise into copyright infringement should not dilute copyright as a property right. This may have the effect of widening the doctrine of copyright infringement beyond the six areas covered by the existing fair dealing defences.

(c) Public Interest Defence

In addition to statutory defences, the CDPA also recognises a more general defence of public interest, which is reaffirmed under s 171(3) of the Act. It states that nothing in this part of the statute 'affects any rule of law preventing or restricting the enforcement of copyright, on grounds of public interest or otherwise'. Before Brexit, it was controversial whether this provision survived the passing of the Infosoc Directive.[43] This is because Recital 32 of the Infosoc Directive states that the Directive provides an exhaustive enumeration of exceptions to copyright infringement, meaning that the member states are not free to introduce defences of their own. A court can interpret public interest in whatever manner the context of a case requires and go on to restrict or deny the enforcement of copyright on this basis. Taken to its logical end, this can become an additional mechanism through which a court can recognise a defence in addition to those specifically listed as such under the CDPA. However, Recital 32, like all recitals of a directive, is used as an interpretive tool.[44] It is noteworthy that this statement does not find expression in the CDPA or in the

[43] Directive 2001/29/EC of the European Parliament and of the Council of 22 May 2001 on the harmonisation of certain aspects of copyright and related rights in the information society [2001] OJ L167/10, p 10–19.

[44] This recital will have to be read in the context of other recitals. The idea of fair balance in the copyright context is enshrined in Recital 31 of the Infosoc Directive. In addition, Recital 3 of the Infosoc Directive identifies the protection of intellectual property, freedom of expression, and public interest as the fundamental principles of law, pointing to the main interests that need to be balanced in a specific case.

assimilated case law. However, s 5(A1) of the European Union (Withdrawal) Act 2018 states that the supremacy of EU law is no longer part of UK domestic law and therefore, in interpreting the provisions of the CDPA, courts need not follow Recital 32. As such, s 171(3) can be interpreted in a manner that makes sense for the United Kingdom.[45]

The law that can restrict or prevent copyright enforcement can originate in common law, a statute other than the CDPA, or a law that is more fundamental than that, such as human rights. Let us consider common law, to begin with. This will mean that the court itself formulates a rule based on public interest and enforces it as a matter of precedent on subsequent cases. The legislative history of s 171(3) points to a conscious decision on the part of law makers to preserve what was known before the enactment of the CDPA as the public interest defence.[46] This was a defence that was originally developed in response to an action for breach of confidence but was extended to copyright infringement in cases where copyright was asserted to thwart the publication of information in public interest. Therefore, courts initially enforced the public interest defence only in cases where both confidentiality and copyright infringement were claimed.[47] However, in later cases courts have enforced this defence even where only copyright infringement had been claimed, although not specifically stating that they were recognising a public interest defence.

The open-endedness of the public interest does not grant an entirely unguided discretion to the judges. The United Kingdom is subject to the international treaty obligation under art 9(2) of the Berne Convention, which provides that a defence to copyright infringement can only be recognised for special cases, provided that such reproduction does not conflict with the normal exploitation of the work and does not unreasonably prejudice the legitimate interests of the author. Although this provision has not been enacted expressly within the CDPA, it is possible to use this as a guiding light to shape the impact of public interest on copyright. This author has discussed elsewhere a number of cases where the courts were implicitly engaging with the public interest defence, and demonstrated how the three-step test can guide decision-making in these cases.[48]

[45] For further discussion on controversies surrounding CDPA, s 171(3), see Mysoor, *Implied Licences* (n 19) 57–61, and Chapter 8.

[46] Poorna Mysoor, 'Capturing the Dynamism of Fairness—a Common Law Perspective' in Daniel Gervais (ed), *Fairness, Morality and Ordre Public in Intellectual Property* (Edward Elgar 2020) 10–12.

[47] *Lion Laboratories Ltd v Evans* [1985] QB 526.

[48] Mysoor, *Implied Licences* (n 19) 200–09.

An example of a statute getting in the way of enforcing copyright can be seen in *Attorney General v Guardian Newspapers*.[49] An ex-employee of the British Secret Services had published a book disclosing certain matters covered by the Official Secrets Act. The book had been banned in the United Kingdom, but the author managed to have it published in Australia. The defendant newspaper entered into a contract with the author to publish the book in the United Kingdom in serial form in its newspaper. The claimant approached the court for an injunction on the basis of the violation of the Official Secrets Act, among other grounds. The court granted the injunction, noting that it is within its powers not to enforce the author's copyright in the work for its violation of this law.[50]

An illustration of a court reading human rights into the public interest can be seen in *Ashdown v Telegraph*.[51] Here, the publication of certain minutes of a confidential meeting authored by the plaintiff had been published, with extensive quotations by the defendant newspaper. The issue was whether the right to freedom of expression of the newspaper to report it verbatim in the public interest overrode the author's copyright. The Court of Appeal held that copyright only protects expression and not the information, which means that protecting copyright still enables the free circulation of information. Accordingly, in this case the court held that a summary of the minutes reporting the information contained in it would have been sufficient, and that the defendant's verbatim reproduction did amount to copyright infringement. However, the court recognised that there may be exceptional cases where literal reproduction might be relevant. In this sense, the court held that copyright could be antithetical to freedom of expression in some cases.[52] In relation to s 171(3), the court held:[53]

> Now that the Human Rights Act 1998 is in force, there is the clearest public interest in giving effect to the right of freedom of expression in those rare cases where this right trumps the rights conferred by the 1988 Act. In such circumstances, we consider that section 171(3) of the Act permits the defence of public interest to be raised.

[49] [1990] 1 AC 109.
[50] ibid 275–76, 294.
[51] [2001] EWCA Civ 1142.
[52] ibid [30]–[31], [43].
[53] ibid [58].

Reading the Human Rights Act 1998 into s 171(3) of the CDPA opens up the application of the European Convention on Human Rights (ECHR). Freedom of expression and information is enshrined in Art 10(1) of the ECHR. In an appropriate case a person, say P, may be able to successfully claim that the enforcement of copyright of another person, say Q, should be restricted or prevented, in order to uphold P's right to freedom of expression and information. However, in response to this Q can assert that their copyright is protected under Art 1 of the First Protocol of the ECHR (A1P1). In human rights discourse only an unjustified interference with a human right is actionable.[54] Article 10(2) identifies these justifications and recognises that the state can restrict the exercise of this freedom 'as prescribed by law and . . . necessary in a democratic society, . . . for the protection of the reputation or rights of others'. Since copyright qualifies as 'rights of others', it may seem to always be able to defeat a defence based on free speech. A1P1 also goes on to say that possessions can be deprived in the public interest and the use of possessions can be denied in the general interest. Since in most cases the dispute is as to an interference with the exclusive use of copyright works rather than the deprivation of the very subsistence of copyright, the justification that is more appropriate is the general interest. Ultimately, the difference between public interest and general interest may be a matter of degree. But we circle back to where we started in that only if the protection of freedom of expression is in the general interest can the enforcement of copyright be prevented or restricted. In most cases, the domestic courts have a wide margin of appreciation in balancing between the right to freedom of expression and right to property.[55]

It may be argued that human rights are engaged in vertical disputes, that is, disputes between the state and private actors. However, intellectual property cases have made far greater advances in bringing human rights into horizontal disputes, that is, disputes between private parties. In specific relation to freedom of expression, the European Court of Human Rights (ECtHR) has affirmed that the member states have a positive obligation to protect Art 10 against interferences by private persons or corporate organisations.[56] In this context, the Court of Justice of the European Union (CJEU) has had many opportunities to apply the Charter of Human Rights in the context of disputes

[54] Laurence Helfer, 'How Intellectual Property and Human Rights Can Live Together' in Paul Torremas (ed), *Intellectual Property Law and Human Rights* (3rd edn, Wolters Kluwer 2015) 39.

[55] Henning Grosse Ruse-Khan, 'Overlaps and Conflict Norms in Human Rights Law' in Christophe Geiger (ed), *Research Handbook on Human Rights and Intellectual Property* (Edward Elgar 2015) 86–87.

[56] *Wojtas-Kaleta v Poland* App no 20436/02 (ECtHR, 16 July 2009).

between essentially private actors such as internet service providers (ISPs) and collecting societies. While in *Promusicae v Telefonica* the issue was whether an ISP could be required to reveal the identity of the infringers,[57] in *Telekabel*, the issue was the validity of website blocking injunctions issued against the ISPs by collecting societies representing copyright owners.[58] In these cases, the right to protection of intellectual property under Art 17(2) of the respective content owners was in conflict with the right to conduct business of the ISPs under Art 16 and the right to freedom of information of the internet users under Art 11. While categorically stating that the right to property protected under Art 17(2) is by no means absolute or inviolable, the CJEU refused the grant of relief in *Promusicae*.[59] In *Telekabel*, the CJEU outlined the measures that may be taken which will not violate the ISP's rights under Art 16 and the user rights under Art 11.[60] The UK courts have followed the CJEU's rulings in *Promusicae* and *Telekabel* while considering the issue of granting injunctions against ISPs to block websites containing infringing content,[61] making them part of the assimilated law in the United Kingdom. This may further be supplemented by the ECtHR's ruling, which has recognised the importance of the internet in enhancing the public's access to and dissemination of information, and as 'the principal means by which individuals exercise their right to freedom of expression and information'.[62]

Another point worth noting here is that the ability of a law to affect the enforcement of copyright has generally only resulted in denial of injunction, leaving the copyright owner to pursue other remedies such as damages or account of profits. Section 171(3) speaks of restricting or preventing the enforcement of copyright. While preventing the enforcement of copyright would mean that all remedies are denied, restricting the enforcement means that only some remedies are refused, such as injunction. This was clearly the approach recommended in *Ashdown* where the court observed *obiter* that, in an appropriate case, a court may deny an injunction but can go on to award damages or account of profits. It noted that 'freedom of expression should not normally carry with it the right to make free use of another's work'.[63]

[57] Case C-275/06 [2008] ECR I-271, paras 29–33.

[58] Case C-314/12 *UPC Telekabel Wien GmbH v Constantin Film Verleih GmbH* [2014] ECR I-0083, para 42.

[59] *Promusicae* (n 57) para 33.

[60] *Telekabel* (n 58) paras 52–53, 56–57.

[61] eg *Twentieth Century Fox Film Corporation v BT plc* [2011] EWHC 1981 (Ch) [163]–[177]; *EMI Records Ltd v BSB Ltd* [2013] EWHC 379 (Ch) [91]–[95].

[62] *Times Newspapers Ltd v UK* (Nos 1 and 2) App nos 3002/03 and 23676/03 (ECtHR, 10 March 2009); *Ahmet Yildirim v Turkey* App no 3111/10 (ECtHR, 18 December 2012).

[63] ibid [44]–[46].

A question may be asked if this is very different from the defences to property torts. Property torts, and especially trespass and nuisance, do have a defence of lawful authority. Does this defence speak of laws that operate to restrict or prevent the enforcement of property rights in the public interest? In relation to trespass the authors of *Winfield* note that there are 'innumerable instances' where officers of the law are authorised to enter land for various reasons, including to search, to take goods, or to arrest a person. They regard these as belonging more to public law than to private law. They provide examples from the Police and Criminal Evidence Act 1984.[64] Beyond these, common law also recognises private persons' ability to enter premises to prevent crime or to arrest a person.[65] Examples of statutes permitting entry onto land include s 2 of the Countryside and Rights of Way Act 2000. There are also defences against a claim of private nuisance under s 122 of the Railways Act, so long as the defendant conforms to the requirements of the statute in using the land for the purpose set out. It is not inconceivable that a person would be able to challenge their A1P1 right against a state action that deprives them of the use of chattels or land. It may well be that the conceptualisation of public interest is better defined, and more formally enshrined within statutes than it is in copyright. But to the extent that these statutes also embody public interest in one form or another, these do not operate very differently from the manner in which CDPA, 171(3) operates.

Might it just be that in copyright the defences are all enumerated in one statute, and in relation to land, these defences are scattered around in different statutes? Might it also be that, in general, there are a similar number of defences that can be pressed into service for both copyright and land? Copyright only exists in the statute and has existed in this form for about three hundred years. In a codified system of property such as copyright it is expected that most defences find expression within the code. When seen together, these do seem too many. But the defences to property torts are spread out broadly in common law and statute. Not seeing them within a single statute makes one believe that the defences are not numerous.

It may well be that public interest guiding defences to both land and copyright operate similarly. However, there is a particular defence to private nuisance which does not find a place in copyright. It is the defence of prescription.

[64] Police and Criminal Evidence Act 1984, ss 17 and 18, under which a police officer can enter premises to conduct a search.

[65] *Handcock v Baker* (1800) 2 Bos & P 260.

It would be worth considering whether a case can be made for this defence also to find a place in copyright.

(d) Prescription

If a nuisance has been carried on for twenty years, then under certain circumstances the right to continue to undertake the action causing nuisance can be legally acquired as an easement by prescription.[66] The action causing nuisance should be performed as of right,[67] meaning without violence, without secrecy, and without permission.[68] For example, in *Lawrence v Fen Tigers Ltd*,[69] the defendant was creating noise which gave rise to a liability in private nuisance. When the claimant sued them, the defendant put forward the defence of prescription. Difficult questions arose as to the time at which the twenty-year period could start running and the certainty in relation to level of noise the creation of which the defendant could be said to have acquired by way of prescription. On the facts it was held that the level of noise had not been sufficient throughout the period of twenty years for the easement by prescription to arise, although in principle it was accepted that an easement of this kind could arise by prescription.[70]

For copyright infringement, there is no defence equivalent to easement by prescription. No matter how long a person uses another person's copyright work, no matter how audacious the use, no defence akin to prescription can be claimed. The doctrine of prescription in land law is based on the policy that land deserves to be used to the best advantage of all persons. If a landowner does not guard against the effects of others around them using their respective lands, then the law does recognise the user's interest as worthy of protection, even if it is to the detriment of the landowner. Beyond the balancing act that takes place for the liability for private nuisance to arise, this policy supports the defence, tipping the balance in favour of the person who in the eyes of the law has a better claim to the continued use of the land.

In copyright this may be useful as an additional solution to the problem of orphaned works. Chapter 3, Section 4(d) put forward an analogy with finders

[66] Jonathan Gaunt and Paul Morgan, *Gale on the Law of Easements* (22nd edn, Sweet & Maxwell 2025) paras 4-175–4-178.

[67] *Bright v Walker* (1834) 150 ER 1057, (1834) 1 Cr M & R 211.

[68] *Gardner v Hodgson's Kingston Brewery Co* [1903] AC 229, 238.

[69] [2014] UKSC 13, [2014] AC 822 [28]–[46].

[70] ibid [140]–[147].

of goods to deal with the issue of orphaned works. An analogy of prescription in copyright could provide an additional and more targeted solution. To remind readers, the Copyright and Rights in Performances (Licensing of Orphan Works) Regulations 2014 define orphan works as works the owner of which cannot be found after a diligent search. A person interested in the work which has become orphaned on these terms can apply to the Comptroller for a licence to exercise one or more rights in it at a fee set by the Comptroller, paid into an account with the government. If the author does not claim the fee within eight years, the Comptroller may use the funds for the advancement of arts and culture.[71]

This regime can easily be modified into a prescription type of arrangement. The law can designate a length of time during which the user will have to have made use of the work, say fifteen years, after which the person acquires a non-exclusive licence to use the work for the remaining term of copyright. The advantage of prescription over finders of goods is that the privilege acquired can be limited to the specific use made of the orphaned work. On the contrary, in finders of goods the claim will be to the entire copyright ownership because of the finder's conduct being regarded as acting like an owner in relation to the orphaned work. Furthermore, no right acquired by prescription is exclusive. Anyone else can acquire that right by the same method. In the same way, any other person might begin publishing a book that may have become orphaned or be out of print. To this extent, a regime akin to prescription will have a similar effect to the 2014 Regulations, but the difference is that the acquisition of the licence is automatic after the designated time, just as the acquisition of the easement is in prescription.

3. Limits to Use

In intellectual property statutes, one of the most pressing limitations can be in relation to its exploitation. For example, patents are subject to compulsory licensing under Patents Act 1977, s 48, whereby a person can make an application to the Comptroller requesting the grant of a licence from a patentee. The grounds to be considered are the patentee not working the patent commercially or meeting the demand, and so on. Evidently, there is a public interest underlying each of these grounds. In the United Kingdom this power has been used sparingly in relation to patents. The authors of *Copinger* provide the

[71] Copyright and Rights in Performances (Licensing of Orphan Works) Regulations 2014, regs 6, 10, and 13.

circumstances under which compulsory licences can be granted in relation to a copyright work.[72] However, the power to grant these licences has not been invoked frequently.[73]

A much more prevalent way of limiting the exploitation of the rights is through collecting societies, or what are called licensing bodies under CDPA, s 116(2). These societies consist of membership from copyright owners organised by the nature of the work such as musical work, literary work, and so on, or based on the rights managed. Although these collecting societies are self-governing, the Copyright Tribunal exercises significant control over their operations under Chapter VII of the CDPA. Since these societies are de facto entities issuing licences to users of the copyright works they manage, the Copyright Tribunal has the jurisdiction to decide any complaints as to too high a fee charged, or licence denied. This is an indirect way in which the CDPA exerts control over the exploitation of copyright works.

However, limits on use are not unique to copyright. There are many limitations on the use of land too. Planning laws such as Town and Country Planning Act 1990 are only the beginning. But depending on where a person's land is situated, a landowner can be subject to regulation on listed buildings or other conservation or environmental laws.[74] Personal property can also be subject to use limitations, especially personal property that can cause harm to others. For example, a person who wishes to own guns must follow the Firearms Act 1968. A person who wants to store or use dangerous chemicals must comply with the Health and Safety at Work etc. Act 1974 and Control of Substances Hazardous to Health Guidance, and so on. Again, it might be the same problem that while most of the limitations are found in one place under the CDPA, they are scattered around in several statutes in relation to land and chattels. But, in general, the fact that limitations can be placed on the ability of a property owner to use the thing is common to both tangible things and copyright.

4. Summary

Property theorists speaking of copyright point to the number and nature of defences to copyright infringement to argue that copyright is unlike a property

[72] Gwylim Harbottle and others, *Copinger and Skone James on Copyright* (19th edn, Sweet & Maxwell 2025) paras 32-01, 32-02.

[73] An example is compulsory licences in relation to television guides under Broadcasting Act 1990, s 176. See Bently and others (n 33) 334–35.

[74] See eg Planning (Listed Buildings and Conservation Areas) Act 1990 and Localism Act 2011.

right. This chapter endeavoured to show that both defences and limits placed on use and exploitation of copyright are comparable to those found within land law and personal property law. Section 2 dealt with defences. It argued that there are some defences like licences which are common to both copyright infringement and property torts. There are others, like the fair dealing defences, which offer a great deal of flexibility to the judges in ascertaining whether the defence is established. Although property torts do not have defences of this kind, this chapter demonstrated how the flexibility and balancing of competing interests seen in private nuisance is eminently comparable to the approach to establishing fair dealing defences. It was further argued that the difference is only one of timing—whether before or after the liability arises. The chapter went on to consider the public interest defence to copyright infringement, which allows a court to consider a rule of law that originates in common law, statute, or fundamental human rights, to prevent or restrict the enforcement of copyright. It compared this defence with the defence to trespass and private nuisance that are based on the authority of the law, all of which have an element of public interest underlying them. It moved on to the defence of prescription to private nuisance, which does not find a place in copyright law. It showed how an analogy with prescription could address the issue with orphaned works. Section 3 compared the limits on use and exploitation of copyright with the limits placed on use of land, such as planning laws, and on the use of chattels, such as hazardous substances, firearms, and so on.

7

Derivative Interests in Copyright

1. Introduction

Worthington argues that of all the characteristics, what defines property is 'the possibility that an owner can share with others' by granting 'derivative or secondary interests in their property to others without giving up their own ownership'.[1] She regards this as the essence of sharing, recognising that the owner is constrained as a result of sharing and the person who shares with the owner gains something they did not have before. Derivative interests originate with the initial right holder. One may see this as a natural consequence of the powers and privileges that one acquires. In their discretion, the owner can either exercise the privileges themselves or grant the privilege of use to someone else.[2] If there are no privileges one can exercise but all one can do is transfer the whole interest to someone else, this does not amount to sharing as nothing remains with the initial right holder. While the ability of a resource to be put to use is a vital indicator of a property right, the ability to create a derivative interest for the use of the resource for someone else is an equally vital attribute of a property right.

The number and the variety of derivative interests are influenced by the content of the subject matter of property rights. Content that is more rivalrous lends itself to fewer interests. This is because maintaining exclusivity in the practical sense of the term becomes impossible if other interests are recognised. Land as a resource offers a wider variety of property interests than chattels do because of its relatively less rivalrous nature. One can speak meaningfully of an easement to walk over a person's land as a recognised form of property interest. But one can hardly speak of an easement of any kind over a pencil. While leasehold interests are commonplace in land, the existence of

[1] Sarah Worthington, 'Revolutions in Personal Property: Redrawing the Common Law's Conceptual Map' in Sarah Worthington, Andrew Robertson, and Graham Virgo (eds), *Revolution and Evolution in Private Law* (Hart 2018) 228.

[2] See Chapter 3, Section 3 for a discussion on privileges and Section 4 on powers.

Copyright as Personal Property. Poorna Mysoor, Oxford University Press. © Poorna Mysoor 2025.
DOI: 10.1093/9780191954962.003.0007

chattel leases is not widely accepted.[3] A landowner can grant the whole of the exclusive possession to someone else by creating a lease or choose to grant the use of a walkway as an easement. *Numerus clausus* dictates that the constituents of the interest granted, be it a lease or an easement, be consistent in their definition and remit, so that any obligations they seek to impose on third parties are not whimsical or arbitrary.[4] Does the relatively less rivalrous nature of copyright mean that it is capable of being shared by the copyright owner by creating derivative interests? Can these interests be designed in a manner that complies with the *numerus clausus* principle? These questions have not received much scholarly attention.

As discussed in Chapter 1, Section 6, *numerus clausus* is a principle that informs the ontology of a property right—from its substantive content to the definition of rights and the shape and contours of property interests created. It encapsulates the idea that the number of property interests that can be created is finite, and that it is not up to the property owners to create new property interests. *Numerus clausus* influences all aspects of property rights that affect third parties by imposing duties on them. Until now, this monograph has dealt with ownership interest—the interest that represents the whole of copyright interest as it comes into existence at the time of first and independent acquisition. Chapter 3 of this book showed that as copyright is acquired, there is an exclusionary signal that is sent to the rest of the world requiring them to keep off. Once the copyright owner has acquired the ownership interest in copyright, they acquire the power to scoop out the copyright interest in many different ways at their discretion and grant it to others.

If the interest granted is the entirety of the ownership interest it is called an assignment, whereby the rest of the world will begin to owe the exclusionary duties to the assignee. As such, if P, the copyright owner of a poem, assigns the copyright in the poem to Q, then the rest of the world knows exactly what obligations they now owe to Q because these will be the same obligations as they owed previously to P. There are no surprises here. However, if the copyright owner had the power and freedom to scoop out from the copyright interest any part in any manner whatsoever and grant it to anyone else and if these interests were to be recognised as property interests, then the rest of the world

[3] Some scholars believe that the only legal property interest in chattels is ownership. Simon Douglas, *Liability for Wrongful Interferences with Chattels* (Hart 2011) 33–36. Others believe that it is ownership and possession. Graeme Watt, 'The Proprietary Effect of a Chattel Lease' [2003] Conv 6.

[4] Law of Property Act 1925, s 1(1) is usually pointed out as the statutory embodiment of *numerus clausus* in land in English law.

might be taken by surprise as to how they should keep off from the new interest created. This is why the law of property closely monitors the property interests that are less than ownership to ensure that these can be granted only in defined ways using *numerus clausus* as the guiding principle. This chapter seeks to address what these interests are and the extent to which the principle of *numerus clausus* affects the contours of these interests. It begins with situations where the statute expressly provides for the derivative interests, namely assignments and licences, and security interests as a sub-species of assignments, moving on to interests that arise in equity and due to commercial necessity, such as options and rights of pre-emption and, finally, a possible new interest entailing the right to receive royalties.

It begins in Section 2 to consider copyright assignments. If the copyright statutes had recognised the possibility only of the entire copyright interest being assignable, this section would have been unremarkable. However, s 90(2)(a) and (b) of the CDPA also recognises partial assignments that can be limited as to the exclusive rights or as to duration. This provision grants the copyright owner sweeping powers to slice and dice the ownership interest, which is remarkable in its impact especially on third parties. This section discusses the implication of this, including on the third parties.

Section 3 goes on to consider licences—exclusive and non-exclusive. Land law and personal property law regard licences as a personal interest. In general, there would have been no need for licences to be discussed in this chapter because they are not property interests. However, CDPA, s 90(4) states that a licence is binding on every successor in title except a purchaser for value without actual or constructive notice. Being personal interests, licences granted in relation to tangible things are not binding on successors in title. This, together with other provisions in the CDPA, begs the question how this provision impacts the nature of copyright licences and whether a case can be made for regarding copyright licences as an equitable property interest.

Section 4 discusses security interests in copyright. Some jurisdictions have subsumed intellectual property rights including copyright within a separate statutory regime governing personal property secured transactions as a whole. However, the United Kingdom has not charted this path. This section examines the implications of this. It also considers the possibility of copyright licences being put forward as a security interest and the stumbling block to doing so.

Section 5 moves on to discuss equitable interests of options and rights of pre-emption. These interests are especially popular in the publishing and film industries. Commentators believe that the equitable rules that apply to these kinds of interests in land also apply to copyright, making it an equitable property right. This means that options and rights of pre-emption would be binding on all except a purchaser for value without actual or constructive notice. This section examines what these rules of equity are and what this means in terms of its impact on third parties.

Finally, Section 6 considers the question of what happens to the right to receive royalties if a copyright owner assigns their copyright interest in exchange for the payment of royalties. If this assignee further assigns the interest to someone else, the right to receive royalties has been held to be only a contractual right not binding on the successor in title of the first assignee. This is clearly problematic. This section discusses various methods drawn from other areas of private law to address the problem. Finally, it considers whether it should be a new property interest deserving of recognition.

2. Assignments

Assignability, or the ability to part with the whole of the interest, is one of the most fundamental hallmarks of a property right.[5] It is possible to assign a debt, but not one's friendships. Not all intangible assets may be transferable. Historically, the belief had been that no intangible assets could be transferred. Over time, equity intervened to enable assignments. These limitations have now been overcome in copyright by the copyright statutes expressly providing for the assignability of copyright.[6] Section 90(2) of the CDPA provides for partial assignability of copyright interest, recognising the ability of the copyright owner to divide up copyright interest in seemingly unlimited ways. Subsection (a) below deals with what this means for partial assignments to be property interests. Section 90(3) of the CDPA requires the grant of an assignment to be in accordance with certain formalities, that is, writing signed by or on behalf of the assignor. Where these formalities are not complied with, by the operation of general principles of equity the assignment becomes equitable. In these situations, the legal title remains with the copyright owner with an equitable interest generated in the counterparty. Subsection (b) below deals with some of these situations.

[5] See generally Shyamkrishna Balganesh, 'Alienability and Copyright Law' in Helena Howe and Jonathan Griffiths (eds), *Concepts of Property in Intellectual Property Law* (CUP 2015).

[6] Law of Property Act 1925, s 136 seems to have no application, but doubts remain as to conditional assignments.

(a) Partial Assignment of Copyright

Historically, copyright interest had been thought to be indivisible. This meant that the assignment of only the whole of copyright interest was possible. However, this changed under the Copyright Act 1956. Section 90(2)(a) of CDPA permits the assignment to be partial as to the exclusionary rights and s 90(2)(b) as to the duration. There is no provision for partial assignment as to territory within the United Kingdom, although assignment of rights limited to different countries internationally is possible.[7] Partial assignees have the same powers of enforcement in relation to their interest as their assignor had. They can also access a gamut of remedies available to copyright owners upon a successful finding of infringement. If we are to interpret *numerus clausus* for derivative copyright interests to mean a closed list of these interests within the CDPA, partial assignments do not violate this principle by their mere existence because of the express provisions of the CDPA. But the extensive powers of dividing up the copyright interest are unique and cannot fully be compared with any interest that is known to land or chattels. The unpredictability of the way in which the copyright interest can be divided up makes this an issue of *numerus clausus*. Let us deal with partial assignment as to exclusionary rights and then as to duration.

(i) Partial assignment as to exclusionary rights

This part examines situations where a copyright owner assigns one or more rights to another person where the transfer means that the copyright owner is no longer able to exercise the assigned right for the rest of the duration of the copyright. It follows that the interest that the assignee acquires is also valid for the remaining duration of copyright and the assignee holds the title to this interest, acquiring immunity from challenge by the rest of the world. This means that the interest that the assignee acquires is also a property interest enforceable against the whole world. The partial assignee steps into the shoes of the assignor to the extent of the interest assigned. This gives them the same power to sue for infringement and access remedies as the assignor, but only to the extent of the interest assigned.[8] Since the assignment is provided for by the statute, if the formalities are followed, the assignment will be legal, and the assignee acquires a legal interest good against the whole world. It goes without saying that the partial copyright interest (reversionary interest) of the assignor

[7] The authors of *Copinger* suggest that assignment to different countries within the United Kingdom or smaller areas should not be permitted. See Gwilym Harbottle and others, *Copinger and Skone James on Copyright* (19th edn, Sweet & Maxwell 2025) para 4–115.

[8] The CDPA deals with this by defining copyright owner broadly. See CDPA, s 173(1).

will also be good against the whole world as regards the interest retained. The successor in title of the partial assignor's reversionary interest takes subject to the partial assignee's interest. If the assignor's successor in title who takes after the partial assignment exercises the rights granted to the partial assignee, they may be liable for copyright infringement. The issue is whether the assignee's interest complies with *numerus clausus.*

It helps to understand first the interest being created. Although s 90(2)(a) speaks of the exclusionary rights, in practice copyright owners need not assign each right together with all the different ways in which the right can be exercised. For example, this author, P, having written this monograph, can choose to assign to her publisher, Q, the right to publish the book in hardback. This means that under the CDPA, the specific rights assigned are the right to make copies under s 17(1) and the right to issue copies to the public under s 18(1). But the entirety of these rights is not transferred. Only the part of these rights as it relate to hardback versions of this book are transferred. This assignment will not include publishing the book in paperback or eBook versions. This assignment between P and Q will be valid under the CDPA because s 90(2)(a) speaks of 'things the copyright owner has the exclusive right to do' and does not refer to them by the provisions that enumerate these rights.[9]

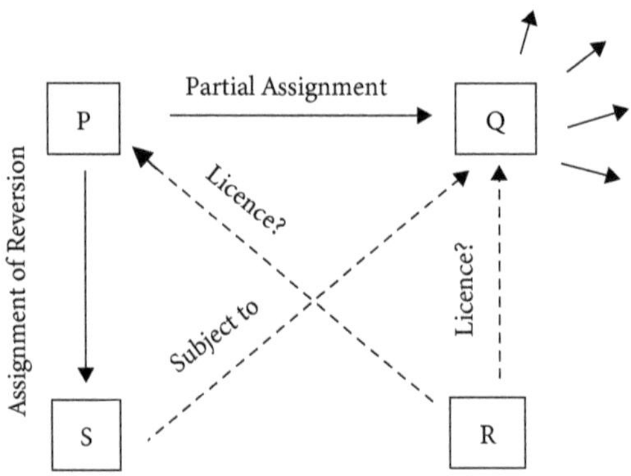

Figure 7.1 Basic property triangle

Figure 7.1 depicts the transactions in the form of a basic property triangle.[10] Upon receiving the partial assignment to publish the book in hardback, Q will

[9] See Harbottle and others (n 7) para 5-108, with references to Parliamentary debates that this was the meaning intended.

[10] This author has drawn inspiration from the work of Ben McFarlane, who uses the property triangle to illustrate many of the issues surrounding property rights. Ben McFarlane, *The Structure of Property Law* (Hart 2008) 3.

be able to enforce these rights against any third party who infringes this right (indicated by arrows around Q in Figure 7.1). P's own ability to enforce all the rights retained against the rest of the world will remain unchanged. Suppose R wants to publish a chapter of P's book in an anthology on personal property. R will need to exercise reproduction and distribution rights in P's book. For this, R will need to investigate who are all the parties from whom R needs a licence. Potentially, both P and Q will need to consent. If R is a potential infringer who is alleged to have copied certain non-literal elements of P's work, then P and Q will both be able to enforce the right of reproduction against R, because P's work is an authorial work whose content and form are both protected. R will be in for a surprise that R is not only liable to P but also to Q, both of whom can enforce any of the powerful remedies against R. Trespassory liability could therefore become problematic.

Strictly speaking, partial assignments do not give rise to successor liability in the true sense of the term in the example above. After granting the partial assignment, suppose that P assigns their reversionary copyright interest to S. S will be a successor in title to P's interest, which already excludes the interest P had assigned to Q. Vis-à-vis Q, S's liability is like any other third party. But a similar analysis can be followed. If S were to proceed with the transaction, S would take subject to Q's rights. This would mean that S will not be able to publish P's book in hardback version. Before proceeding with the transaction, just like R, S as a successor in title to P's interest would be well advised to conduct their own due diligence because S cannot rule out the possibility that P has partially assigned away some rights.

For both R and S, the question is the same—what interest does Q have? Given that P has such an expansive freedom to carve out the partial assignment in any shape or form, R and S will have to expend a great deal of resources in investigating the extent of the reversion P has. Simply knowing that P has granted a partial assignment will not do. R and S will have to examine the assignment document and understand the words used and the extent of their interpretation. In this context, the clarity of the interpretation given to the exclusionary rights by the courts also makes a big difference.[11] The illustration given above is a simpler version of the reality. Suppose P has assigned the right to publish the paperback to Q1 and the right to publish eBooks to Q2. Let us say that the assignment to Q2 is unclear as to the kind of eBooks—whether it is for publication in e-format to go on a database with downloadable chapters or whether it is for publication of the book on an e-reader platform where the text

[11] Chapter 4, Section 2(b) discusses the need for the definition of a right itself having to be clear.

cannot be separated from the platform. R may be in for a surprise to find that they need to seek a licence from so many persons with potentially cryptic descriptions of entitlements. S may also be in for a nasty surprise in ascertaining what it is that they are acquiring from P and, importantly, what they should or should not do to avoid infringing any of the rights of Q1 or Q2. This may yet be simpler than some of the quagmire that surrounds the commercial transactions in the film and music industries. Mulligan's work on the US experience of fragmentation of copyright and the confounding hurdles that it presents is highly instructive.[12]

The best-case scenario for R is to be able to approach only P for a licence, and for S to be able to acquire the entire copyright interest from P. This would mean that no partial assignment would be allowed. Historically, there had been a bar on partial assignments, but this does not reflect the prevailing commercial reality in any of the industries for copyright works, be it publishing, music, theatre, or films. Partial assignments enhance a copyright owner's ability to extract the maximum value out of their work by negotiating precise arrangements with different parties. Would it make things better for the law to prescribe more defined ways of entering into assignment transactions, by requiring that a partial assignment can only be of a right in its entirety? The information costs associated with these transactions would certainly be lessened in comparison. This would mean, in our example above, that P will be required to only assign the entirety of the reproduction right and the distribution right. If this were the case, then R and S could proceed with the certainty that any partial assignment that P may have granted takes a particular form. While R will only have to seek a licence from Q, and S will be looking at a reversion that is minus the rights that P has assigned. However, this might again not match with commercial reality because a person specialised in paper publishing may not have the expertise in publishing eBooks, and the copyright owner will lose out on finding the right kind of publishers for their work. Even if partial assignments give much wider freedom to copyright owners, it may not be possible to do away with partial assignments. One needs to balance coherence and predictability on the one hand, with commercial demand on the other.

One may wonder whether the ability to carve out discrete uses of a resource and granting them to another person is unique to copyright. Is it not also found in the context of land? For example, F, a freeholder, can carve out an easement of right of way on their land and grant it to A, and carve out an easement of a

[12] Christina Mulligan, 'A Numerus Clausus Principle for Intellectual Property' (2013) 80 Tenn L Rev 235.

car park on F's land and grant it to B. Assuming that all other requirements of easement are satisfied, this means that F has granted the same kind of property interest, namely an easement, in relation to different rights over land, namely a right of way and a right to park a car. Indeed, it would be possible to further refine these rights—an easement of right of way only for walking in favour of A1 and for driving vehicles on the same path in favour of A2. Both these easements will be enforceable because these will pass the test of certainty. If the easement arises in relation to a freehold estate, it can last for as long as freehold lasts, that is, indefinitely. How different is F's ability to carve out different rights from P's ability to carve out her copyright in the example above?

It may be argued that an easement has a particular transactional design which is prescribed by the law and encapsulated in the celebrated case of *Re Ellenborough Park*.[13] The need for the existence of definable dominant and servient land, the use having to accommodate the land, and so on imbue the contours of the transaction with predictability. The subject matter of the grant could have been potentially unlimited, but common law requires its expansion to take place incrementally by analogy. McFarlane points this out to be a manifestation of *numerus clausus*,[14] for its ability to bring about coherence and predictability. One may begin with the core uses of land, which could include the ability to walk over it for access, to store things such as vehicles, to engage in recreational activities over it, and so on. If the core uses are rendered predictable, making these uses more specific in the easements (as to walking or driving as above) does not render them an impermissible way of slicing the interest in land. The specific use will not be alien to the core use but can be arrived at by analogy. If one wants to ascertain the specifics of the use permitted by an easement, in any event one must examine the language of the grant even in the context of land. This does not make the easement non-compliant with *numerus clausus*.

An analogy with this mechanism may be possible with partial assignment of rights in copyright. Here, the transactional design is much simpler, requiring only that a right be transferred irrevocably. As to the subject matter of the interest, it requires that a right drawn from the suite of exclusionary rights of the copyright owner be transferred. These rights correspond to the core uses in the copyright context, that is, to copy, to issue copies to the public, to perform, and so on. The core uses are limited by statute as opposed to the common law

[13] [1956] Ch 131.

[14] Ben McFarlane, 'The Numerus Clausus Principle and Covenants Relating to Land' in Susan Bright (ed), *Modern Studies in Property Law*, vol 6 (Hart 2011) 313.

incrementalism as in land law, but bringing a certain predictability all the same. Any refinement (such as paperback or hardback publishing) further limits the core uses such as right to copy and right to issue copies, as opposed to being alien to them. If one wishes to ascertain the specific use permitted by a partial assignment, the need to examine the language of the grant should similarly not make it opposed to *numerus clausus*.

If doubts still remain as to whether the interests to which partial assignments give rise are unpredictably variable, we may also test their ability for compliance with the criteria in *National Provincial Bank v Ainsworth*.[15] Despite scepticism that the criteria have never been used to create a new interest in tangible assets,[16] it may not hold true for intangible assets. The need for definability and identifiability by third parties not only refers to clarity in drafting of the partial assignment but also in ensuring that there are no overlapping rights that are assigned to different parties. Since assignment enables the doing of a thing exclusively (as opposed to licences, which can enable non-exclusive use), the definition of partial assignment without impinging on rights already assigned is crucial. One of the reasons why partial assignment of a right in its entirety does not work is that the right to make copies underlies the exercise of rights such as the right to make an adaptation. The copy made when one makes an adaptation of a work will be a non-literal copy. If the copyright owner partially assigns these rights to different persons, it renders the partial assignment of the right to adapt the work without substance. An assignment of the right to make copies can be implied, but that will be an equitable assignment, which will be discussed in Subsection 2(b) below. To some extent, avoiding overlaps is also a matter of drafting,[17] and the convention in the relevant industry.[18] If the partial assignment has certainty of language,[19] it will be 'capable in its nature of assumption by third parties', enabling its further assignment by the assignee. Therefore, Q in Figure 7.1 should be able to assign the partially assigned interest to someone else. Since these assignments are for the remainder of the copyright term, there is no problem with permanence or stability.

[15] [1965] AC 1175, 1247–48.

[16] William Swadling, 'Property—General Principles' in Andrew Burrows (ed), *English Private Law* (3rd edn, OUP 2013) paras 4.26–4.31.

[17] See Harbottle and others (n 7) paras 4-95–4-102, who speak of interpretation of assignments and other issues that might arise in relation to assignments, such as different versions of a work being assigned to different persons.

[18] In *British Actors Film Company Ltd v Glover* [1918] 1 KB 299, a clause that restricted the assignment to 'provincial professional performances' was held sufficiently clear within the relevant industry to be enforceable.

[19] Morgan J observed *obiter* in *Crosstown Music v Rive Droite Music* [2012] Ch 68 [94] that if the language of a partial assignment under CDPA, s 90(2)(a) satisfies the test of certainty, it should be acceptable for passing the interest.

In any event, despite the analogy, the land law situation may be distinguished from copyright because of the existence of registration, which enables easy access to information on the easement. This will be the case even if partial assignments comply with the *Ainsworth* criteria. It is not difficult to see that the search and verification costs of both R and S in Figure 7.1 can be reduced by a robust registration system for copyright transactions. Benefits of registration, however, should be separated from benefits of *numerus clausus.* Registration can only give publicity to transactions but not eliminate the need for investigation altogether. What *numerus clausus* brings are coherence and predictability to transactions, which registration alone cannot achieve.

Supplementing compliance with *numerus clausus* with the availability of a system of registration of derivative copyright interests might solve the problem. However, as noted in Chapter 1, Section 3, international treaty obligations mean that introducing a registration system is not a matter for individual nations. Article 5(2) of the Berne Convention provides that the enjoyment and exercise of copyright shall not be subject to formalities. A system of registration of transactions might call for creative interpretation of 'exercising' copyright, as it can potentially be argued that granting partial assignment is one of the ways in which the owner exercises their copyright.[20] In the absence of registration, prospective licensees like R and prospective assignees like S in Figure 7.1 will have to depend on the copyright owners like P to disclose the prior interests. Their non-disclosure could vitiate the contract for misrepresentation, which offers some deterrent effect. In many of the modern transactions these can take the form of representations and warranties that the assignors like P will have to provide. Parties like R and S may also consider taking out insurance to deal with the risks arising from the uncertainties of the scope of assignments. A combination of these factors seems to explain why there is a surprisingly low number of cases involving copyright partial assignees that result in litigation (at least those that reach the courts and are reported). Yet, an unavoidable conclusion is that without a robust system of registration, transactions in copyright industries are laden with high costs, which eventually get passed on to consumers.

(ii) Partial assignments limited by time

Section 90(2)(b) of the CDPA provides that an assignment can be of limited duration and does not have to last for the whole of the remainder of the copyright term. This provision seems perplexing. Assignment in general law means

[20] Scholars have argued for reconsideration of formalities in copyright. See eg Stef van Gompel, *Formalities in Copyright Law: An Analysis of Their History, Rationales and Possible Future* (Kluwer Law International 2011).

the irrevocable transfer of an interest.[21] One can see that the statute was trying to capture two ways of slicing the rights—vertically with rights and horizontally with time. Although in equity partial assignments are not unknown, it is difficult to reconcile with the general law the notion of the assigned interest reverting to the assignor after the assigned period expires. In general, the difficulty is not that the interest reverts to the grantor. Even in land law, once a lease expires the leased interest reverts to the landlord. The difficulty is with calling it an assignment and attaching all the incidents of an assignment to it. The horizontal slicing appears more consistent with exclusive licences provided for under CDPA, s 92. Indeed, on the surface a partial assignment as to time seems indistinguishable from a limited term exclusive licence. There are good reasons why the difference must be appreciated. For this reason, it is also important to know how to distinguish between these two. This matter is dealt with under Subsection 3(a) below, once the salient features of an exclusive licence have been laid out.

It is worth examining the scope of a time-limited partial assignment itself, without comparing it to other transactions. It helps to refer back to Figure 7.1, but suppose the partial assignment to Q had also been limited in time for, say, five years. Then the only difference would have been that P's reversion would include the prospect of the interest assigned to Q reverting to P. Thus, when P assigns all of their interest to S, S will be a successor in title. Upon the expiration of five years Q's interest would then revert to S and not P. But if the assignment to S was of all of P's interest but partial in being time limited, say, for seven years, then Q's interest would first revert to S at the end of five years and then S's interest to P after seven years. The ability to grant assignments of indeterminable duration adds another layer of complexity to the problems discussed under Subsection 2(a)(i) above. One such can be seen in the case discussed below.

This was squarely at issue in *Crosstown Music v Rive Droite Music*.[22] The partial assignment in this case incorporated what was called a 'floating reverter' clause. By virtue of this clause the rights assigned would automatically revert to the defendant assignors if the claimant assignee defaulted on material clauses of the assignment and did not cure the default within a specified time of being notified.[23] It was argued that this clause was not in compliance with CDPA, s

[21] It has been held in the context of equitable assignment that the intention required is to divest the thing immediately. See eg *Finlan v Eyton Morris Winfield* [2007] EWHC 915 (Ch), [2007] 4 All ER 143 [33].

[22] [2012] Ch 68.

[23] ibid [2], [24].

90(2)(b) for the following reasons: first, an assignment must be absolute, in a similar way to the assignment of legal choses in action provided for under s 136 of the Law of Property Act 1925. In an assignment for a limited duration under s 90(2)(b), there can be no automatic reversion but only a contractual obligation to reassign. Secondly, even if reversion were possible, the duration of the partial assignment depended on a future uncertain event. As a transaction that transfers proprietary interest in copyright, certainty should be at its centre. However, the Court of Appeal upheld the clause as being compliant with s 90(2)(b) as a partial assignment clause.

Although no mention of it was made, it is clear that this case was about *numerus clausus*. The claimants were trying to convince the court that the clause in the agreement did not fit into a shape that was acceptable under s 90(2)(b). With the first argument, the attack seemed to draw an analogy with mortgages, where a covenant to reassign is required; a conditional assignment will not do, according to the general law.[24] However, the court pointed out that the CDPA, providing clearly for assignment of copyright, makes it impossible to read it in the light of s 136 of the Law of Property Act 1925. It held that the language of s 90(2)(b) is consistent with an assignment for limited duration to automatically revert to the assignor without the need for reassignment. The court referred to the Copyright Act 1911, which had expressly provided for copyright to revert to the first owner of copyright for the last twenty-five years of the term of copyright, to enable copyright owners to renegotiate contracts if their works became commercially successful at a later stage. The court also referred to the case law under the previous copyright legislation where the parties had entered into similar arrangements.[25] What the court failed to see is that the transaction was more in the nature of a conditional assignment than a partial assignment. The issue was not so much on the auto-revert clause as it was on the revert clause being conditional on certain conduct of the assignee, that is, the assignee keeping appropriate accounts.

With the second argument, the claimants seemed to be trying to draw an analogy with leases, although no express mention has been made of this in the judgment.[26] Just as a lease over land cannot have a duration that is dependent

[24] See Section 4 below for more discussion on mortgaging copyright.

[25] [2012] Ch 68 [37]–[38]. The cases referred to were *Messager v BBC* [1929] AC 151, 155–56; *Loew's Inc v Littler* [1958] Ch 650, 663; and *Mother Bertha Music Ltd v Bourne Music Ltd* [1997] EMLR 457, 479–80.

[26] Crosstown did contend that s 90(2) could not cover the assignment of copyright that was 'for a period that was not fixed or certain, was unknown and could not be known at the date of the original assignment', [2012] Ch 68 [19].

on a future uncertain event,[27] the duration of a partial assignment could likewise not be based on an uncertain event. The facts of this case demonstrate why a clause as to uncertain duration can pose difficulties. Certain songwriters entered into the partial assignment at issue with Rive Droite (RD) that incorporated the reversion clause linked to material breach on RD's part. The breach alleged by the songwriters was that RD's accounting was flawed and that under the assignment they were owed higher amounts of royalty. RD later assigned this interest to Crosstown (C) without the floating reverter clause. C rightly argued that RD had a contractual obligation which could not bind C, but did not identify the obligation as such.[28] C should have argued that the obligation breached was contractual, and not the obligation of having to reassign copyright upon breach of this obligation. The court was right that automatic reversion makes reassignment unnecessary. But C had not assumed responsibility for the accounting irregularities that led to breach of accounting obligation. It is even more telling that RD went into administration subsequent to the assignment to C, which may speak of mismanagement within RD. The court went by the reason that C took the assignment from RD having knowledge of this reverter clause. Regarding the duration of the partial assignment, Mummery LJ's view was that nothing in the wide language of s 90(2) is there a requirement insisting on the assignment duration to be fixed or certain or known to the parties at the date of the original assignment.[29] The other judges agreed with Mummery LJ in holding that the language of s 90(2)(b) does not allow the courts to place any further restrictions on the certainty of the duration. Overall, in giving this kind of interpretation to s 90(2)(b), *Crosstown* may have gone too far.

If one were to defend this decision, one might argue that what C acquired was an interest with the vulnerability for reversion for material breach. One may cite the *nemo dat* rule here—no one can give more than they have. However, this statement is only partially correct. Vulnerability for reversion is built into s 90(2)(b) in that the interest under an assignment that is for a term less than the copyright term will have to revert upon the expiration of that term. A person who acquires an interest under a partial assignment as to time cannot complain about the reversion. It is not an obligation impressed on the assignee, but simply that the term of the assignment expires. There is no issue with the *nemo dat* rule applying to partial assignments limited by term. But the issue is the term being dependent on a future uncertain event.

[27] eg *Prudential Assurance Co v London Residuary Body* [1992] 2 AC 386, 392, where a purported lease granted over land until it was required for road widening was held not to be a lease.

[28] [2012] Ch 68 [24], [27].

[29] [2012] Ch 68 [36].

Even if s 90(2)(b) does not say so, partial assignments with duration measured by uncertain events should not be permissible as a matter of *numerus clausus*. A partial assignment as to duration is not the same as a conditional assignment, especially if the condition is based on an uncertain event. Commentators regard conditional assignments as not compliant with s 90(1) and therefore giving rise to only an equitable assignment.[30] Furthermore, making the duration of partial assignment dependent on the contractual breach of the original assignee cannot have been contemplated by the language of s 90(2)(b).

In *Crosstown*, C had also received notice to remedy RD's breaches. C argued before the court that the notice for curing breach was out of time, with which the court disagreed. It was an established fact that RD had gone into administration and therefore was not going to cure the breach. In effect this meant that even if C was not itself in breach, if it wished to prevent reversion it should have done everything to cure the breach by setting the accounts right. Even if C had been capable of curing the breach, forcing this obligation upon C seems to suggest that in the guise of enforcing the terms of a partial assignment, the court was in reality trying to enforce a contractual obligation against a non-party to the contract (C instead of RD). It just so happened in this case that the third party was aware of the contractual obligation,[31] and it was objective enough for them to assume. If the obligation happened to be such that only the original assignee could perform, making it binding on a non-party could create problems of its own. For example, if L, a lyricist assigns the copyright in their lyrics to a singer M so long as M remains L's employee, and if M assigns this interest to N without this clause and quits employment with L, then N has no way to cure this breach to retain the copyright interest even if N had notice of this condition.

Even if a conditional assignment is regarded a new property interest, it does not meet the *Ainsworth* criteria. The definability and identifiability may be achieved by clear drafting to some extent, but the duration rendered uncertain because of a future uncertain event will, by its very nature, make the interest being assigned uncertain. It makes no difference if the uncertainty is caused by an event not within the contracting parties' control (eg a period until the war ends) or if it is within the original assignee's powers to not let the uncertain event happen (as in this case, the breach of a term of the assignment). The term

[30] Harbottle and others (n 7) para 4–231, fn 786.
[31] Even if it had been an equitable assignment, it would have been binding on C, who was a successor in title of the interest with notice. More on equitable assignments in Subsection 2(b) below.

will fall foul of definability and identifiability. Therefore, it should be possible to interpret the 'part' in s 90(2)(b) to mean a part that is certain, based on the general law that underpins certainty as a fundamental requirement of all property interests. After all, it is based on general law that courts come to the conclusion that an exclusive licence is not a property interest, although the statute says nothing to this effect.

(b) Equitable Assignments

There are many instances where assignments become equitable. The most obvious is where the formalities of an assignment are not complied with, but the intention to assign is clear. Based on the doctrine of advancement, the court will treat as done what ought to have been done.[32] Courts can order specific performance to perfect the title of the equitable assignee. This is a relatively straightforward application of equitable principles which arise after the work has been created. The more complicated scenarios arise in relation to copyright entitlement of commissioned works where the work has yet to come into existence.

In general, the statute determines the authorship of a work. Section 11(1) of the CDPA states that the author of a work is the first owner of the work, and under s 9(1) states that an author is the person who creates it. Under s 11(2), it is possible for authors to alter the first ownership rule under an employment contract. If a person commissions a work to be created by another person, the default rule of the author being the first owner applies. If the person commissioning wishes to acquire the copyright in the work, to the extent that the commissioned work comes into existence on the occurrence of a future event, copyright in it can be regarded as future copyright under CDPA s 91(2).[33] It is possible to grant a legal interest in future copyright under s 91(1) to the person commissioning if the assignment is in writing and signed by the person assigning, that is, the future author. This assignment is normally incorporated within the commissioning agreement. If the agreement is unclear, then the rule of author as first owner applies. However, having given consideration and being the reason for the work to have come into existence, the person

[32] An illustrative case being *Walsh v Lonsdale* (1882) 21 Ch D 9.

[33] Future copyright should be distinguished from future assignment of an existing work. While CDPA, s 91(1) makes the assignment of future copyright legal, future assignment is equitable. See Harbottle and others (n 7) para 4-219.

commissioning could be excluded from exercising any of the rights in relation to the work. Courts see this as pointing to an implied intention of the parties to permit the person commissioning to exercise some rights in relation to the commissioned work. Depending on the unexpressed joint intention of the parties and the surrounding circumstances, courts may imply a non-exclusive licence, an exclusive licence, or, in rare cases, an assignment.[34] By definition, an implied assignment will lack writing and therefore it becomes an equitable assignment.

Another way of putting this is that the first ownership rule vests the legal title in the owner, but the beneficial ownership of the work will remain with the person commissioning the work. In this sense, one may also argue that the author holds the work on an implied trust for the person commissioning the work. The nature of the trust that comes into existence is more akin to constructive trust because it is arguable that the law imposes this trust to avoid situations of unconscionability.[35] Whereas the implied assignment reasoning grounds the result in the intention of the parties, the implied trust reasoning grounds it in unconscionability. Courts have preferred the implied assignment approach.

Consider *R Griggs v Evans*,[36] depicted in Figure 7.2. It illustrates how an equitable assignment arises in practice and what the consequences are for the different parties involved. Griggs (G), the claimant, was the manufacturer of the well-known 'Doc Martens' footwear. They commissioned the first defendant, Evans (E), a freelance designer, to combine the design of G's trade marks and create a single mark. G also owned copyright in each of these trade marks. E created the combined logo, which was essentially a derivative work of the copyright works in the two trade marks. Once the combined logo was created, E assigned it to C, the second defendant, who was G's competitor. G approached the court for a declaration that G was the equitable owner of the combined logo. It was common ground that C took assignment of the combined logo with the actual knowledge of the claim by G.[37] The High Court implied an assignment in G's favour, holding that they needed more than simply a right to use, and no copyright could be retained by E although the statute

[34] Lightman J in *Ray v Classic FM* [1998] FSR 622, 640 has laid down detailed criteria. For a further discussion of commissioning contracts, see Poorna Mysoor, *Implied Licences in Copyright Law* (OUP 2021) 103ff.

[35] See generally Poorna Mysoor, 'The Jurisdiction of Implying' in Henry E Smith, Shyamkrishna Balganesh, and Poorna Mysoor (eds), *Intellectual Property and Private Law* (CUP 2026 forthcoming).

[36] [2003] EWHC 2914 (Ch).

[37] ibid [11]–[14].

regarded E as the author of the commissioned work.[38] This meant that the legal title which E had assigned to C had to be restored to G to perfect G's title.

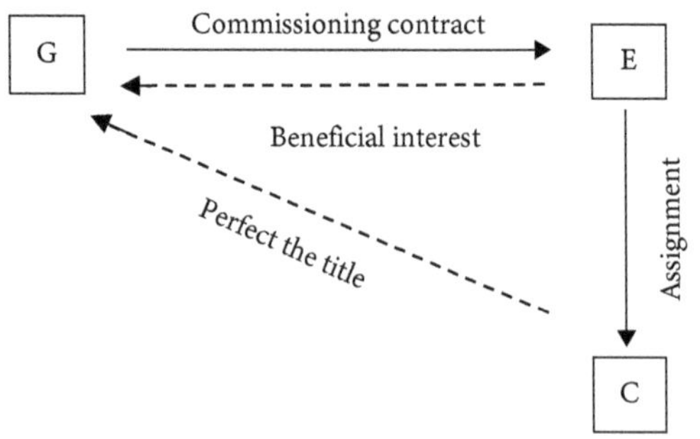

Figure 7.2 An illustration of equitable assignment

The fact that the combined logo owed its existence to the commissioning instructions from G was not a sufficient reason to let G retain the equitable interest in it. The commissioning fee, the nature of the work, and the purpose of commissioning can all influence the interest that the commissioner acquires. A strong reason why E could not have retained copyright in the combined logo was because it contained a trade mark and copyright that belonged to G. Further, the combined logo was going to be used by G to identify the origin and build goodwill in its shoes. G needed every freedom to be able to use the combined logo and prevent everyone else, and competitors in particular, to refrain from using the logo. Under the circumstances, G's beneficial interest arose when the combined logo was created, that is, prior in date to the assignment to C. An equitable interest is binding on all successors in title, except those who take in good faith for valuable consideration without actual or constructive notice.[39] However, C was a successor in title who did not satisfy these criteria, since he was aware of G's interest. Therefore, G's beneficial interest was binding on C.

Another instance of this from popular culture is *Lucasfilm v Ainsworth*.[40] As in *Griggs*, here the commissioned work was the stormtrooper helmet used in the Star Wars films. The helmet owed its origin to an artwork, the copyright to which was owned by Lucasfilm. Therefore, when the helmet was created

[38] ibid [36]–[37], [51]–[52]. The Court of Appeal confirmed this finding, [2005] EWCA Civ 11 [10]–[11], [19]–[25].

[39] Lionel Smith, 'Fusion and Tradition' in Simone Degeling and James Edelman (eds), *Equity in Commercial Law* (Lawbook Co 2005) 32–33.

[40] [2011] UKSC 39, [2012] 1 AC 208.

by Ainsworth, Ainsworth could not claim copyright in it and start his own business in stormtrooper merchandise. The beneficial interest belonged to Lucasfilm, and Ainsworth was ordered to perfect this title. In general, if the person commissioning gives something proprietary to a person to be used to create the work being commissioned, it is more likely that the commissioner will have an implied assignment.

Commentators enumerate the circumstances in which courts imply assignments.[41] These instances include where the person commissioning lends its employees to create the new work, or when the author stands in a fiduciary relationship to the person commissioning as a director of a company. These factors have the effect of retaining a beneficial interest in copyright with the person commissioning.

3. Licences

Licences have confounded jurists for centuries. Hohfeld described licences as a word of 'convenient and seductive obscurity'.[42] The CDPA reaffirms the ability of a copyright owner to grant licences but gives licences additional characteristics that make them even more of a mystery. These licences owe their origin to the powers acquired as part of the first ownership of copyright. The licences can be exclusive or non-exclusive. Different consequences follow with each of these, not only in the general law but also because of the provisions in the CDPA. Each will now be dealt with in turn.

(a) Exclusive Licences

An exclusive licence is defined under CDPA, s 92(1) as a licence 'authorising the licensee to the exclusion of all other persons, including the person granting the licence, to exercise a right which would otherwise be exercisable exclusively by the copyright owner'. The licensor must not only ensure that no one else is granted what an exclusive licensee is granted but also exclude themselves from exercising what is granted to the exclusive licensee. Although the provision speaks of exercise of right and not doing of a thing, in practice the content of an exclusive licence can also be in conformity with the commercial need and does

[41] Harbottle and others (n 7) para 4-207.
[42] Wesley N Hohfeld, 'Faulty Analysis of Easement and Licence Cases' (1917) 27 Yale LJ 66, 92.

not have to conform to the boundaries of specific exclusive rights.[43] Again, although it is not specifically provided for, it should be possible for the licensor to grant an exclusive licence that does not extend to the whole of the term of copyright but is limited in duration. Let us examine the implications with the help of Figure 7.3.

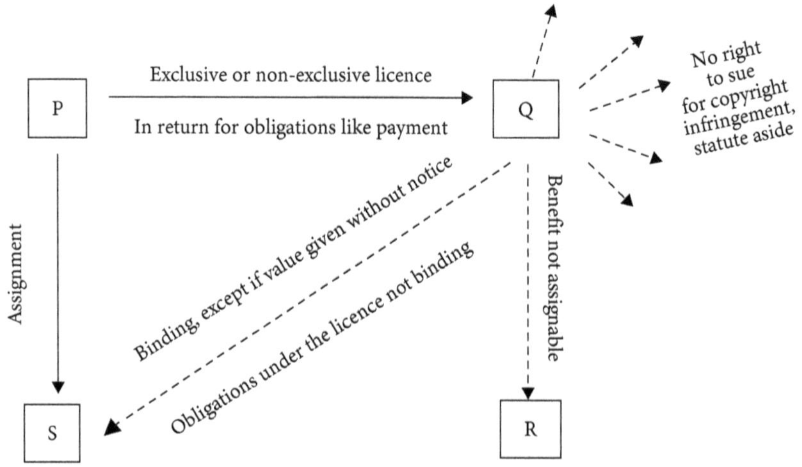

Figure 7.3 Nature of licences

One may immediately notice a striking resemblance of exclusive licences with assignments. Commentators insist that the primary difference between them is that assignments grant proprietary interests, while exclusive (and non-exclusive) licences do not. The CDPA has modified the nature of exclusive licences in many different ways. Therefore, it is apposite to examine the similarities and differences between partial assignments and exclusive licences. In Figure 7.3, suppose P grants a licence (exclusive or non-exclusive) to Q. There are certain consequences that follow. Beginning with differences, first, P will continue to have the residuary copyright interest which P can assign to others, say S here. P would not have been able to do this had they granted Q an assignment instead. Even if P grants a partial assignment to Q, P cannot assign the same interest to S, but an interest minus the interest granted to Q. Secondly, Q cannot assign the benefit of their interest to R without the licence permitting such assignment. Nor can they sub-license it. Again, if Q had received a complete or partial assignment, Q would have been able to assign their interest or any part thereof to R, as we saw in our discussions of Figure 7.1.

[43] *Sega Enterprises Pty Ltd v Galaxy Electronics Pty Ltd* (1998) 39 IPR 577.

Now on to the similarities. First, successor liability. Land law and personal property law tell us that licences are not binding on successors in title.[44] However, s 90(4) states that Q's licence will be binding on S except where S has given valuable consideration in good faith for the assignment and has no actual or constructive notice of Q's licence. This makes copyright licences look like equitable interests, but only because of this statutory provision. Interestingly, what is binding is only the licence. If Q had been subject to an ongoing obligation such as payment of royalties, then P assigning the overall copyright interest to S would not automatically entitle S to the payment of royalties. More on this under Section 6 below. Secondly, trespassory liability. In general, licensees are unable to sue third parties in property torts.[45] However, if Q is an exclusive licensee, s 101 of the CDPA enables Q to sue third parties for infringement and seek remedies in the same way as if Q had been granted an assignment.[46] If Q had taken a partial assignment instead, as was explained in Figure 7.1, it would have been possible for Q's interest to be binding on the whole world. Thirdly, licences generally do not need any formalities for their creation. However, s 92(1) states that an exclusive licence must be in writing signed by the person granting it, in the same way that assignments are required to be in signed writing. In summary, exclusive licensees would have been wholly distinguishable from assignees if not for the statutory provisions transforming them in certain significant ways.

Having ascertained that there are some differences between exclusive licences and assignments, our next quest is how we are to identify them when we see an agreement. Third parties like R are affected by this difference because an assignment to them from Q may not be valid if Q turns out to be an exclusive licensee without the authority to assign its benefit. The difference is a matter of construction, but both courts and commentators acknowledge that the distinction can be a fine one.[47] While the use of words such as assign or licence, if not conclusive, might be an indication,[48] the presence of ongoing obligations may prompt a court to veer towards an exclusive licence rather than an assignment. This is on the basis that assignments generally give a clean break, and licences can be an ongoing transaction. However, the recognition of partial

[44] *King v David Allan* [1916] 2 AC 54, 61 (Lord Buckmaster LC).

[45] *Hunter v Canary Wharf* [1997] AC 665, 702–03 (Lord Hoffmann).

[46] If the exclusive licensee and an assignee have concurrent rights of action against a third party, an action brought by one must join the other, unless the court grants leave otherwise, under CDPA, s 102(1). The policy behind this is to reduce multiplicity of proceedings.

[47] *Western Front Ltd v Vestron Inc* [1987] FSR 66, 75–76.

[48] Commentators provide a list of considerations one must look for. See Harbottle and others (n 7) paras 4-244, 4-245.

assignments limited by time may make this deduction much less straightforward. Regardless of lack of clarity as to the distinction between assignments and exclusive licences, the uncertainties themselves should not mean non-compliance with *numerus clausus*. Even in land law, we see the perennial debates rage on regarding the difference between a lease and a licence. These uncertainties do not threaten *numerus clausus* in land law, nor should they in copyright law.

There is a sense in which one may argue that the statutory provisions enabling exclusive licensees to acquire similar rights to an assignee may also make exclusive licences behave like a property interest. Since the statutory provisions have successfully created partial assignments as a property interest that do not exist in land law or personal property law, why could it not be the case that the statutory provisions also make exclusive licences become property interests? The fear is that that this would make exclusive licences almost entirely indistinguishable from assignments.

Commentators insist that there are benefits to exclusive licences being contractual, on the basis that this gives the copyright owners the maximum freedom to choose between proprietary or contractual consequences for their transactions.[49] If licences are regarded as proprietary, the licensees will be able to freely assign their interest. The first argument is that free assignability of exclusive licences will make the copyright owner lose control over the person to whom the exclusive licensee assigns the licensed interest. If no assignment of the exclusive licensee's interest were possible, then this would give additional control to the copyright owner to terminate an exclusive licence if the exclusive licensee assigned the licence to an incompetent person to exploit the rights.[50] A possible rejoinder to this is that the market may take care of it. An exclusive licensee would assign their licensed interest to an undesirable licensee at their own peril. To the extent that this affects the copyright owner's moral rights, the copyright owner should be able to enforce this against the new assignee.

The second argument is that licences normally have ongoing obligations such as payment of royalties (more on this under Section 6 below). Even if the law recognises the power of the exclusive licensee to assign their interest, under the general law, only the benefit of an interest can be assigned. The ongoing obligations attached to the interest will be regarded as contractual only. This is

[49] Christopher M Newman, 'An Exclusive License Is Not an Assignment: Disentangling Divisibility and Transferability of Ownership in Copyright' (2013) 74 La L Rev 59, 76.

[50] Newman presents this as both a threat and an opportunity, ibid 115.

the same with partial assignments. If there is a breach of an ongoing obligation, the copyright owner can terminate the exclusive licence, taking back control over the licensed interest. If the copyright owner had given a partial assignment instead, they would not have been able to terminate it. Even if this is correct, by the same token, these ongoing obligations will not be enforceable by an assignee from the copyright owner against an exclusive licensee. Exclusive licences remaining contractual, therefore, may benefit copyright owners but not their assignees.

It may bring greater clarity to the available property interests in copyright if exclusive licences are recognised as property interests but in a slightly different version. The exclusive part of exclusive licences is much like leases in that the landowner is also excluded from the land together with the rest of the world. In addition, exclusive licences should be for a limited term which is certain. Of course, copyright is not spoken of in terms of estates the way land is. Historically and doctrinally this analogy cannot be drawn lightly. Copyright itself is for a limited duration. However, if the maximum duration that copyright statutes grant is recognised by analogy as being co-extensive with freehold, any amount of time that is less than this would be acceptable for an exclusive licence, so long as there is certainty to this term. The statute should no longer provide for partial assignments as to duration. Instead, this should be replaced by redefining exclusive licences as interests with limited and certain duration.

There are several advantages to this. First, the copyright owner can take comfort from the fact that the interest licensed will come to an end at some point. Currently, the fear is that if exclusive licences become proprietary then the copyright owner will lose control in the same way as they would lose control with assignments. In the words of Newman, an assignment allows a copyright owner to split some part of the copyright interest 'relinquishing all authority over it and effectively creating an entirely separate object of ownership'.[51] With an exclusive licence, on the contrary, a copyright owner 'signals the intent to retain ultimate residual authority over the use rights granted'.[52] But this is not inconsistent with an argument that an exclusive licence should be a separate property interest. In land, when a freeholder grants a lease, the freeholder retains residual control over the land. Limiting the duration of exclusive licences makes it possible for copyright owners to rest assured that the

[51] ibid 61.

[52] To be sure, Newman does not advance an argument that an exclusive licence should not be a property interest. Indeed, he compares exclusive licences to easements over land, which are proprietary, ibid 71.

reversionary interest still belongs to them and that the interest licensed will come to an end someday.

Secondly, there would be no compromise as to content of the exclusive licences. What is being proposed here is only to introduce a different transactional design for exclusive licences. The content of exclusive licences can remain the same. Just as in partial assignment, an exclusive licensee would be able to slice and dice the content of their rights. Although the suggestion is for the currently contractual rights to be recognised as property rights, the immutability associated with *in rem* rights that Merrill and Smith argue for does not have to follow.[53] This proposal does not tie down the copyright owners' hands any more than when they partially assign their rights. As already argued, by analogy with easements, it is possible to balance flexibility and immutability also when the transactional design is that of an exclusive licence as proposed here.

Thirdly, imposing a term and insisting on its certainty would help distinguish the interest from partial assignment once partial assignment is limited only to the exclusionary rights and not to duration. Exclusive licences can otherwise have exactly the same scope as partial assignments. If there were no difference in the transactional design of exclusive licences from partial assignments, these would be indistinguishable. Limiting the term gives exclusive licences a definitive attribute that can help avoid all the litigation that surrounds the assessment of this distinction.[54]

Fourthly, exclusive licences defined this way will be *numerus clausus* compliant both as to content and as to transaction design. As to the scope of the content, the arguments that support the compliance of partial assignments with *numerus clausus* under Subsection 2(a)(i) also support the scope of exclusive licences. Limiting the exclusive licences to a term that is certain avoids the difficulties explained in Subsection 2(a)(ii) above in relation to partial assignments limited by time.

Fifthly, making exclusive licences a property interest brings coherence to the law. Currently, if an exclusive licence is not in writing but the intention is manifest otherwise, then one can speak of an equitable exclusive licence. It seems to be possible for equitable exclusive licensees to require the licensor to transform their equitable interest into a legal exclusive licence. If exclusive licences

[53] Thomas W Merrill and Henry E Smith, 'The Property/Contract Interface' (2001) 101 Colum L Rev 773, 800–09, where they argue that *in personam* rights are flexible and *in rem* rights are more rigid and are determined by law.

[54] One such is the celebrated case of *Chaplin v Leslie Frewin (Publishers) Ltd* [1966] Ch 71, which involved an agreement with the minor son of Charlie Chaplin to write his biography by a ghost writer.

themselves are only contractual and not property interests, it is unclear in what sense there could be an equitable exclusive licence.[55]

Finally, and most importantly, any ongoing obligations of the exclusive licensee can be made binding on their assignees by analogy with leasehold covenants. More on this in Section 6 below.

(b) Non-Exclusive Licences

As the name suggests, non-exclusive licences can be granted to any number of licensees. It follows that some of the provisions in the CDPA that give special status to exclusive licences do not apply to non-exclusive licences. Regarding trespassory liability, s 101A(1) of the CDPA provides that a non-exclusive licensee can sue for infringement if the licence is in signed writing and expressly provides for the non-exclusive licensee to have the power to sue. Regarding assignability, the same rule applies as for exclusive licensees. Non-exclusive licensees cannot assign the benefit of their license to third parties freely, unless their licence provides otherwise. However, successor liability applies in relation to non-exclusive licensees in the same way as it applies to exclusive licensees. Section 90(4) of the CDPA is worded broadly enough to include non-exclusive licensees. Going back to Figure 7.3, even a non-exclusive licensee's interest can be binding on all successors in title, except those who take in good faith for valuable consideration without notice.

Nevertheless, an argument to make non-exclusive licences proprietary would be far weaker than for exclusive licences. Non-exclusive licences that are bare licences arise in very many different circumstances, just as land licences arise in informal circumstances. In many of these instances, the copyright owner may not even be aware of copyright having come into existence. A poet may write a song to help a friend develop a career as a singer.[56] A producer might write the outline of the first scene to get a playwright started on writing the rest of the play.[57] It would be difficult to argue that these informal licences could be property interests. They might not comply with the *Ainsworth* criteria of being capable of assumption by third parties and of stability,[58]

[55] Harbottle and others (n 7) para 4-247, who cite *Wrenn v Landamore* [2008] EWCA Civ 496 [46] (Mummery LJ), although this point was not specifically decided.
[56] *Banks v CBS Songs* [1996] EMLR 440.
[57] *Bright v Jones* [2004] EWHC 1157 (Ch).
[58] *National Provincial Bank v Ainsworth* [1965] UKHL 1.

because these bare licences can be withdrawn just as freely as they were granted.[59]

It still begs the question as to what might have been the reason why all licences, whether exclusive and non-exclusive, whether bare or contractual, are binding on successors in title. It does appear out of place that while licences over land do not bind successors in title, copyright licences do, even if it excludes bona fide purchasers for value without notice. Even if this provision does not imbue licences with proprietary character, there must be an explanation for its existence. The historical context might also explain whether the intention was to make licences proprietary. The Copyright Act 1911,[60] introducing express provisions for the grant of voluntary licences, and recognising it as the grant of an 'interest' in copyright, left it ambiguous as to whether it meant property interest. Subsequently, s 36(4) of the Copyright Act 1956 went on to provide that copyright licences do bind successors in title. This provision was carried not only into the current law in the United Kingdom but also into the copyright statutes of other common law countries such as Australia.[61]

A plausible explanation is that, in the early twentieth century, technological innovation enabling the making of sound recordings and cinematographic films had begun in larger scale, followed by radio broadcasting. All these involved great investment on the part of willing entrepreneurs and held great promise for authors in enabling wider dissemination of their works. Whilst events such as coronations or sporting spectacles required no copyright licences, a significant part of other content, such as songs, films, and so on, required licences from their authors. The business model of the producers of sound recordings and cinematographic films depended extensively on authors assigning or at least licensing their works. There is no gainsaying that these entrepreneurs as substantial licensees of these authorial works were powerful players at the forefront of law reform in the run-up to both the 1911 and the 1956 Acts. It seems plausible that the 1956 Act enacted the provision favouring copyright licensees, so that if authors assigned their copyright interest, their assignees would still be bound by the licences authors had granted. This may have been thought to give some stability to the powerful licensees such as record companies, film producers, and broadcasters who depended on the rights licensed not disappearing at the whim of the authors. Neither the Parliamentary

[59] For further discussion on implied bare licences, see Mysoor, *Implied Licences in Copyright Law* (n 34) ch 4.

[60] Copyright Act 1911, s 5(2). This provision still remains in Canadian law under the Canadian Copyright Act 1985, s 13(4).

[61] ACA, s 196(4), which extends the binding effect not merely to those without notice, but to all purchasers.

debates of the time nor the submissions made by powerful actors like the BBC give much information about this. But the timing of this provision being inserted in the statute and the birth of entrepreneurial works together add some credence to this explanation.[62]

4. Security Interests

It is possible to put forward copyright as a security for a loan or some other obligation. The more common forms of security interests created are mortgages and charges. There is no express provision in the CDPA that permits putting forward copyright as a security. One will have to rely on assignment provisions under CDPA, s 90. Commentators argue that it is not possible to create a legal mortgage based on a conditional assignment, with the mortgaged interest automatically reverting to the mortgagor, and that this will only be effective in equity.[63] However, as we saw in Subsection 2(a)(ii) above, in *Crosstown*, courts did accept what was effectively a conditional assignment under the guise of a partial assignment limited by time. The better view seems to be

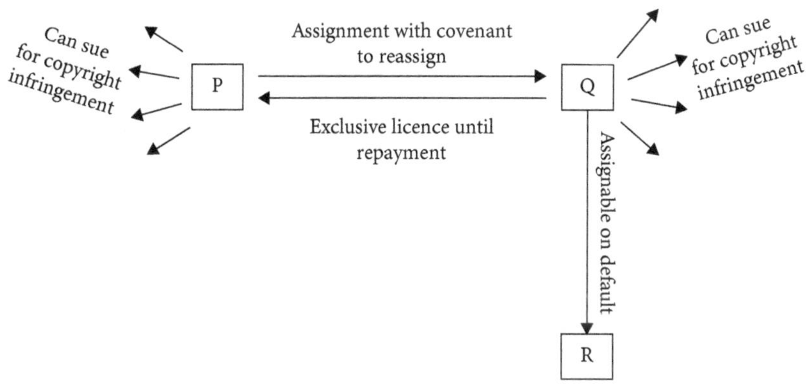

Figure 7.4 Nature of mortgages

that conditional assignments should only take effect in equity, if at all. To be effective a legal mortgage should involve an absolute assignment of copyright with a covenant to assign it back to the mortgagor once the debt is paid, to comply with s 90(1). It is possible for a legal or equitable mortgage to come into

[62] This author thanks Professor William Swadling for helping her develop her arguments in this direction.
[63] Harbottle and others (n 7) para 4-231, fn 786.

existence, depending on whether the underlying assignment is legal or equitable. Let us again examine this with the help of Figure 7.4.

If P is a copyright owner, say of their film, they can mortgage the copyright in the film by granting an assignment to Q with a covenant in the assignment that Q will assign back the copyright once P repays the loan. It seems possible for P to put forward only partial assignment to Q, such as the right to distribute the film on online streaming platforms, but no other rights. Commentators believe that partial assignments that make the assignment conditional upon a future uncertain event (eg upon default) will not be acceptable as a valid assignment. It is suggested here that the assignment may be valid as an assignment need not be absolute under s 90(1) of the CDPA. However, commercially such an assignment may be unattractive to a mortgagee.

The assignment which P grants with a covenant to reassign appears to be unlike other kinds of assignment. This is because commentators believe that it is possible for P to continue to have the standing to sue for copyright infringement even through copyright has been assigned to Q. Under the general law, P will retain the equity of redemption, which apparently gives sufficient standing for this purpose.[64] However, this equity of redemption does not allow P to continue exploiting copyright. For this purpose, P requires a licence from Q, and preferably an exclusive licence, so that it comes with all the statutory powers like those of an assignee,[65] at least until the loan is repaid. If P fails to repay the loan, Q will have the power to assign the secured interest to third parties, say to R, to realise the loaned amount. Since the condition of the covenant to reassign would not have been fulfilled, R will receive a good title when they take an assignment of the copyright interest from Q.

P's ability to grant an assignment presupposes that P has the copyright interest. What if P is an exclusive licensee? Since the scope of an exclusive licence can be the same as an assignment, it should be equally valuable commercially. However, since exclusive licences are not freely assignable, it would not be possible to put it forward as a security if the terms of the exclusive licence does not permit assignment of this interest. Commentators believe that this is a lost opportunity for the copyright licensee to be able to capitalise on their licensed interest.[66]

There are, however, certain issues that surround giving security of personal property in general. Most prominent is the absence of a register where these

[64] ibid 4-232.
[65] ibid 4-230.
[66] See generally Andrea Tosato, 'Intellectual Property License Contracts: Reflections on a Prospective UNCITRAL Project' (2018) 86 U Cin L Rev 1251 <https://scholarship.law.uc.edu/uclr/vol86/iss4/4> accessed 22 December 2024.

transactions can be recorded. The due diligence required of mortgagees to assess whether the copyright owner has given any conflicting prior interests in copyright would be terribly onerous.[67] Furthermore, since mortgagees do not exercise any of the rights of a copyright owner outwardly, their own security interest in copyright can remain hidden from commercial transactions. For certain high-value copyright works such as films and sound recordings, the copyright owners may want to put forward the same work as security for multiple loans. The mortgagees need to know their priority vis-à-vis each other before they agree to the transaction. Again, as in partial assignments discussed above, the absence of registration to record copyright ownership or transactions poses a hurdle for the discoverability of these interests. However, if the copyright owner is a company (which in most cases it will be), then the Companies Act 2006 requires that all security interests are registered on the Companies Register within twenty-one days of entering into the transaction. Commentators believe that the absence of registration in copyright can be advantageous because this avoids discrepancies in the entries made in the specialised registers (such as the Patents Register) and the Companies Register.[68]

Another type of security interest possible in copyright is an equitable charge.[69] An equitable charge comes into existence when a copyright owner simply agrees to put forward copyright interest as security for a loan or other obligation. Since the CDPA makes no provision for this, the charge is a creature of equity under the general law. In the example in Figure 7.4, if instead of a mortgage, P gave an equitable charge over their film, then Q's equitable charge would be binding on all successors in title of P, except those who take in good faith for valuable consideration without actual or constructive notice. It is more common for undertakings to grant a charge of this kind as part of a floating charge over their entire undertaking, and not separately over copyright. No assignment is necessary between the chargor and chargee. If the debt is not repaid, the chargee has a right to have the charged interest sold and the debt realised. The absence of assignment also makes it possible to create an equitable charge over the interest of an exclusive licensee. However, the same issues may arise as to record keeping, publicity, due diligence, and the priorities between successive chargees.

[67] David MR Townend, 'Intellectual Property as Security Interests: Technical Difficulties Presented in the Law' (1997) 2 IPQ 168, 187–89.

[68] ibid 190–94, for more detailed solutions; see also Andrea Tosato, 'Security Interests Over Intellectual Property' (2011) 6 JIPLP 93, 100.

[69] Harbottle and others (n 7) para 4-233.

5. Options and Rights of Pre-emption

Just as options and rights of pre-emption are equitable property rights that arise in relation to land, in the same way these can arise in relation to copyright. The statute says nothing about these, but it is possible to use the analogy with land law. For example, suppose P writes a novel. A film producer, Q, might enter into an option agreement whereby Q may agree that if Q manages to find the required funding within three years, then Q should be given the option to be assigned the relevant rights to make a film based on the novel. The right of first refusal also works in a similar way. Instead of defining the period for looking for finances, if Q enters into a pre-emption agreement, Q will be agreeing with P that if P ever decides to assign the relevant rights, then they should offer them to Q first. Only if Q does not take up the assignment will P then be free to offer the rights to someone else. P may never decide to assign their copyright, which would mean the right of pre-emption would never accrue.

It is important to mention here that whether the transaction seeks an option or pre-emption, it must be for purchase, that is, a partial or complete assignment from P. This is because only an assignment is a property interest under the general law currently, and an agreement to assign a property interest creates an equitable interest of its own. An option will be enforceable on all successors in title of the copyright owner except those who give value in good faith without actual or constructive notice. If the option is for an exclusive licence, the option agreement will only operate in contract. This means that, in the above example, if the copyright owner P enters into an option agreement with Q for Q to take up an exclusive licence, and if P then assigns copyright to R, Q will not be able to enforce their option against R, compelling R to exclusively license the relevant rights. Q will be left with having to sue P in breach of contract for damages. No specific performance may be given. The same consequences seem to follow if P assigns to R in breach of a pre-emption right previously granted in favour of Q.

6. Right to Receive Royalties

When copyright owners assign their copyright, often the consideration for the assignment is not a one-off payment, but a periodic payment of royalties. One can see the attraction of ongoing payment of royalties for both copyright owners who do not wish to lose out on the success of their work subsequent to assignment, and for assignees who do not wish to take a risk on the success of the work after assignment. While assigned interest from the copyright owner to the assignee is regarded as a property interest, the copyright owner's right to receive royalties is not. The right to receive royalties is regarded merely as a contractual right between the parties to the original assignment. This means that the right to receive royalties will not be binding on the successors in title of the assignee. Let us examine this with the help of Figure 7.5.

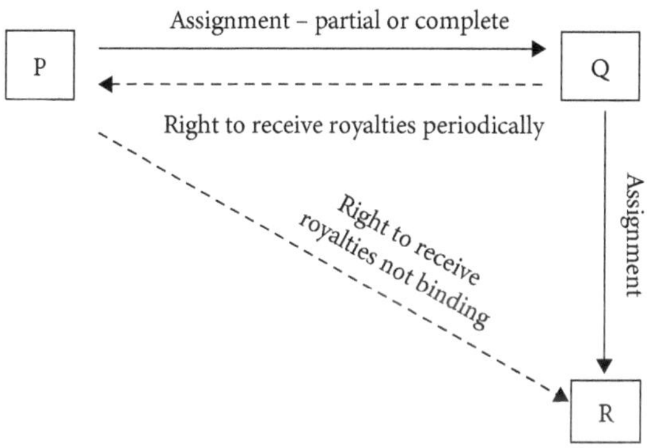

Figure 7.5 Right to receive royalties currently

Suppose P, a novelist, assigns their right to publish their new novel to Q in return for royalties to be paid periodically, say, based on the sales. Having taken the assignment, Q then transfers this copyright interest to R. If Q stops paying royalties because they no longer have the rights to publish the novel, P will not be able to enforce this right against R. The right to receive royalties has been regarded by the courts to be only a contractual right enforceable between P and Q, the original parties to the contract.[70] Therefore, only an action in breach of contract would lie against Q. But if Q goes bankrupt, and the receiver sells Q's interest to R, R can refuse to pay royalties to P. This is what happened in *Baker v Stickney*.[71] R in the meantime, having received the assignment, can publish the novel paying nothing to P—a shocking outcome for P!

If P's assignment was partial as to use, say publishing in paperback, P may still be able to exploit their right to publish the novel in other formats, such as eBooks. If P's assignment was partial as to duration, say for ten years, Q will only have been able to assign R this very interest or an interest further carved

[70] Depending on the language of the agreement and the relationship, courts have sometimes held publishers to be in a fiduciary relationship to the authors. See *John v James* [1991] FSR 397, 433–34, which was about the legendary artist Sir Elton John in relation to agreements entered into when he was a minor.

[71] [1919] 1 KB 121.

out from it, say for five years. But at the expiry of ten years, the assigned interest will revert to P. There may be some opportunity for P to make good the royalties they lost during the period of assignment to Q, although there is an opportunity cost associated with this. If P's assignment was for the remaining duration of copyright in the right to publish the novel, then P will have lost out on being justly remunerated for the exploitation of their work. Adams has warned that this is not merely a theoretical problem but a practical one too, because more and more publishers insist on outright assignments rather than exclusive licences.[72] He has also put forward several arguments to address this, by analogy with land law and personal property law.[73]

One may argue that this problem could be dealt with by incorporating a floating reverter clause with the assigned interest reverting to the copyright owner, as we saw in the discussion of *Crosstown* above under Subsection 2(a)(ii). Helpfully, the breached obligation in *Crosstown* also related to giving accounts for royalties, and was therefore a relevant precedent. Despite the difficulties with its reasoning and its problematic conclusion, it is still good law at least until it is overturned.

One may argue that P has an unpaid lender's lien on the assigned interest. This was raised in *Baker* itself and rejected because it was found that there was no intention of the parties to this effect.[74] Adams has pointed out that, to this extent, *Baker* is incorrectly decided because an unpaid seller's lien is a matter of law and not a matter of intention of the parties.[75] Even if a lien arose, it is doubtful whether P would be able to enforce it against R. Further, lien is a right exercised by sellers who lawfully retain physical possession of chattels until they are paid the contracted sum. Since physical possession is not possible in copyright, the analogy with lien may be difficult.

It may be possible to construe the agreement as giving rise to an equitable charge. This is a matter of intention of the parties discerned from the construction of the agreement. This was also rejected in *Baker* as there was no intention.[76] It may be somewhat artificial to construe a provision in an assignment agreement providing for payment of royalties on a periodic basis that the assigned interest is to act as security for the obligation of paying royalties. If the language does not show this to be the natural meaning, this argument too will fail.

[72] John N Adams, 'Barker v Stickney Revisited' [1988] IPQ 113.
[73] John N Adams, 'The Passing of the Burden of Royalty Payments' [2007] IPQ 403, 405ff.
[74] [1919] 1 KB 121, 125–26.
[75] Adams, *Passing of the Burden* (n 73) 408.
[76] [1919] 1 KB 121, 126–28.

Adams has also argued that one can draw an analogy with *Tulk v Moxhay*.[77] In his view, the decision in *Tulk* was based on the defendant's notice of the claimant's right in the land when he purchased the land.[78] However, the comparison is incomplete. The covenants in *Tulk* were enforceable because of the ownership of the neighbouring lands by the covenantors and the covenantees and the benefit to the land retained by the covenantees. In copyright, this will translate to the duty to pay royalties as the covenant, with the copyright owner P in Figure 7.5 as the covenantee (with the benefit to receive royalties) and the assignee Q as the covenantor (with the burden to pay royalties). However, unlike land, upon assignment, P does not retain an interest in copyright that can benefit from the covenant. All that can be said of P is that P has the authorial connection with the work, which is not the same as arguing that P has an interest in copyright. In any event, even if there is enforcement of covenants in equity, it is only of negative covenants.[79] It is also argued that, for personal property, the result is similar in that if any covenants are enforceable because of notice, these can only be negative.

Other arguments include the benefit and burden principle in *Halsall v Brizell*.[80] Again, this depends on the intention of the parties. In our example, R needs to show an intention of taking the benefit of the copyright interest together with the burden of having to pay the royalties. It is not going to be common for R to manifest such an intention when the law allows them to get away with not having to take on the burden. Yet another argument is that R holds the royalties on constructive trust for P, if he takes with notice of Q's obligation to pay. However, a court will likely not impose constructive trust lightly and unconscionability alone may not be a sufficient basis for this. Finally, one may argue that R will be unjustly enriched if they exploit P's work without paying royalties to P.[81] Each of these mechanisms might be deserving of independent exploration.

One might argue that perhaps an assignment was not the correct transaction for P to enter into if P wanted to ensure an uninterrupted flow of royalties. To the extent that P could negotiate,[82] P should have only granted an exclusive

[77] (1848) 2 Ph 774.

[78] Adams, *Passing of the Burden* (n 73) 405–06.

[79] See Molly Shaffer Van Houweling, 'Technology and Tracing Costs: Lessons from Real Property' in Shyamkrishna Balganesh (ed), *Intellectual Property and Common Law* (CUP 2013) 390–95, for a discussion of the role of covenants in copyright by analogy with land law in the US context.

[80] [1957] Ch 169.

[81] Adams, *Passing of the Burden* (n 73) 411–13.

[82] Commentators argue that large corporations insist on assignments which are often in standard form contracts. Adams, 'Barker v Stickney Revisited' (n 72) 113.

licence to Q. Of course, if the transaction was unclear as to the intention of the parties, in view of the existence of the ongoing obligation to pay royalties, a court might have held the transaction to be more consistent with an exclusive licence. However, if the language used in the document is clear about the transaction being an assignment, then the existence of ongoing obligation alone will not make a court conclude that it is an exclusive licence.

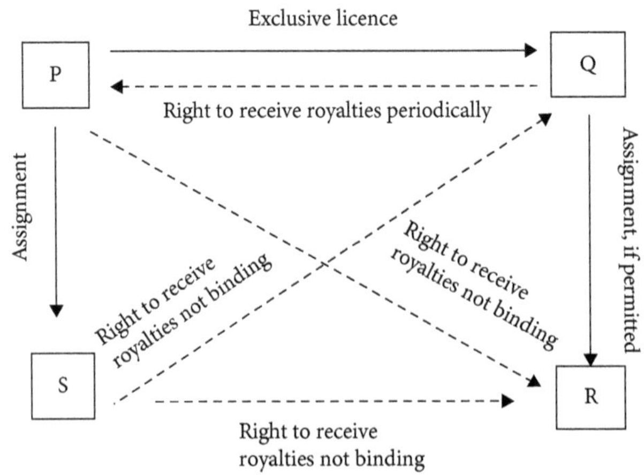

Figure 7.6 Right to receive royalties

See Figure 7.6. Suppose the transaction that P entered into was an exclusive licence. As discussed in Subsection 4(a) above, in the first place, Q will not have been free to assign the copyright interest licensed to them. Suppose the exclusive licence permits free assignment of the licensed interest as a matter of contract. Since Q cannot assign the obligation to pay royalties to R for being merely contractual, the obligation stays with Q. If Q stops paying royalties because Q has assigned the licensed rights, P can terminate the contract with Q. P would not be able to terminate if P had assigned the rights to Q. Assigning rights has a finality to it in the sense of parting with the assigned interest (even if partially), which is not the case if the rights are licensed (even if exclusively). Since P retains the residual ownership of copyright, upon termination of the licence P can sue R for infringement.[83] Since R's interest was derived from Q and the grant to Q has been terminated, R's further exploitation of the licensed interest amounts to infringement. P can seek an injunction to stop R from exploiting,

[83] This is what distinguishes *Crosstown*, where the transaction was a partial assignment and not an exclusive licence.

or specific performance compelling R to pay the royalties to P, though both are at the discretion of the court. Furthermore, if P assigns their residuary interest to S, the right to receive royalties is not binding on either Q or R.

It is submitted that an alternative solution could be achieved by first drawing an analogy of exclusive licences with leases as argued under Subsection 3(a) above. If exclusive licences are recognised as a property interest with certain and limited duration, then any ongoing obligations that they impose can be enforced as leasehold covenants. A limitation of the contractual argument of exclusive licences is that the right to receive royalties will also continue to be a contractual obligation. Just as P cannot enforce it against R as the assignee from the exclusive licensee, S cannot enforce it against Q as the assignee of the residual interest from P. As a benefit of the contract between P and Q, the right to receive royalties is assignable from P to S. But if P does not assign this right in its assignment of copyright to S, S will not receive royalty payments from Q automatically. P's ability to terminate the exclusive licence with Q in an effort to render R an infringer will not work in the same way for S. S has no recourse to P because P has parted with their interest. S cannot take free of the exclusive licence on the basis that S was not a party to the licence which was entered into between P and Q because it is binding on S under s 90(4).

In land law, a positive leasehold covenant (say to pay rent) is enforceable against the assignees of a leasehold interest, based on privity of estate. Although one cannot speak of estate in copyright in the same way as in land law, the interest created by the first exclusive licence can be the defining interest from which all subsequent interests are derived. In other words, this helps connect in a chain the assignees who are taking under the exclusive licence. The statute can provide that all obligations in an exclusive licence that relate to copyright exploitation should be binding on the subsequent assignees of exclusive licensees and enforceable by the copyright owner's assignees. All those taking under it as assignees will be subject to the same positive obligations that the first exclusive licensee was. This will ensure that the copyright owner does not have to depend on the discretion of the courts to enforce the payment of royalties or be left with having to resort to termination. This will also ensure that an assignee from the copyright owner (S) will be able to enforce obligations associated with licences and not simply be bound by the licences granted by their predecessors in title.

Eventually, if none of these avenues is acceptable, it may be worth exploring whether the right to receive royalties can be an independent property right. To the extent that this is being proposed as a new entrant into copyright law and not mentioned as one of the interests under the statute, its compliance with the

Ainsworth criteria is worth considering. The right to receive royalties is certainly definable and identifiable by third parties. It is also capable of assumption by third parties because it is objectively discernible and it also has a degree of permanence and stability.

7. Summary

This chapter dealt with the derivative interests in copyright. It discussed partial assignments as to rights and partial assignments as to time as the expressly stated legal derivative interests under the CDPA. Since the CDPA provides for legal assignment, it appears to be possible to create legal mortgages, but charges being derived from the general law would be equitable. Equitable assignments which come into existence for various reasons, options, and rights of pre-emption were discussed as well recognised categories of equitable interests. Exclusive licences, despite benefiting from numerous statutory provisions making them resemble assignments, are not regarded as property interests. This chapter argued for making exclusive licences property interests and for limiting them by duration of a certain period. It argued that this would make them more clearly distinguishable from partial assignments. Being limited by duration can make exclusive licences analogously equivalent to leasehold interest, which in turn can enable the enforcement of ongoing positive covenants in the like manner as leasehold covenants. The discussion surrounding the right to receive royalties demonstrated the myriad areas of private law that influence the workings of copyright law. The analogies of exclusive licences with leases and leasehold covenants show that the solutions developed in the land law context can inspire creative solutions for the problems facing copyright law.

Final Remarks

This monograph set out to achieve two objectives: first, to demonstrate that examining and strengthening the attributes of copyright as a property right limits the scope of copyright and curbs its undue expansion; and secondly, to examine what this means for copyright to be located within the larger context of personal property. It sought to achieve both these objectives by drawing analytically appropriate analogies between copyright and property rights in tangible things. It would be opportune here to evaluate whether these objectives were achieved.

Let us begin with the first objective—have the analogies with property rights in tangible things helped limit copyright? The most foundational analogy drawn in this monograph was in relation to thinghood. It was sought not only to establish that copyright relates to a thing but also to establish the characteristics of the thing by analogy with tangible things—in particular with parts and products of the human body. Chapter 2 analysed the thing in copyright—the work—as consisting of (i) the substantive content, that is, the resource that copyright protects; (ii) being separable from human body, the legal system, and the rights themselves; and (iii) having a form that demarcates the boundary of the thing in copyright. With the substantive content, the application of *numerus clausus* meant that the list of categories of works that can exist within the Copyright, Designs and Patents Act 1988 (CDPA) is closed, thereby limiting copyright protection only to the resources that can be objectively perceived. Separability helped confine copyright protection only to expressions that exist outside the human body, and not to thoughts or ideas. The boundaries drawn by the form were shown to help not only to exclude the rest of the world but also to prevent the owners from overclaiming that which lies beyond the boundaries. To the extent that the requirement of form was not met, broadcasts were identified as an outlier and a product of political and international pressures. But, on the whole, this chapter helped establish that each of the characteristics of the thing helps limit the scope of the work. If instead copyright was conceptualised as a chose in action, the teleological

Copyright as Personal Property. Poorna Mysoor, Oxford University Press. © Poorna Mysoor 2025.
DOI: 10.1093/9780191954962.003.0008

significance of these characteristics would not have been understood, nor their ability to perform the limiting role.

The thinghood of copyright facilitated the examination of the rules of first acquisition of copyright in Chapter 3, by analogy with first acquisition of title through the accession of a thing by manufacture and by taking possession of a thing. Copyright in authorial works is acquired by expressing the author's thoughts in an original way and in entrepreneurial works by creating a record that is not a copy of an existing entrepreneurial work. The perspective offered by the analogies with accession and possession helped reassess the level of originality required to justify copyright to subsist in a work. This is particularly helpful in the current state of play in copyright law because the case law sets the bar for originality very low, making it too easy to acquire copyright as also to infringe copyright. It is clear that if copyright had been conceptualised as a chose in action, no analogy with any title acquisition methods in land law or personal property law would have been possible. Not seeing the need for originality by analogy with accession or taking possession would regard originality simply as one of the requirements for subsistence of copyright. The slightest intellectual or entrepreneurial input would enable the acquisition of copyright. Surely, the title to tangible things cannot be acquired by actions that are too slight or ambiguous, such as merely grazing land without enclosing it or simply touching an apple without grasping it. By drawing an analogy with the signalling behind the manner of acquiring title to a tangible thing, an effective argument can be made for raising the bar for originality, making it harder for copyright to be acquired and infringed.

Separating the thing from the manner of its acquisition enables an independent appreciation of the thing itself. In the copyright context, separating the work from the requirement of originality enables an independent understanding of the work. Historically, the recognition of different types of works for copyright protection has been based on the works satisfying certain definitional requirements. If a work is to be regarded a work of artistic craftsmanship, there should be both artistry and craftsmanship in the work. Insisting on artistry as a requirement ensures that not every object of craftsmanship acquires copyright, thereby limiting the conduct which attracts copyright protection. If one were to follow the CJEU's case law which conflates originality with the work, it could potentially lead to an expansion of copyright protection that would lack legitimacy, conceptual coherence, and historical justification. It would be doctrinally problematic in that it would make it too easy for works to come into conflict with each other. Therefore, separating the work from originality by analogy with separating the thing from its acquisition helps limit acquisition of copyright to more deserving subject matter.

Establishing the existence of a thing and that it can be acquired independently helps the proposition that property rights arise in or in relation to the thing, and this is what Chapter 4 dealt with in relation to copyright. The misunderstanding in relation to exclusionary rights of copyright is perhaps the gravest because of the chose in action conceptualisation of copyright—that copyright is simply a collection of rights. There is a belief that exclusionary rights in the context of property rights can only mean one thing—exclusion from the thing itself. This chapter considered trespass to land and private nuisance to see what interest is protected. It found that in aerial trespass there is no 'thing' from which one may exclude oneself, and in private nuisance the exclusion is from doing something unreasonable on the neighbouring land, and not an exclusion from the land itself. Since land law is open to an interpretation of exclusionary rights different from the exclusion from the thing itself, there is no reason why in copyright too the exclusionary rights cannot be understood differently. Together with demonstrating that upon acquisition of ownership a copyright owner becomes able to exercise exclusive powers and exclusive privileges, this chapter helped copyright to decisively move away from the chose in action conceptualisation.

While on the issue of exclusionary rights, the interpretation given by the Court of Justice of the European Union (CJEU) and followed by the UK courts of the right of communication to the public at present is wholly contrived and unjustifiable. A dividend of closer analogy with property rights is the insistence on closer adherence to *numerus clausus*. Whenever there is a duty arising from a property right imposed on the rest of the world without their consent, *numerus clausus* can help sharpen the scope and interpretation of the exclusionary rights, particularly the interpretation of rights that have no bearing on the words describing the right. The issue of the botched interpretation of the right of communication to the public could not have been seen as a *numerus clausus* problem if copyright was not regarded a property right. The only manner in which any change could occur would have been to wait for the legislature to amend the statute, providing some clarity. Instead, principles drawn from property theory such as *numerus clausus* might help courts to see the problem and roll back some of the artificiality in the interpretation of the rights.

Another significant limiting impact that can be achieved from an analogy of copyright law with land and personal property law is in the enforcement of rights, powers, and privileges. Chapter 5 was able to show that direct voluntary interference as in trespass is analogous to literal infringement of copyright, whereas indirect voluntary interference is analogous to non-literal infringement, and involuntary interference to subconscious infringement. Clearly, the fault element changes from trespass to private nuisance to negligence in land law. On this basis, this chapter called out the unfairness of copyright infringement in being a singular immutable tort with the strictest fault element whether the infringement is direct or indirect, voluntary or involuntary. The strangeness of recognising analogy with property rights for remedies but not for the method of enforcement of property rights was also pointed out in this chapter. The chapter revealed the irony that the paradigmatic property rights such as those relating to tangible things would be enforced in a kindlier and more nuanced way than copyright infringement. This cannot even be justified by characterising copyright infringement as an economic tort because economic torts are intentional torts, but copyright infringement can be entirely subconscious. The chapter proposed the manner in which copyright infringement can be made less prone to unjust outcomes.

Defences to copyright infringement and limitations on the exploitation of copyright play a significant role in balancing competing interests. Some scholars point to these, especially the defences of fair dealing, to argue that the flexibility offered by these defences undermines the nature of copyright as a property right. This argument is a product of the mistaken view that copyright is nothing but a right, a chose in action. This is why it appears to these scholars that the defences shift the boundary of copyright. Chapter 6 sought to demonstrate that the flexibility incorporated by the fair dealing defences is no different from the flexibility within the analysis of the undue interference in private nuisance. The difference is only a matter of timing. In this sense, it sought to argue that a closer analogy of copyright with property rights in tangible things will not weaken the limiting role already played by the defences to copyright infringement. It may indeed be argued that the relatively less rivalrous nature of copyright works is a strength that makes them capable of being used by many simultaneously, enabling a greater number of defences to be recognised. Chapter 6 further pointed to various defences to trespass and private nuisance scattered around in different statutes giving lawful authority for the state and public authorities to curtail property rights in land. To the extent that public policy is the underlying justification, these defences play a similar role in enabling sharing the use of land among multiple people at the same time.

A major benefit of examining copyright as a property right by analogy with property rights in tangible things is that one can undertake a closer examination of the derivative interests to which copyright gives rise. Chapter 7 showed that copyright does demonstrate the ability to create lesser interests in the thing and exercises the power to grant these to others, while retaining the residuary rights to the thing. It analysed not only those derivative interests mentioned by the statute, namely licences and partial and complete assignments but also security interests by implication, and equitable interests such as options and the rights of pre-emption. It examined the problematic nature of partial assignments limited by duration and exclusive licences not being regarded as property interests. It proposed to bring about transactional simplicity and clarity by abolishing partial assignments limited by duration, but instead making exclusive licences be limited by duration, more akin to leases. It finally examined the case for the right to receive royalites as a standalone property interest. Chapter 7 showed that analysing these interests through the lens of *numerus clausus* enables a clearer, sharper, and more certain definition of these interests, thereby helping limit their impact on successors in title, as well as in imposing trespassory liability on the rest of the world.

In addition to the individual chapters showing the limiting effect of property rights, on the whole, the very approach facilitated by the analogy with property rights to tangible things deserves highlighting. Taking a bird's eye view, this monograph sought to liberate copyright from the conceptualisation as a chose in action and identified the attributes of the thing in copyright. Analysing copyright by analogy with property rights in tangible things helped copyright to be benchmarked against the concepts, principles, and doctrines in land law and personal property law. If, in contrast, copyright were conceptualised as a chose in action, no such benchmarking would be possible, because other choses in action such as debts and shares have nothing in common with copyright except their intangibility. Since copyright is regulated by statute, it would be convenient to come to the conclusion that Parliament does not need to acknowledge any theory and that, in its sovereignty, Parliament can enact anything—including a move away from avowed common law principles, their historical and conceptual origins. It would also be simpler to make any issue with the copyright regime a matter of political lobbying or a product of statutory interpretation, without the need for any guidance from any theory or indeed any analogy. If there is no yardstick against which the copyright regulatory regime can be measured, copyright would end up growing in the direction decided by the loudest politico-economic voice. We have seen this happen in the case of broadcasts where, despite not adhering to anything that one can conceptualise as a 'thing', they were granted protection as a copyright work.

In addition, if the conceptualisation of copyright as a chose in action were to prevail, none of the limiting effect brought about by the analogy with property rights to tangible things would benefit copyright. From the discussion in the foregoing chapters, it is clear that the divergences from property logic have led to unjustified expansion. The salient indicators of expansion pointed out in this monograph are: making any product of human mind a copyright work regardless of how uncertain its boundaries or how subjective its perception or how impervious it is to the definitional requirements of a work; granting the protection of a copyright work to broadcasts despite not satisfying the requirement of form; abolishing most formalities as a matter of international treaty law, for copyright to subsist in a work, and not even to require the registration of any transactions involving copyright; lowering the bar for originality; giving contrived interpretation to exclusionary rights; making copyright infringement a needlessly severe tort with no consideration for types of interferences; and making copyright transactions unnecessarily complex and confusing. These are the reasons why this book argued that it is essential to underpin copyright in the logic drawn from property theory and conceptualise it by analogy with property rights in tangible things.

From the perspective of property theory, together with each chapter demonstrating the limiting role of property regime, the principle of *numerus clausus* anchors the whole of the monograph and acts as an overarching limiting principle. The lack of consensus as to the existence of an 'intangible thing' has resulted in its weaker conceptualisation in relation to copyright. It is the intangible things which need the backbone support in the form of *numerus clausus* to hold their conceptual structure together, ever more so than tangible things. Property theorists do not have any issue applying *numerus clausus* to property interests when it is quite clear that these interests themselves are intangible. Even if these interests eventually relate to a tangible thing like land, the thing does not really make much difference to the design of these interests which typically involve rights and duties that are also intangible. In many ways, it may be argued that the need for *numerus clausus* arises because the duties imposed on third parties without their consent are invisible to them, regardless of whether the duties relate to a tangible or an intangible thing. This monograph took up the challenge of applying *numerus clausus* at every step of the analysis of the nature of copyright, the exclusionary rights, and the derivative interests, reaping the fullest benefit of it as a guiding principle.

From a doctrinal perspective, adverse possession, finders of goods, and prescription do not find a place in copyright. These are some of the most important doctrines that limit the powers of the property owner, enabling the person who has demonstrated an ability to make better use of the thing to gain precedence over the property owner. The magic of relativity of title in relation to tangible things ensures that the person demonstrating a better use of the thing gets the title as against everyone except the true owner. The adverse possessor's taking control of the land involves putting the land to use in a manner akin to a landowner. These actions over time topple the title of the paper title holder (if the land is unregistered in the United Kingdom). A person becomes a finder of a chattel because its true owner is not currently using the chattel. The acquisition of an easement based on prescription is entirely based on persistent use of the easement, confirming the argument that land law favours those who use the land. When use is given precedence over the owner, the law achieves this by limiting the owner's rights, powers, and privileges. Bringing these doctrines into copyright by analogy can help shape the contours of the copyright owner's rights, powers, and privileges in a more balanced way.

Limiting the remit of copyright ownership is not for its own sake, but for the sake of the welfare-enhancing results it brings about. If we take the objective of copyright to be incentivising greater creativity, making sure that copyright works conform to thinghood as discussed herein in turn ensures that the law does not make infringers out of those who may otherwise be innocent in being unable to ascertain what the work is or where the boundaries lie. Raising the bar for the acquisition of copyright leaves much more content in the public domain from which newer and more creative works may be created. It also ensures that infringement is not found too readily. Instead, if greater output stays outside the realm of protection, it improves the expanse of the public domain. Access to a healthy public domain without the fear of infringement can lead to greater creativity and innovation. Ensuring that the exclusionary rights are clearly defined prevents overlapping rights, reducing risk of infringement whilst promoting transactional efficiency. By making use of the less rivalrous nature of copyright works to its best advantage through the recognition of many defences addressing legitimate uses of copyright works, fair access to information can be maintained. Allowing human rights arguments to be read into these defences can help limit state action interfering with free speech in the guise of asserting copyright.

With the recent amendments to the EU (Withdrawal) Act 2018, one of the most important consequences has been that the supremacy of EU law is no longer required to be recognised. Further, higher courts in the United Kingdom will have the jurisdiction to reconsider the CJEU jurisprudence that has been part of domestic law. The UK courts will have a choice between continuing to affirm EU law or change it to reflect what is a much more natural fit for the interpretation of the CDPA. Some of the most crucial decisions will be the interpretation of a work and the separation of the work from the method of acquisition, as discussed in Chapters 2 and 3, and in the interpretation of the right of communication to the public discussed in Chapter 4. The benefits of interpreting the provisions of the CDPA by analogy with property rights in tangible things established in this book can help UK courts make an informed choice in this regard.

Let us move to the second objective that this book sought to achieve, namely, to locate copyright within the larger context of personal property rights. Throughout the monograph, an attempt was made to show how the analogy with property rights in tangible things is the most natural fit for copyright, starting from thing-relatedness to derivative interests in copyright, from a conceptual, doctrinal, and historical perspective. Based on this, one can demonstrate that property rights can be conceptualised along a spectrum, with copyright being located closer to the property rights in tangible things than to other intangible assets such as debts and shares. To achieve this, the resources being considered need to be mapped on the horizontal axis. Since chattels are more rivalrous than land, and land more rivalrous than copyright, these resources can be placed on the horizontal axis in that sequence. The vertical axis can be plotted with the attributes drawn from each of the chapters, forming the metrics for the spectrum. The discussions in this monograph have revealed these to be necessary for benchmarking a resource for its eligibility to attract property rights. Whether these are also sufficient as metrics depends on the purpose for which the spectrum is being considered. A possible visualisation of this is given in Figure F.1 below.

Starting with thinghood, one can observe the fluidity of the spectrum. Whilst all three resources have a separable subject matter, chattels (say, a bracelet) have a form naturally defined by their shape and configuration which the law can enforce; for land the boundaries have to be defined by building walls, fences, and so on, to which the law will ascribe meaning for the purposes of enforcement; and for copyright again the boundaries have to be defined by recording the work, to which the CDPA ascribes meaning for the purposes of enforcement, as argued in Chapter 2. With the first and independent acquisition of title, factual physical control is all that is required of chattels (say, wearing the bracelet); with land, securing boundaries like building fences and locking gates will be regarded as legally sufficient control even if factually it may not be; and with copyright, the analogy can be more fluid, with both manufacture (similar to chattels) and securing boundaries (similar to land), as argued in Chapter 3. With exclusionary rights, in chattels these impose a duty on the rest of the world of exclusion from the chattel itself or be substantially deprived of its use; in land, the exclusion can be from the land, but equally from the space above where there is no physical thing from which one is required to exclude oneself; in copyright work, the exclusion is from an activity, as argued in Chapter 4. In this way, the spectrum can be developed in relation to each of the attributes discussed in this book as a separate metric. Chattels being most rivalrous have the least number of derivative interests, followed by land, and then copyright. Chattels score highest on each metric for exclusion and exclusivity, being situated closer to the top left-hand corner, with each subsequent resource scoring less on each metric, giving the spectrum a downward curve.

If the idea of a spectrum is found convincing, the horizontal axis can be fine-tuned further within the zone of things that count as chattels. Given their diversity spanning, say, a diamond ring to an aircraft, from perishable agricultural produce to artefacts of cultural heritage that have survived millennia, it may be possible to test the generalisations one makes in relation to chattels, by reference to the metrics on the spectrum. Even within the zone for copyright a distinction can be made between authorial works and entrepreneurial works. The spectrum can be extended by considering other resources such as other types of intellectual property—patents, trade marks, registered and unregistered designs, and so on. The more resources with which one tests the spectrum, the more robust the metrics on the vertical axis will become, which enables more borderline resources, such as confidential information, to be analysed more astutely. An effort can be made to plot the newer and more esoteric kinds of intangible resources, such as digital assets and raw industrial data. Some digital assets might be different from copyright works in being more rivalrous and therefore might take up the spot between land and copyright. By analogy with copyright statute, it may be possible to see how a statutory framework, if one is envisaged, can be designed around the metrics of the spectrum.

Resources that are normally classified together with intellectual property as choses in action or as pure intangibles, such as contractual debts, can also be plotted against these metrics. With contractual debts there is no subject matter that is separable from the right itself, and therefore it fails this aspect of the thinghood requirement. Since thinghood affects everything from acquisition of the right, the nature of the rights, exclusive privileges and powers, enforcement, remedies, defences, and even derivative interests, debt will not respond to most of these metrics. To the extent that debts are assignable and chargeable as a security, there may be some place for them on the spectrum limited to these metrics. This pushes its positioning towards the right-hand bottom end of the spectrum at the tapering point. Drawn this way, the spectrum could show visually how far removed debts are from copyright and how unsatisfactory the category of chose in action or even pure intangibles is.

The spectrum is a more sophisticated way of explaining the resources than the existing taxonomy. To begin with, it is not binary—everything that is not one thing does not have to be the other. There are no brightline distinctions, but mapping against the same metrics for different resources, recognising that some resources respond to certain metrics more than the others. The metrics can be general or specific, depending on the purpose for drawing the spectrum. For example, if the purpose is to examine the conduct required to take control of the resources to acquire rights in them for the first time, the metrics for this can narrow down specifically to the relational and exclusionary signalling discussed in Chapter 3. If the purpose is to examine how patent rights compare with chattels, much more generic metrics, such as those of thinghood, acquisition, enforcement, and so on, can be utilised to give a general picture. Because of its inherent fluidity, the spectrum makes it acceptable for concepts, principles, and doctrine to move from resource to resource, with the required modification by analogy. The label of specialism would become much less of a barrier for examining these resources. For example, the consideration of a doctrine similar to adverse possession in relation to trade marks should not seem implausible when one considers it in the light of the metric on the spectrum that deals with the conduct of first acquisition of title independently, and its analogy with possession in land.

Overall, the monograph sought to give a new perspective from which to view land and chattels—the perspective being that of copyright. Neither personal property lawyers nor land lawyers may have paid much attention to unpicking the components and the characteristics that make up the thing. Personal property lawyers may not have noticed what the rules of manufacture can mean for products of the human mind. Land lawyers may not have seen the benefit of distributive logic of land law being relevant by analogy to intangible things in the knowledge economy. In general, neither land lawyers nor personal property lawyers may have given close consideration to all the different ways in which rules that govern property rights in tangible things limit the rights of the owner and balance them with the interest of others. This monograph sought to open the debates around the topics that are familiar to land and personal property lawyers and show how much of what is discussed in copyright has a close proximity to land and personal property law.

To sum up, intangible assets make up a substantial part of modern economies and it is likely that newer forms of intangible assets might have to be considered for protection in future. If these intangible assets are to be bestowed with the attributes of an intangible thing, it would be sensible to turn to the existing laws that made it possible for other intangible assets to be regulated.

The CDPA is one such example which illustrates how copyright works came to be conceived as intangible things. An investigation into the reasons underlying the design of the CDPA, including those drawn from property theory and copyright history, could help inform meaningfully the manner in which newer forms of intangible things can be conceptualised and regulated. Given the reality of a growing economy in intangible assets, the analogical reasoning here may herald a move towards a pluralistic, progressive, and dynamic approach to property rights befitting the times we live in today.

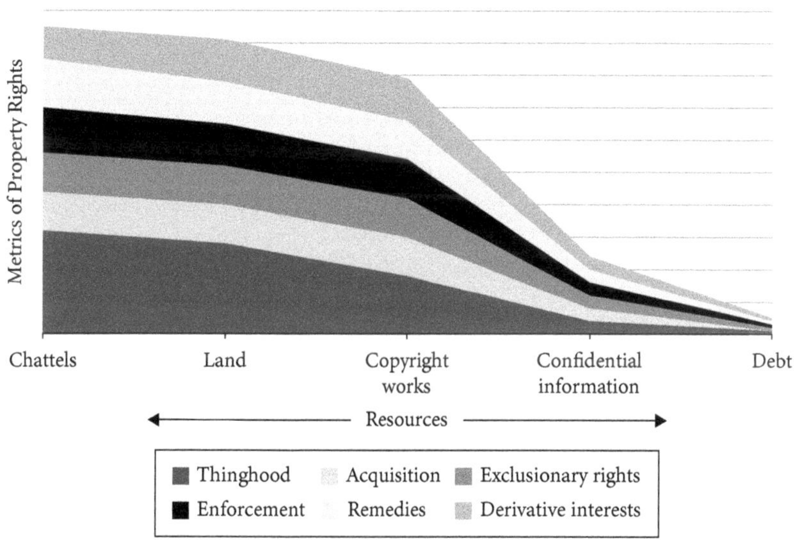

Figure F.1 Visualisation of spectrum of property rights

Bibliography

Adams JN, 'Barker v Stickney Revisited' [1988] IPQ 113
Adams JN, 'The Passing of the Burden of Royalty Payments' [2007] IPQ 403
Akkermans B, 'The Numerus Clausus of Property Rights' in M Graziadei and L Smith (eds), *Comparative Property Law: Global Perspectives* (Edward Elgar 2017)
Aplin T, 'Subject Matter' in Estelle Derclaye (ed), *Research Handbook on the Future of EU Copyright* (Edward Elgar 2009)
Authors Licensing and Collecting Society <www.alcs.co.uk/>
accessed 10 December 2024
Balganesh S, 'The Social Costs of Property Rights in Broadcast (and Cable) Signals' (2007) 22 Berkeley Tech LJ 1303
Balganesh S, 'Foreseeability and Copyright Incentives' (2009) 122 Harv L Rev 1569
Balganesh S, 'Alienability and Copyright Law' in H Howe and J Griffiths (eds), *Concepts of Property in Intellectual Property Law* (CUP 2013)
Balganesh S, 'Causing Copyright' (2017) 117 Colum L Rev 1
BBC Memorandum, 'A Copyright in Broadcasting' (June 1949), submitted to the Broadcasting Committee (copy with the author, taken from the National Archives)
Bently L, 'Account of Profits for Infringement of Copyright. Potton v Yorkclose and Others' (1990) 12(3) EIPR 106
Bently L, 'Accounting for Profits Gained by Infringement of Copyright: Where Does it End?' (1991) 13(1) EIPR 5
Bently L and others, *Intellectual Property Law* (6th edn, OUP 2022)
Bevan C, 'The Doctrine of Benefit and Burden: Reforming the Law of Covenants and the Numerus Clausus "Problem"' (2018) 77 CLJ 72
Birks P, 'Before We Begin: Five Leys to Land Law' in S Bright and J Dewer (eds), *Land Law Themes and Perspectives* (OUP 1998)
Boulier W, 'Sperm, Spleens, and Other Valuables: The Need to Recognize Property Rights in Human Body Parts' (1995) 23 Hofstra L Rev 693
Breaky H, 'Properties of Copyright' in H Howe (ed), *Concepts of Property in Intellectual Property* (CUP 2013)
Brewer S, 'Exemplary Reasoning: Semantics, Pragmatics, and the Rational Force of Legal Argument by Analogy' (1996) 109 Harv L Rev 923
Bridge M, *Personal Property Law* (4th edn, OUP 2015)
Bridge M and others, *The Law of Personal Property* (3rd edn, Sweet & Maxwell 2022)
Brodhurst S, 'Is Copyright a Chose in Action?' (1895) 11 LQR 64
Burrell R, 'Abandonment, Copyright and Orphaned Works: What Does It Mean to Take the Proprietary Nature of Intellectual Property Rights Seriously' (2011) 35 Melb U L Rev 971
Carrier M, 'Limiting Copyright through Property' in H Howe and J Griffiths (eds), *Concepts of Property in Intellectual Property* (CUP 2013)
Chan T, 'The Nature of Property in Crypto-assets' (2023) 43 LS 480
Ciolino DS and Donelon EA, 'Questioning Strict Liability in Copyright' (2002) 54 Rutgers L Rev 351

Crawford M, *An Expressive Theory of Possession* (Hart 2020)

Cronin C, 'Law and Odor: Elusive Copyright and Other IP Protection for Fragrances' in E Bonadio E and N Lucchi (eds), *Non-Conventional Copyright* (Edward Elgar 2018)

Deazley R (2008) 'Commentary on the *Statute of Anne* 1710' in L Bently and M Kretschmer (eds), *Primary Sources on Copyright (1450–1900)* <www.copyrighthistory.org>

Deazley R (2008) 'Commentary on *Tonson v. Collins* (1762)' in L Bently and M Kretschmer (eds), *Primary Sources on Copyright (1450–1900)* <www.copyrighthistory.org>

Derclaye E, 'Debunking Some of UK Copyright Law's Longstanding Myths and Misunderstandings' [2013] IPQ 1

Douglas S, *Liability for Wrongful Interferences with Chattels* (Hart 2011)

Douglas S, 'Kuwait Airways Corporation v Iraqi Airways Company' in S Douglas, R Hickey, and E Waring (eds), *Landmark Cases in Property Law* (Bloomsbury 2015)

Douglas S and Goold I, 'Property in Human Biomaterials: A New Methodology' (2016) 75(3) CLJ 478

Douglas S and McFarlane B, 'Defining Property Rights' in J Penner and H Smith (eds), *Philosophical Foundations of Property Law* (OUP 2013)

Drassinower A, 'Capturing Ideas: Copyright and the Law of First Possession' (2006) 54 Clev St L Rev 191

Edelman J and others, *McGregor on Damages* (22nd edn, Sweet & Maxwell 2024)

Elphinstone HW, 'What is a Chose in Action' (1893) 9 LQR 311

Epstein R, 'Possession as the Root of Title' (1979) 13 Ga L Rev 1221

Epstein RA, 'Notice and Freedom of Contract in the Law of Servitudes' (1981) 55 S Cal L Rev 1353

Essert C, 'Property in Licences and the Law of Things' (2014) 59 McGill LJ 559

Finnis J, 'Some Professional Fallacies about Rights' [1972] Adelaide L Rev 377

Fuller LL, 'Consideration and Form' (1941) 41 Colum L Rev 799

Gaunt J and Morgan P, *Gale on the Law of Easements* (22nd edn, Sweet & Maxwell 2025)

Giblin R and Weatherall K, 'If We Redesigned Copyright from Scratch, What Might it Look Like?' in R Giblin and K Weatherall (eds), *What if We Could Reimagine Copyright?* (ANU Press 2017)

Goldberg J and Zipursky B, 'The Strict Liability in Fault and the Fault in Strict Liability' (2016) 85 Fordham L Rev 743

Goold P, *IP Accidents: Negligence Liability in Intellectual Property* (CUP 2022)

Gordon W, 'Copyright as Property' (1989) 41 Stan L Rev 1343

Goudkamp J, *Tort Law Defences* (Hart 2013)

Goudkamp J and Nolan D, *Winfield and Jolowicz on Tort* (20th edn, Sweet & Maxwell 2020)

Gray K, 'Property in Thin Air' (1991) 50 CLJ 252

Green S, 'To Have and to Hold? Conversion and Intangible Property' (2008) 71 MLR 114

Green S, 'Time for a Tertium Quid' (University College London 25 May 2023) <www.ucl.ac.uk/laws/events/2023/may/recording-time-tertium-quid> accessed 24 November 2024

Green S and J Randall, *The Tort of Conversion* (Hart 2009)

Grey K and Grey SF, *Elements of Land Law* (6th edn, OUP 2009)

Guadamuz A, 'Can the Monkey Selfie Case Teach Us Anything about Copyright Law?' (*WIPO Magazine*, 21 February 2018) <www.wipo.int/wipo_magazine/en/2018/01/article_0007.html> accessed 20 November 2024

Hansmann H and R Kraakman, 'Property, Contract, and Verification: The Numerus Clausus Problem and the Divisibility of Rights' (2002) 31 JLS 373

Harbottle G and others, *Copinger and Skone James on Copyright* (19th edn, Sweet & Maxwell 2025)

Harris JW, *Property and Justice* (Clarendon Press 1996)

Hawes C, 'Conversion by Detention' [2009] LMCLQ 188

Helfer L, 'How Intellectual Property and Human Rights Can Live Together' in P Torremas (ed), *Intellectual Property Law and Human Rights* (3rd edn, Wolters Kluwer 2015)

Hohfeld WN, 'Some Fundamental Legal Conceptions as Applied in Judicial Reasoning' (1913) 23 Yale LJ 16

Hohfeld WN, 'Fundamental Legal Conceptions as Applied in Judicial Reasoning' (1916) 26 Yale LJ 710

Hohfeld WN, 'Faulty Analysis of Easement and Licence Cases' (1917) 27 Yale LJ 66

Honoré AM, 'Ownership' in AG Guest (ed), *Oxford Essays in Jurisprudence* (OUP 1961)

Hudson E and Burrell R, 'Abandonment, Copyright and Orphaned Works: What Does It Mean to Take the Proprietary Nature of Intellectual Property Rights Seriously' (2011) 35 Melb U L Rev 971

Hugenholtz B, 'Works of Literature, Science and Art', in B Hugenholtz and others (eds), *100 Years of Dutch Copyright Law: Auteurswet, 1912–2012* (deLex 2012)

Hughes J, 'The Philosophy of Intellectual Property' (1988) 77 Geo L J 287

Katz L, 'Exclusion and Exclusivity in Property Law' (2008) 58 U Toronto LJ 275

Law Commission, *Digital Assets: A Consultation Paper* (Law Com No 256, 2022)

Law Commission, *Report on Digital Assets* (Law Com No 412, 2023)

Lemley M, 'Property, Intellectual Property, and Free Riding' (2004–05) 83 Texas L Rev 1031

Llewelyn D and Aplin T, *Cornish, Llewelyn & Aplin Intellectual Property: Patents, Copyrights, Trademarks & Allied Rights* (10th edn, Sweet & Maxwell 2023)

Locke J, An Essay Concerning Human Understanding, Book II, Chapter I: Of Ideas in General <www.gutenberg.org/files/10615/10615-h/10615-h.htm> accessed 10 November 2024

Marinotti J, 'Possessing Intangibles' (2022) 116 Northwest Univ L Rev 1227

McCutcheon J, '*Levola Hengelo BV v. Smilde Foods BV*: The Hard Work of Defining a Copyright Work' (2019) 82 MLR 936

McFarlane B, *The Structure of Property Law* (Hart 2008)

McFarlane B, 'The Numerus Clausus Principle and Covenants Relating to Land' in S Bright (ed), *Modern Studies in Property Law*, vol 6 (Hart 2011)

McFarlane B, 'Tulk v Moxhay (1848); Hill v Tupper (1863)' in C Mitchell and P Mitchell (eds), *Landmark Cases in Equity* (Hart 2012)

McFarlane B and Douglas S, 'Property, Analogy, Variety' (2022) 42(1) OJLS 161

McKendrick E, *Contract Law* (7th edn, OUP 2014)

Megarry R and others, *The Law of Real Property* (10th edn, Sweet & Maxwell 2024)

Merrill TW, 'Property and the Right to Exclude' (1998) 77 Neb L Rev 730

Merrill TW, 'Ownership and Possession' in Y-C Chang (ed), *Law and Economics of Possession* (CUP 2015)

Merrill TW and Smith HE, 'Optimal Standardization in the Law of Property: The Numerus Clausus Principle' (2000) 110 Yale LJ 1

Merrill TW and Smith HE, 'The Property/Contract Interface' (2001) 101 Colum L Rev 773

Mossoff A, 'What is Property? Putting the Pieces Back Together' (2003) 45 Ariz L Rev 371

Mulligan C, 'A Numerus Clausus Principle for Intellectual Property' (2013) 80 Tenn L Rev 235

Munzer SR, 'An Uneasy Case Against Property Rights in Body Parts' (1994) 11 Soc Phil & Pol'y 259

Mysoor P, 'Unpacking the Right of Communication to the Public: A Closer Look at International and EU Copyright Law' [2013] IPQ 166
Mysoor P, 'Does UK Really Have a "Closed" List of Works Protected by Copyright?' [2019] EIPR 474
Mysoor P, 'Capturing the Dynamism of Fairness—a Common Law Perspective' in Daniel Gervais (ed), *Fairness, Morality and Ordre Public in Intellectual Property* (Edward Elgar 2020)
Mysoor P, 'Form in Conceptualising Copyright as a Property Right' (2020) 67(1) J Copyright Soc'y USA 79
Mysoor P, *Implied Licences in Copyright Law* (OUP 2021)
Mysoor P, 'Possession in Copyright by Analogy' (2024) 140 LQR 277
Mysoor P, 'Licence Fee Damages and the Nature of IP Rights' [2025] Harv J L & Tech (Forthcoming)
Mysoor P, 'The Jurisdiction of Implying' in HE Smith, S Balganesh, and P Mysoor (eds), *Intellectual Property and Private Law* (CUP 2025 forthcoming)
Netanel NW, 'Why Has Copyright Expanded? Analysis and Critique' in F MacMillan (ed), *New Directions in Copyright Law* (Edward Elgar 2008)
Newman CM, 'An Exclusive License Is Not an Assignment: Disentangling Divisibility and Transferability of Ownership in Copyright' (2013) 74 La L Rev 59
Newman CM, 'Vested Use-Privileges in Property and Copyright' (2017) 30 Harv J L & Tech 75
Newman CM, 'Using Things; Defining Property' in J Penner and M Otsuka (eds), *Property Theory: Legal and Political Perspectives* (CUP 2018)
Nimmer D, *Nimmer on Copyright* (Matthew Bender 2020)
Oliar D and Stern JY, 'Right on Time: First Possession in Property and Intellectual Property' (2019) 99 BUL Rev 395
Oliphant K, 'The Structure of the Intentional Torts' in Jason Neyers (ed), *Emerging Issues in Tort Law* (Hart 2007)
Penner J, 'The Bundle of Rights Picture of Property' (1996) 43 UCLA L Rev 711
Penner J, *The Idea of Property in Law* (OUP 2000)
Performing Rights Society <https://www.prsformusic.com/> accessed 21 September 2024
Pila J, *The Subject Matter of Intellectual Property* (OUP 2017)
Pollock F, 'What Is a Thing' (1894) 10 LQR 318
Pollock F and RS Wright, *An Essay on Possession in Common Law* (Clarendon Press 1888)
Pretto-Sakmann A, *Boundaries of Personal Property: Shares and Sub-Shares* (Hart Publishing 2005)
Rahmatian A, *Copyright and Creativity* (Edward Elgar 2011)
Rognstad O-A, *Property Aspects of Intellectual Property* (CUP 2018)
Rose CM, 'Possession as the Origin of Property' (1985) 52 U Chi L Rev 73
Rose CM, 'The Law Is Nine-Tenths of Possession: An Adage Turned on Its Head' in Y-C Chang (ed), *Law and Economics of Possession* (CUP 2015)
Rostill L, *Possession, Relative Title, and Ownership in English Law* (OUP 2021)
Rudden B, 'Economic Theory v. Property Law: The Numerus Clausus Problem' in J Eekelaar and J Bell (eds), *Oxford Essays in Jurisprudence: Third Series* (Clarendon Press 1987)
Ruse-Khan HG, 'Overlaps and Conflict Norms in Human Rights Law' in Christophe Geiger (ed), *Research Handbook on Human Rights and Intellectual Property* (Edward Elgar 2015)
Sganga C, *Propertizating European Copyright* (Edward Elgar 2018)
Sheehan D, *The Principles of Personal Property Law* (Hart 2017)

Sherman B, 'What is a Copyright Work?' (2011) 12 Theoretical Inq L 99

Sherman B, 'Public Ownership of Private Spectacles' in B Sherman and L Wiseman (eds), *Copyright and the Challenge of the New* (Kluwer Law International 2012)

Sherman B and Bently L, *The Making of Modern Intellectual Property Law* (CUP 1999)

Simone D, 'Pay No Attention to that Man Behind the Curtain!: Copyright, Authorship and Artificial Intelligence' [2023] AIPJ 120

Smith HE, 'Exclusion Versus Governance: Two Strategies for Delineating Property Rights' (2002) 31 J Legal Stud S453

Smith HE, 'Intellectual Property as Property: Delineating Entitlements in Information' (2007) 117 Yale LJ 1742

Smith HE, 'Property is Not Just a Bundle of Rights' (2011) 8(3) EJW 279

Smith HE, 'Property as the Law of Things' (2012) 125 Harv L Rev 1691

Smith HE, 'The Elements of Possession' in Y-C Chang (ed), *Law and Economics of Possession* (CUP 2015)

Smith L, 'Fusion and Tradition' in S Degeling and J Edelman (eds), *Equity in Commercial Law* (Lawbook Co 2005)

Speck A and others, *The Modern Law of Copyright* (5th edn, LexisNexis 2018)

Spence M, *Intellectual Property* (OUP 2007)

Stiglitz JE, 'Economic Foundations of Intellectual Property Rights' (2008) 57 Duke LJ 1693

Swadling W, 'Property—General Principles' in A Burrows (ed), *English Private Law* (3rd edn, OUP 2013)

Sweet C, 'Choses in Action' (1895) 11 LQR 238

Tettenborn A and others, *Clerk & Lindsell on Torts* (24th edn, Sweet & Maxwell 2024)

The Gowers Review of Intellectual Property (December 2006)

Tosato A, 'Security Interests over Intellectual Property' (2011) 6 JIPLP 93

Tosato A, 'Intellectual Property License Contracts: Reflections on a Prospective UNCITRAL Project' (2018) 86 U Cin L Rev 1251 <https://scholarship.law.uc.edu/uclr/vol86/iss4/4> accessed 22 December 2024

Townend DMR, 'Intellectual Property as Security Interests: Technical Difficulties Presented in the Law' (1997) 2 IPQ 168

van Erp S, 'Ownership of Data: The Numerus Clausus of Legal Objects' (2017) 6 Brigham-Kanner Prop Rts Conf J 235

van Gompel S, *Formalities in Copyright Law: An Analysis of Their History, Rationales and Possible Future* (Kluwer Law International 2011)

Van Houweling MS, 'Technology and Tracing Costs: Lessons from Real Property' in S Balganesh (ed), *Intellectual Property and Common Law* (CUP 2013)

Van Houweling MS, 'The New Private Law and Intellectual Property: Calibrating Copyright on the Common Law Continuum' in A Gold and others (eds), *The Oxford Handbook of the New Private Law* (OUP 2020)

Vitoria M and others, *The Modern Law of Copyright and Designs* (4th edn, LexisNexis 2018)

Waldron J, *The Right to Private Property* (OUP 1988)

Watt G, 'The Proprietary Effect of a Chattel Lease' [2003] Conv 6

Watts PG and Low KFK, 'The Case for Cryptoassets as Property' in S Agnew and M Smith (eds), *Law at the Cutting Edge* (Hart 2024)

Weil EV, 'Stability and Change in Property Law: A Comparative Approach to the Principle of Numerus Clausus' (PhD thesis, University College London 2022) <https://discovery.ucl.ac.uk/id/eprint/10147462/> accessed 28 August 2024

Weinreb LL, *Legal Reason: The Use of Analogy in Legal Argument* (CUP 2005)

Williams TC, 'Property, Things in Action and Copyright' (1895) 11 LQR 223

Worthington S, 'Revolutions in Personal Property: Redrawing the Common Law's Conceptual Map' in S Worthington, A Robertson, and G Virgo (eds), *Revolution and Evolution in Private Law* (Hart 2018)

Yen AC, 'Restoring the Natural Law: Copyright as Labor and Possession' (1990) 51 Ohio St LJ 517

Index

For the benefit of digital users, indexed terms that span two pages (e.g., 52–53) may, on occasion, appear on only one of those pages.

Tables and figures are indicated by an italic *t* and *f* following the page number.

The manufacturer's authorised representative in the EU for product safety is Oxford University Press España S.A. of el Parque Empresarial San Fernando de Henares, Avenida de Castilla, 2 – 28830 Madrid (www.oup.es/en or product.safety@oup.com). OUP España S.A. also acts as importer into Spain of products made by the manufacturer.

www.ingramcontent.com/pod-product-compliance
Ingram Content Group UK Ltd.
Pitfield, Milton Keynes, MK11 3LW, UK
UKHW022230160426
470018UK00004B/40
* 9 7 8 0 1 9 2 8 6 4 4 2 0 *